D1569685

CARL ROHNE

I Can Do This!

RVing where the Moose and the Caribou Play

For Sandra CH Smith, my beloved wife and enduring travel companion, whose inspiration, support, encouragement and example have led me to believe I really can do this!

I Can Do This!
RVing where the Moose and the Caribou Play

©2021 Carl Rohne

print ISBN: 978-1-09837-220-0
ebook ISBN: 978-1-09837-221-7

Contents

CHAPTER 1

On The Road

Slumped in disbelief, I watched the highest Pacific tide of the month close in on the huge rear tires of our RV. Our 38-foot home on wheels was deeply stuck in the sands of an Oregon beach and the water was rising – fast. We had been told that beach driving was possible (and even legal) here so my bride of six months, Sandra, and I had decided to take the RV out for an afternoon on the sand. We had high hopes of camping overnight at the magical edge of the Pacific.

We had motored slowly onto the beach, Sandra skillfully piloting the big rig. She had turned the RV south along the wet sand paralleling the Pacific and I had gotten into the beach scene, cranking up an old *Mamas and Papas* CD and opening all the windows to let the sound flow. Glancing sideways, I noticed that Sandra was suddenly gripping the steering wheel very tightly and her eyes were narrowed in concentration. I took these as signs of impending trouble and asked her what was happening. She replied that the RV was behaving oddly, losing traction. To be safe, we decided to turn sharply left, heading up shore onto drier sand that might provide better traction. Bad choice! The coach instantly sank to the hubs in some of the softest sand we had ever encountered.

We both got out to assess the situation, which didn't appear promising at first blush. Being embedded was bad enough, but making matters much worse (and more tense) was the rapidly rising tide. This was the point at which a stomach-tightening fear set in. If we couldn't figure out what to do – and quickly - there was a distinct possibility we would lose the rig to the ocean. Fortunately, we owned a shiny new camp shovel, bought after a prior debacle (that time in thick, rich Alaskan mud). I unlimbered my new toy and discovered what I really needed was a construction-grade backhoe.

The faster I shoveled the sand from around the rear wheels, the faster it seemed to flow back into the hole I had just made. Shovel, shovel, pant, pant, shovel, shovel! There seemed no way my 70-year old straining muscles and my little shovel were going to free those fat rear tires. Once this dawned on me and I ran out of energy (pretty much simultaneous events) I decided to find out if my cell phone would work on the beach. Yes! I had bars. Should I call 911? Being a guy, there was a brief battle between pride and tide. Tide quickly won. I called.

The very bored dispatcher explained, between yawns, that being stranded in the sand was my problem, not that of the local gendarmerie. She did, however, relent and give me the name of a towing company experienced in beach removals. I thanked her and called the haul-out service. My mind visualized rescue arriving in the form of a gigantic wrecker similar to those featured on reality TV shows such as *Highway Through Hell* or *Heavy Rescue* - a multi-axle, always-shiny, chromed monster with a rotator that could move bridge girders without breaking a sweat. After all, our diesel condo tipped the scales at over 17 tons of impressive bulk. And our obese girl was getting more stuck by the moment.

When succor finally did show up, it came disguised as a battered Toyota pickup, a vehicle whose better days were several decades in the past. A rusty red color, with bits of wire and tape holding the important mechanicals together… was this truck to be our Galahad? Lacking only the obligatory high-mount machine gun, it strongly resembled those trucks shown on cable news plowing through Mid-Eastern deserts loaded down with bearded combatants. The driver, a young man with the nonchalance of one who has seen and heard it all from dumb, stuck tourists, jumped down and surveyed the problem. I was incredulous as to how this little four-banger was going to move Regina Victoria, but he had a solution immediately at hand. We would remain where we were – trapped - with the tide rising. Well, that sounded encouraging!

But wait, not to worry… he would come back in three hours or so to "see how y'all are doin.'" If the situation hadn't deteriorated any further, he would then effect a rescue. Three hours, he explained, would allow the tide to crest and then recede. Once it had ebbed a bit, he could, as he put it, "Just winch 'er out… no sweat". My eyebrows were now raised slightly above my receding hairline. Mildly put, I was dubious but we had no other choice. Our greatest concern was that the RV would majestically and slowly tip over sideways, becoming a massive, inert insurance claim. Or, it might sink in further as the tide rose, likely destroying its large and expensive engine now located just inches above the very salty Pacific.

The next three hours passed very slowly. I feigned disinterest, walking our Chihuahua, Smokey, up and down the busy beach and furtively glancing every three seconds at the RV to see if the ocean had yet claimed it. Sandra, of course, remained calm as she always did in such situations, preparing a lunch for us to enjoy while watching the waves lap at the beach .At high tide, as we nibbled on curried egg salad sandwiches, the ocean was caressing the double rear tires with the last eight feet of the coach sitting squarely over a great puddle of very corrosive water.

Just as promised, our tow driver returned after three hours and once again surveyed the situation while figuratively scratching his chin. With a couple of words of instructions, he backed his truck up about 30 feet, then performed a surprising maneuver. Gunning his engine, he buried all four wheels of his truck in the wet sand. Tires spinning, engine whining into higher octaves, sand flying madly in all directions, his truck sank deeper and deeper. Once satisfied he had created a solid anchor at his end, he unwound his winch cable and attached its big hook to a tow point on the rear of the motorhome. Next, our rescuer told us to start the engine in the RV as we were going to have to add some backup power. Arrangements complete, the tow driver started his winch, the line tightened, Sandra hit the gas pedal and ....nothing happened!

This came as a bit of a surprise to all of us. Reconsidering, the driver instructed Sandra to keep her foot *off* the throttle this time. The idea was to let "diesel creep" work for us, and it did! Slowly we began to inch backwards. We moved at the speed of a geriatric snail on crutches, but with deliberate inevitability. The coach just kept reversing at this incredibly slow pace until the rear tires were free of their deep ruts and resting on firmer damp sand. At this point, we were able to reverse delicately under our own power. Then we used the RV as an anchor for the little Toyota to extract itself from its voluntary entrapment.

Success! We were all jubilant. Even our laconic tow operator seemed pleased with the results, and we were delighted the bill came to far less than we would have paid had the truck of my dreams come to save us.

Later that evening, watching the sun set over the ocean, I reflected on how far Sandra and I had come since our marriage back in the late spring. Just after our wedding we had left St. Louis, my home of many years, on our Grand Adventure. We wanted to take our shiny motor coach first to Michigan, then to the central Canadian provinces. We would explore Canada's bread basket, using the Trans-Canadian highway to get us over to the Canadian Rockies. We planned to meander slowly, pausing often, through those spectacular mountains and then our plans were open, with the proviso we get to Alaska before winter would make travel too difficult in a big RV. After that, as they say in the military, the situation would become more fluid. Beyond Alaska, I reckoned nearly any direction that included the word "south" would be a good one.

Sandra and I had met just over a year before on the internet, and we quickly became inseparable. I am a man of numerous careers - retired academic medievalist/marketing manager/real estate broker – a classic white collar guy. For the last 13 years, my life had been largely "go to the office, work, come home from the office" and care for a very sick wife. A strong and courageous woman, she battled a list of illnesses that ran to several pages and a prescription drug intake that sometimes topped 20 different prescription drugs per day. In the end, her body could not fight any longer. Just when it looked as though she might be emerging from another cardiac-related hospitalization, she suffered an early morning massive heart attack.

I received an urgent call from the hospital and rushed to her bed-side, only to discover that she had been transferred to the ICU. Her former room was a mess - all the debris of a resuscitation littered the floor. The nurses and residents had done their best, but to no avail. Her cardiologist took me aside and very gently explained that she was, indeed, brain dead. Throughout the remainder of that long, grim day I had to consider the options. Knowing my wife, I finally choked out the directive that I never thought I would be forced to utter - stop the life support. This was a decision made suddenly easier at the very end when she went into cardiac arrest once again.

On December 20, at 7:05 p.m, I was alone.

In time, I found myself wandering through museums, taking short out-of-town trips for the first time in many years, going to magnificent Powell Hall in St. Louis to attend symphony concerts, and even dating again. I signed up for Match, but the very pleasant women I would meet for coffee or movie dates often seemed far more interested in their grandchildren than in any new relationship.

And then Sandra discovered *me.*

My on-line bio had specified a dating radius no more than 30 miles from St. Louis. Sandra had somehow gotten my information, even though she lived a good 200 miles away in Springfield, Missouri. She had seen my picture on the very day she had finally decided to resign her job as Director of the Springfield Regional Arts Council. Sandra and I found early on we had many interests and life experiences in common, including a shared love of travel, good food and classical music, especially opera. I mention opera because I had found in previous dating forays that Grand Opera was not an art form beloved of some eligible Mid-Western women. Mentions of Siegfried or of the Marchellin in *Der Rosenkavalier* drew blank looks. One of Sandra's first emails to me included, "So, Carl, are you going to let a few miles spoil our chance of enjoying a great aria together?" I was hooked.

I also discovered in reading Sandra's bio that she did not drink. It was a great relief to learn that my potential new friend and I had both consumed 'way too many Manhattans in our earlier lives and that now we shared years of sobriety.

Not drinking on first dates could be a bit tricky, as I had discovered. The conversation often went something like:

"Oh, you're not having a drink?"

"No, I gave it up a long time ago"

"Health issues, huh? Do you have a bad heart (liver? stomach? pick your body part)."

Knowing that Sandra was in recovery was important because our shared experience provided a focal point for deepening our relationship in ways both of us understood.

We began an intensive, personal, and often funny email and telephone exchange, culminating Memorial weekend when I drove to meet my new friend for the first time. I was so excited that I called or emailed her a a number of times during that 200 mile journey. Her responses were delightful: "I'm so nervous I want to hide under the bed, but there are too many dust bunnies under there." and "I can't escape out the back door: I can't find the damned key!"

For me, at least, it was love at first sight, and we spent a delightful weekend getting to know each other better and letting Smokey, her handsome blue Chihuahua, get to know me without feeling he either had to bite my ankle or hide under the couch.

After a splendid dinner and a top-down drive around Springfield in Sandra's vintage, extremely red 1988 Alfa Romeo Spider Veloce, we returned to her house tired and ready for sleep. I was to have the guest bedroom and I somewhat timidly undressed and made ready for bed. Sandra came into the room clad in a cute nightshirt. On impulse I moved to hold her at the end of the bed and we shared our first real kiss. We stood clenched until, somewhat breathlessly, Sandra said, "I've got a much bigger bed in my bedroom."

In the morning, Sandra made a wonderful breakfast. While we were lingering over coffee, she mentioned that she knew of a charming Victorian artists' village called Eureka Springs, about 90 miles south in Arkansas. I had not been there for many years, so I was very eager to go and explore. Suiting action to words, we were soon ensconced in Sandra's bright chartreuse Jeep, my new pal Smokey riding comfortably on my lap. Once we entered the delightful little town, Sandra mentioned that she knew of a really good B&B and would we like to stay there for the weekend? Of course, I was all in with that idea.

As Sandra drove through town, she gave me a history lesson of Eureka, complete with anecdotes about a number of the locals. This surprised me a bit, as she had not before mentioned a familiarity with anything Arkansan. In a few minutes we arrived in front of a lovely Victorian style B&B. Instead of parking in front where I assumed guests normally park, Sandra raced straight up the steep driveway and parked her Jeep in the empty carport beside the main building. At this point I rather belatedly began to suspect that there was more going on here than I knew about. To my delight, Sandra produced the key to the back door of the inn and with a huge grin announced that she was, indeed, the proud owner of the most popular inn in Eureka Springs.

She explained to me, as we toured the grounds and the other cottages of the inn, that she had built the business from scratch after sailing alone in the Pacific for seven years. She had created her beloved inn with little money and a great deal of chutzpah. I also came to understand how tirelessly she worked to promote the inn and pamper her guests. It would take several crises in our life together before I understood the emotional attachment she had to the inn, her art collection and her heirloom antiques. Her Inn, made up of the Victorian replica she had designed in her logbook while anchored somewhere off Guatemala and then built in Eureka, and her collection of historic houses she had restored all along the same street downtown (her Monopoly game, as she called it) would be a *leit motif* throughout our early days together, most often a positive force, sometimes a divisive wedge between us.

The best part of our first date weekend (or at least the most revealing) was when Sandra arranged a canoe trip on the White River near her inn. I had not, I confess, been in a canoe since my childhood summer camp days, and I am not a strong swimmer, but Sandra seems to bring out the adventurous in me. The parting words of advice from the canoe rental manager were,

"Don't forget now, they just opened the dam so the water is going to be real fast and real, real cold".

With that encouragement, we set off. Once underway, I let my hand drag in the water and discovered it was, indeed, cold enough to cause severe hypothermia in about four seconds flat! All was going well for the first 20 minutes. I was getting into some semblance of a paddling rhythm, Sandra was trying her best to look " boop-boop-be-doo" cute sitting at the bow and we were enjoying the scenery when I looked up, startled, to see a low-hanging tree branch directly in our path. I began to paddle more vigorously to avoid it, but the current was quite strong and as contact with the tree branch became inevitable, I made a bad mistake. Ducking sharply to my right, I overturned the canoe and dumped us into the swift, bone-chilling current.

I was very, very scared…panicked, in fact. I have a nearly phobic fear of water, something that has been with me since childhood and, while I can swim, I often feel a real sense of distress in water where I can't touch bottom. "Oh Jesus", I thought as I rolled under the canoe and deep underwater for the first time in many years. "I don't want to die here". In seconds I came bobbing up (I am blessed with buoyancy of a cork!) but I was coughing up water and realized that the current was taking us away from the bank and back out into the middle of the river.

Smokey and I were lucky that day. Sandra is a muscular swimmer and managed to hang onto me and the boat. With strong leg kicks and with me shamed into trying my best to swim with her, we managed to get back to the rocky shore. Treading water, we realized the next challenge would be getting the boat up on the rocks, filled as it was with freezing water. Breathing spasmodically and shivering, we finally managed to shove the canoe onto the lower rocks, where we emptied most of the water. Taking stock, we discovered we had lost one of the paddles and had nearly lost Smokey (fortunately his lead was tied to the mid ship thwart). The little dog's eyes were like saucers and he has never liked water since.

After resting and trying to get some circulation back into our frozen extremities, we re-floated the canoe and proceeded – very watchfully! – downstream. That we were soon able to laugh about this spoke well for our new relationship. Of course, there was more to come that afternoon. Returning the canoe, we discovered the keys to Sandra's Jeep were presently whirling down the White River, having fallen out of my pocket when we went upside down. We called the local locksmith, who opened the Jeep but couldn't start it because of its electronic keying system. The locksmith gave us a ride back to Sandra's inn, where we changed clothes and took another car back to her house in Springfield (two hours each way) to get the spare Jeep keys. The day turned into a very long one, but we happily joked about our misadventures, a quality I hoped would stand us in good stead in what I was already secretly hoping might turn into a lasting relationship

There is something to be said for long distance romances: you get to listen to all of your favorite CDs as you cruise the otherwise boring interstates running between home and your new heartthrob. I-44 passes through beautiful, rolling parts of the Ozarks where it was possible to actually receive classical/jazz stations. It's a treat to scan the dial while driving through small-town America and suddenly hear Stravinsky or Brahms. All praise to those stations for keeping a tradition of classical music alive!

During our early months together as a "couple", we twice tried a limited version of the RV life. In August of the year we met, Sandra asked if I would join her in her 30-foot motor home for a trip to Door County, Wisconsin. Naturally, I jumped at the chance. I had seen her RV in the driveway of her home in Springfield, but had never even driven it, let alone thought of living in it for a month. Being with Sandra has taught me to jump at new challenges. Plus, the idea of visiting this very artsy part of Wisconsin in August with a new girlfriend sounded irresistible. I hadn't been to Wisconsin since attending the University of Wisconsin (Madison) summer music camps in high school, but I remembered it would likely be cooler than the steamy lower mid west.

The trip did not start auspiciously.

Tasked with filling the RV's big fresh water tank, I connected the garden hose to what seemed the right inlet (RV plumbing is a mysterious science best understood by elderly wizards and Ph.D.s in hydraulic engineering). Something quickly went wrong. Within a few minutes, water was cascading enthusiastically from under the side door and down the coach's steps. I took this as a bad sign, immediately turned off the hose and ran to the house to tell Sandra. She burst out laughing. Many other people I have known would have been caustic or angry. Sandra was neither, and it was a quality I came to appreciate many times in our relationship. Relieved I had not been banned from the trip (or from her life, come to think of it), I began sopping and mopping.

When we ran out of dry towels, I headed off to the nearest big box store to buy a wet/dry vac, then spent the next two hours patiently sucking up water and emptying the ever-heavier canister. Eventually, with everything under control and connected correctly and no faucets open anywhere inside the RV, I finally filled the tank. I had learned a valuable first lesson. RVs are complex, they have many systems, and it is always a good idea to read the manual before starting an operation.

Our trip to Wisconsin was a wonderful success. I learned to drive the motor home with something akin to confidence, at least on the long, straight stretches through rural Illinois and Wisconsin. I could even back it into a campground parking spot if it wasn't too narrow. The first time I was able to do that unassisted was a cause of quiet celebration for me. It was the first of many opportunities to prove I could master something I had never thought I could do. Successfully backing Sandra's rig into that Wisconsin space was an "I Can Do This" moment.

We spent most of our time in Peninsula State Park with frequent trips into the charming little hamlet of Fish Creek to savor the local delicacies and snack on ice cream treats at what was possibly the busiest ice cream venue either of us had ever seen. This part of Wisconsin gets snow - a *lot* of snow - so most of the shops try to make all the money they can during the short summer season. However, we did find snow mobile trails clearly laid out and marked, with tall snow poles, so there is clearly some winter tourism as well. One of the highlights of the trip was attending a cookout of a type I had never seen before - a Door County Fish Boil.

Hours before the dinner hour, huge cauldrons of water are set a-boil over open fires. Fish and spices are added to the pots and then, just before serving time, the cook throws kerosene on top of the boiling water, sets it alight, and basks in the oohs and ahhs from the assembled diners. I'm not sure this improves the flavor, but it certainly makes for a spectacular presentation and some grand photo ops.

One of the glories of this trip was being able to see the famed Perseid meteor shower from a Northern vantage point. When the showers were at their most visible, we spread blankets under the stars and watched this celestial fireworks display for the better part of the night. Tired but exhilarated, we slept very late the next day. Our first RV excursion together went so well we decided on another RV vacation, this time to Florida after Christmas, when all the inn- keeping and family obligations would have been satisfied.

During our winter trip we took a huge plunge. Not yet married, but increasingly committed to a life together, we took Sandra's RV for an oil change in Panama City. While we were waiting at the dealership, we thought it would be innocent fun to "just take a look at what was on the market in our price range", as we told the salesman there. We wandered through travel trailers, fifth-wheels and a range of motor homes. The next day we were signing papers to buy our dream RV!

We were captivated by a Holiday Rambler Endeavor – a large diesel pusher, nearly 40 feet long with two big TVs, lovely leather seats and a comfy couch, a cockpit resembling a jumbo jet for instrumentation, and – best of all – an air horn! The horn got me – I just had to have that coach, and Sandra concurred. Friends have pointed out that it might have been cheaper to buy an air horn for my Prius, but that would have taken away the drama, the sense of command that comes with sitting high up behind a huge steering wheel with the horn button just inches from my left hand. Plus, I discovered that my bride also secretly enjoys the air horn. She loves to salute her friends in quiet suburbs with it!

I didn't realize from my limited test drive just how big a challenge driving this behemoth would be. After we took formal possession, I somewhat nervously got behind the bus-sized steering wheel to take us the 50 or so miles back to our Florida campsite. As soon as I exited the dealership I realized that I was in a cul-de-sac and had no real idea of where the turning points were on this RV. With the wheels actually behind the driving position, one has to develop a new set of references for navigating in close quarters. At crawling speed, I just managed to clear curbs and parked cars. I even had to back up once but, without a tow car, that proved to be relatively easy: simpler, in fact, than backing Sandra's old RV, as our new toy was possessed of an abundance of huge mirrors.

The months after we acquired the Holiday Rambler were times of growth and change for us both. On the way back from Florida we decided that full-time RVing was one possible future for us We began planning a really long trip to Canada and Alaska, to explore areas both of us had always dreamed of seeing. Additionally and without much fanfare, the idea of marriage began to creep into our thinking and our conversation. Commitment to each other was becoming more important as we began to envision whatever was ahead of us. After several marriages each, using the 'M' word was a bit scary for both of us, but we somewhat nervously got used to it.

Finding the perfect engagement ring was great fun, especially at our age. We were a bit starry-eyed as we went through the looking/ buying/wearing process. All my relatives enthusiastically approved of Sandra, and I had met her twin brother, his wife, and Sandra's adult son at Thanksgiving when we travelled to North Carolina to be with her family. I had thoroughly enjoyed her small clan and the long holiday weekend had given us all a chance to get to know one another better. So now we planned an intimate wedding in St. Louis' gorgeous botanical gardens.

What amazed both of us was how quickly, as two older adults, we were able to make decisions, send e-mails, follow up with phone calls and arrange the entire event (which turned into a 3-dayer) in a matter of hours on two late-winter afternoons. Of course, buying a pretty new outfit for Sandra and a spring suit for me took more time than all the other arrangements combined!

To make matters more interesting, we had already decided on a trip to Prague with my sister Karen, my travelling companion to Europe on previous trips during my years as a widower. All three of us had a grand time in late April exploring that most architecturally magical city. A highlight of that trip was a long bus journey to the stunning medieval city of Cseski Krumlov. As a medievalist, I was in Gothic Heaven! This is one of the most complete medieval cities imaginable and, like Prague itself, remained relatively untouched by the savage scarring of 20th century warfare.

Returning home, we realized that we had but one week until our nuptials! Mild sense of panic, but…with everything done, why be concerned? We relaxed and welcomed Sandra's family to St. Louis.

Our wedding day dawned brilliantly clear and sunny but with enough wind to turn Sandra and her new broad brimmed hat into Sister Bertril, the flying nun. Luck, hatpins, and a realization that no hat would *dare* disappoint Sandra on her wedding day combined to keep my bride firmly on the ground. The wedding went swimmingly (we had written our own vows) with my sister Karen acting as celebrant. All of my small family showed up to wish us well. We spent the rest of the day eating, sightseeing, socializing, and ending with a carriage ride and dinner cruise on the Mighty Mississippi. The next day we had a sumptuous, white-tablecloth brunch and sped all the out-of-towners on their way. Happy, married, and dead tired, we rested, then began the push to get our big new play toy ready for our upcoming live-aboard adventure to our Northern Neighbors.

Preparing to travel for an extended period turned out to be more complicated than anticipated because Sandra had to transition day-to-day operation of her inn to a newly-hired manager. While I continued to sort out the St. Louis house, Sandra was deeply involved in teaching her new-hires the complexities of running her inn. It is (and I speak from later experience) not an easy operation to master. There are endless details, from how the towels are folded and stacked on the Jacuzzi tubs, to where each special item goes on the silver breakfast trays. Then there is the wine inventory, the luxurious soaps and shampoos, the large garden areas to be tended, plus the ongoing maintenance of buildings that are a century or more old. Only later did I really appreciate how much effort the inn took and how hard Sandra was working in order to for us to go travelling together

Finally, a few days prior to our departure date, Sandra returned to St. Louis. The last days turned into a scramble of packing, discarding, and making my house ready for a friend who had agreed to rent it in our absence. There were – inevitably – tensions between us as we grew weary and came to realize how limited the space was going to be even in this generously proportioned motor home. Both of us had differing wants and needs in terms of what we were going to be able to take.

I am a minimalist is some ways but I must admit that I wanted to carry aboard far too many clothes. My motto has always been, "You never know when you may need your tuxedo." Sandra, on the other hand, learned her cooking skills in Provence, and wanted to bring what appeared to be trunks full of exotic herbs and spices, special cooking wines, magic ingredients, and items at whose use I couldn't even guess In the end we reached a compromise because we discovered that this was too important to us to fail. I left (mostly) the dress clothes at home, and Sandra agreed not to bring a number of her beloved *objets de cuisine*.

In the final few days before departure, I became frustrated with the RV's many systems and their occasionally arcane operation, culminating in my failing to realize that the on-board, home-size refrigerator had to be kept level to work properly. I had parked the RV on an incline in front of my home…very bad idea! The result of that error was the loss of hundreds of dollars of fresh and frozen foods when the big side-by-side fridge/freezer decided to pack it in for the duration. My new wife, who lives by "waste not, want not", was not pleased!

I could only apologize and promise to read the thick operations manual more carefully in the future. She was not mollified. She suspected, quite correctly, that her new hubby hadn't bothered to read the book in the first place. Sandra reminded me that she had spent a good deal of time in the midst of all her own preparations making up menus and selecting foods to keep our trip interesting and provide us with really good eats. I appeared blissfully unaware of this, which provoked a strong reaction on her part.

Our first real argument, and it was a very tense one, took place departure morning upon discovery of the errant 'fridge. I thought my apology was perfectly adequate and felt that she was making too much of this. Sandra became more and more upset as we talked, squared off in the middle of the bedroom. At one point, she declared that she should probably return to Springfield and seek a divorce.

This stunned me and I simply stood mute. We just stared at each other and I realized, with a bad feeling deep in my stomach, that there was more going on than the loss of frozen food. It became clear that I had taken what our recovery program refers to as "the easier, softer way" in dealing with the RV. This is a long-ingrained tendency with me and even after years of being in our program, I realize that it is a defect I will always have to deal with. And I had been blithe about the loss of the food, passing it off far too lightly and not taking sufficient responsibility for my role in this debacle.

After moments of tense silence, Sandra reached out to me. "Smokey says that I should give you a hug", she whispered through tears. I hugged her tightly. The moment passed, the tension drained, but I realized that the effort to leave her inn and commit to a life on the road was much harder on her than I had dreamed. I was going to have to be more thoughtful in dealing with issues that mattered to my new wife.

I had been Mr. Enthusiasm, eager to be on the road after years of caring for a sick wife and a career that kept me tied to my phone and to clients who thought nothing of calling at midnight. Sandra, I suddenly perceived, was giving up control of her beloved inn, a place where she felt fulfilled, contented, surrounded by the "pretty things" she so enjoyed. As I would discover during our journey together, there were other factors at work, including the very real fear that she was taking off with another impractical "academic" husband. That morning of our departure I swept much of this under a convenient mental rug, but I knew inside that these conflicts could, and likely would, return again down the road.

As painful as that morning's lesson was, it was salutary in making me aware of just how little I knew about our new vehicle (and my new wife, for all of that) and how important it was to "do things by the book" when living in a motor home. I was going to have to become more knowledgeable (and quickly!) about all the systems in this big, complex rig. Perhaps I thought the RV came with a riding mechanic. It did not! Maybe RV repair centers would be clustered thickly along our route? They were not!

It was suddenly urgent to read the fat instruction manual that came tucked into its own special cabinet in the RV. I needed to be smarter about how and why you used the generator (big box in front) rather than the inverter (little box in back) or, for that matter, what all those electrical panel controls did. How did the hot water heater *really* work? Why was determining tire pressure for the six big donuts such a complicated process that it required whole pages of charts and numbers in the ops manual? The list of things I didn't know was daunting but I didn't have time to read my way fully into expertise. It was going to have to be "learn by doing" on top of "learn by reading".

The process of stocking the big RV left us with tired backs, sore knees, and a greater appreciation of why the English always had scores of porters to carry their supply of Sherry and other such essentials when they went "on safari". By the afternoon of departure day, we were both exhausted, grumpy and doubting the wisdom of this whole scheme. But as the late May sun began sinking, Sandra, our better driver, slid behind the steering wheel, turned the key in the ignition, and fired the diesel to life, beginning our Grand Adventure. With 330 horses warmed up and rumbling in our ears, Sandra hit the drive button, popped off the air brake, pulled out into the street (nearly running over one of my nosier neighbors) and began what we hoped would be a satisfying new experience for both of us.

As we left St. Louis and headed eastbound on I-70 we couldn't stop looking at each other with huge grins on our faces, realizing that at long last we were finally on our way. "Can you believe we're really doing this?" we kept asking each other in voices tinged with wonder. I don't think it really sank in until later that evening, somewhere in the middle of yet another Illinois corn field, that we actually were off and running "North to Alaska". The current scenery was uninspiring, the temperature high and we were both dead tired, BUT... we had achieved the first goal that we had set for ourselves as a married couple. We were on our way and we had done it by ourselves. That was especially important to me, a white collar, pay-to-have-it-done sort. Never before had I been in a situation where I had to use my hands as well as my head, where I might be well beyond the reach of people I could count on to bail me out, even if the bailout came with a price.

My deeply ingrained stereotypes about myself were already beginning to change. "They had better," I thought to myself," if this is going to work." It occurred to me that travelling in this fashion over very long distances might require that I develop a bit more ingenuity and mechanical aptitude than any of my previous careers had required. I had a lot to learn but getting the RV ready made me feel better about myself than I had in quite some time. I wasn't even upset to admit that I really hadn't figured out how to check the various fluid levels in the dauntingly large engine compartment. I would, I thought - there's got to be a page on that somewhere!

As darkness descended on this, our first night on the road, I thought of how our lives had changed over the past year, of how much richer I felt for the challenges faced. The glow of the instrument panel softened our tired faces and we reached across the big cabin to touch and hold hands as we motored steadily eastward. Finally, in Effingham, Illinois we pulled into a friendly Walmart for the night, our very first stop on what would be a long journey…not glamorous, not scenic, but so restful after this day of heavy schlepping and serious emotional stress.

Soon I had the generator going, both the roof A/Cs on and the plumbing system working. We were ready for the night. Smokey, our faithful travelling companion, took this all in stride. He is a seasoned *voyageur* and after a bit of supper and his evening walk he – like us – was more than ready to snuggle into the comfy queen bed in the aft cabin.

CHAPTER 2

Northbound

The promise of cooler weather as we travelled north spurred us to action early the next day. We turned the RV sharply left at Effingham and spent the day with the dash A/C running full blast. For our second night on the road, we stopped at a pleasant rest stop operated by the Michigan Department of Highways just inside the state border. We came to love these big rest areas as we travelled. Generally we shared them with 18-wheelers, so we felt quite safe and secure. The only downside was the noise of idling trucks or, worse, the racket from refrigerated trailers. The upside was they were free, had clean restrooms, and featured parking spaces designed for rigs even longer than our 60 feet.

Feeling considerably more refreshed and with some of our aches and pains beginning to ease, we were eager to pick a good sightseeing route. After putting our heads together over morning coffee at a Mickey D's (with the necessary big parking lot), we decided we would most enjoy the scenic route around Michigan's thumb. We hoped that we would reach a specific (and uncrowded) state park that night. I used my cell phone to make a quick reservation, so we wouldn't feel we had to push too hard. And here came an interesting tidbit of new self-knowledge - I am far more likely than my wife to be stressed if we don't have a place lined up for the evening.

I had wondered why I had this vague sense of unease when we would set out in the morning and gradually it dawned on me that I am a creature of too-much regularity. As much as I would like to shed that concern for stability and control, it continues to haunt me. Of course, to make myself feel better about this character defect, I tell myself that the motor home is actually so big, especially with the tow, that one can't simply pull in just anywhere. Every turn in to, or out of, a parking lot has to be thought out in advance. Not thinking a few moves ahead can result in having to remove the tow car, a bothersome process.

That said, I began to realize that here was another personal issue that I was going to have to work on if I were to get maximum fun out of this adventure. And so I began trying not to worry about what the end of the day would bring. Rather like Sandra, I started to live more in the moment. She has a much more profound sense than I do of the "right now". It is a mindset she gained while single-handing in the Pacific and one I hoped to acquire on this journey.

The drive through Central Michigan and on to "The Thumb" was routine. The RV was running smoothly and I did my share of the driving on this stretch, but a new adventure soon awaited. Some things about a big diesel pusher take getting used to. For one, since they require diesel (a *lot* of diesel) truck stops are the preferred fill-up venues. I have always loved truck stops and truckers (even with a PhD, my secret job choice has always been over-the-road, long-haul trucker) but as a car driver, I had always been looking in on the world of huge trucks and their mahouts. With a diesel-powered motor coach, I suddenly acquired a passport to enter that magic kingdom.

There are, however, things to learn about truck stops. The first is that diesel fuel is inherently messy and filling the rig is best done in old hobby clothes (the kind that smell permanently of turpentine or fish or wet dog). It also helps to wear gloves (most truckers do) since diesel aroma has about the same half-life as plutonium. After a few embarrassing tries at pumping fuel, I learned that it is a good idea to go into the fuel-pay area before you begin. The pumps, particularly those in the huge truck plazas along the interstates, are often programmed to ask trick questions involving obscure meter-readings and ICC identifiers, none of which RV owners have. Trying the pump first can result in considerable confusion as you shout questions to whichever trucker is nearest to you, usually over the rumble of about a dozen huge engines all idling at once. Some truckers pretend acute deafness, others shake their heads, and a few will patiently suggest that, since you are not driving a truck, you should probably go inside to sort it all out.

When you *do* go inside, you will often be asked the same questions as the inanimate pump asked, but with less patience. However, once the pump-side miracle of video technology shows your RV, the questions abruptly stop and your money (usually a large sum of it) is cheerfully taken in advance of filling. Then you are allowed to go back out, stick the huge nozzle in and begin the filling process. Actually, this doesn't take nearly as long as one might think as most truck stop pumps could easily fill a jumbo jet in about five minutes flat. Plus, our RV, just like the big 18-wheelers, can be filled from both sides at once, making topping off the 100 gallon tank even quicker. Once full, you can go back into the pay area and retrieve your credit card or get (a tiny amount of) change back. Since there is usually a queue, this is also the time to observe your fellow diesel jockeys.

These knights, and often ladies, of the road come in a complex variety of shapes and sizes. Some are classically burly and look as though they could easily dispense with such silly add-ons as power-steering. Others are short, wiry, wear glasses and look as if they would be at home in academia (like me, some of them probably were....I suspect trucking pays better). And then there are the ladies…more of them than I had realized are driving professionally. They, too, are an interesting amalgam. Many drive with hubbies or boyfriends, a few drive solo and some with another woman. They generally appear to be no-nonsense pros and are usually treated that way as well. Plus, they often have a better selection of decorative and informative tattoos, more attractively displayed, than their male counterparts.

One of the bonuses of driving a diesel RV is that sometimes you buy enough fuel to get a great perk…a free shower. With the shower comes a washcloth, a clean towel, plenty of hot water and a little cubicle that you get to call your very own. Having just bought about 90 gallons of best-quality diesel, I found out at my second truck stop that I was entitled to one of those free showers. I decided I would pass at this point as I was not yet really gamey. Sandra wouldn't be able to take one as well and I was blocking a line of trucks at the pump. If I left and wanted to come back in to shower, I wasn't certain I would be able to find a place to park the rig since you DO NOT back up a motorhome with a car in flat-tow mode (all four wheels on the ground).

This is another major lesson to be learned and it took some getting used to. Unlike anything else I have ever driven, a motor home dragging a car behind on its own wheels does not know reverse. Before we started our trip it was darkly hinted by our local RV specialist (with much muttering and squinting at our expensive new tow bar) that extremely dire things would occur if we so much as *thought* of putting the big Allyson transmission into the "R" position. I came away feeling that lots of mechanics were making a good living from older duffers like me who suddenly panic and stab the gear selector's reverse setting. One positive … RV drivers become adept quite rapidly at selecting "best path" solutions to pull in/ pull out problems. Those who fail to plan properly (guilty, as charged, on more than one occasion) will have the chance to enjoy the healthy outdoor exercise that comes with removing the tow car, backing it away from the RV, maneuvering the big motorhome out of the dead-end it is in, and then re-attaching the tow car.

This can be highly entertaining to locals anywhere and especially so at small-town service stations where a ubiquitous row of local retirees, sitting in chairs at the front of the garage, will watch you hook and re-hook with the intensity of Bobby Fisher on Move 26. The reason you are providing this amusing local entertainment? You failed to realize that the large lot behind the station you had planned to use as your way out is, in actuality, a field of very small soybeans. Driving through them would greatly upset the owner, a respected and (usually) kindly gentleman sitting squarely in the middle of the station's front porch.

Piloting the RV around the top of Michigan began to make all three of us feel as though we had finally entered fully into our trip. The waters of Lake Huron were sparkling bright and U.S. 23 is simply a delightful road with almost constant vistas of the lake shore. For Sandra and me, it meant that we were once again in close contact with a large body of water. I had discovered (although Sandra already knew it) that we are what she terms "water people". Her years of Pacific sailing have made being on or near water an essential for her. And I have found that I am happiest when I can see, hear, and – importantly – smell water. This is something of a mystery to me, because I am not blessed with a particularly discriminating sense of smell. I nonetheless seem capable of discerning all sorts of aromas associated with oceans and lakes.

Smells are also an important part of my travel memories. I can recall much about my favorite European city, Barcelona, if I but think of how the water around the big marina smells. Those sensory impressions open a catalogue of other aromas that can take me around the city from the statue of Columbus at the water end of the Ramblas (popcorn, corndogs, calamari) to Park Guell with its commanding view of the city (sardine tapas, strong espresso and Fanta orange pop). Back in the here and now, driving around Lake Huron, the air just began to feel and smell cleaner and certainly cooler. We even saw our first seagulls, entertaining us by skylarking above the rocky beaches.

An evening highlight to the day's refreshing drive was a stop at the top of Michigan's Thumb for a good dinner. We had agreed before embarking that we were not going to eat "bad road food" or our own cooking exclusively. There were to be times when we would stop for a special dinner or a leisurely lunch, generally just because we felt like it. This was such a time. We found a charming restaurant (part of a B&B) near the water in a town small enough that we could just park the rig along Main Street, a block from our targeted eatery. The inn had a cozy bar and a very nice back room with bay windows where we were seated among a few other dinner guests. The meal was quite good and we both had the perch which is locally caught, very fresh and well-prepared.

One of the revelations on this trip is that I found out I like more kinds of food than ever I realized. Growing up in the Midwest, fish was not a part of my family's cuisine. Mother disliked fish and only served it when it didn't look or smell like fish, generally in the form of unidentifiable fish sticks, heavily slathered with tartar sauce to further disguise their aquatic origin. Occasionally, if she was feeling especially brave (or if the pressure cooker, her favorite cooking tool, wasn't working) she would make baked fish with an amazingly thick tomato sauce. The sauce served to hide the fish smell and she would always have all the kitchen windows thrown wide open, even in the dead of a St. Louis winter. Now, here in Michigan, I was actually ordering fish …odd what a change 60 years could make in one's dietary choices.

Sandra and I took time to have dessert and linger over coffee, before continuing to drive for a few more hours in the glorious fading sunshine. Of course, we snuck out a tiny treat for Smokey who always waits patiently to see what we have brought him. If he sees a white paper napkin in Sandra's hand, his joy is boundless. Curly tail wagging at top speed, he leaps from the driver's seat to the big dash board to get a better view. Once we are inside the coach, the little fellow bounces up and down enthusiastically until Sandra finally delivers his cherished snack.

The following morning, we continued up the Michigan mainland to Harrisville State Park, a very pleasant Michigan campground. Half the population of Michigan, however, appeared to arrive at the same time. It was Memorial weekend, a fact whose implications had escaped us in our mad flight out of St. Louis. But it turned out to be a wonderful chance to relax (the first time, really, since our wedding) and to people-watch. It is amazing how teenaged girls (boys, too, come to that!) can find ways in a campground to continue working on looking either "cute" or "cool" or sometimes both. Several young ladies, camped with their (shudder!) parents, managed to change outfits and hairstyles at least three times a day over the course of the weekend.

Harrisville and Lake Huron worked magic on my bride and me. Bracing water invited some serious shoes-off, hand-in-hand strolling along the shoreline. We also began what became for us a ritual…reading each day from the literature of our 12-step program and searching for meetings so we could "trudge our happy road of destiny". The sharing which followed our readings over our morning coffee went far towards keeping us focused and certainly made a difference in how we came to view each day. Paying attention to our programs was another life lesson learned early in this trip. We each have had long-term success against our respective demons and we found that our marriage worked best when we understood the need for quiet times apart or shared reflections on where we had been (metaphysically) and where we hoped to go.

After Memorial weekend, we headed Regina Victoria (as we had named our rather regal condo on wheels) north to Michigan's Upper Peninsula. Here again, we were fortunate to be able to stay in state parks, but real adventure came with the side trips. It dawned on me that we had made a really good choice in deciding to take a tow car (a Jeep Grand Cherokee of considerable mileage), even though that made driving more difficult at times. Our very first excursion away from the RV was to Mackinaw City to sample local pizza and collect brochures about area attractions.

We had both heard of Mackinac Island so, after reading the brochures, we decided the Island would be our next day's destination. To be on the safe side, we pre-checked ferry company parking lots and settled on the ferry to the island that had largest acreage of blacktop. Our plan was to keep the RV in the lot the nights before and after our trip to Mackinac Island rather than travelling miles backwards to our current camp ground. (A side note about Mackinac Island…both the island and the town of Mackinaw are pronounced the same way, "aw". The spellings were differentiated simply for mail-delivery reasons)

The ferry ride takes less than an hour and we were deposited at the island docks just steps away from the main drag through town. The ferry itself presented an interesting panorama of people and cargo. Several European nations and quite a few Asian countries were represented and the soft admonitions of parents to children in Hindi, German, French, Mandarin and several other languages was a very welcome sound after white-bread rural Michigan. For cargo (and there is always cargo on any island ferry) there were numerous bicycles, huge crates of fresh produce for the island's restaurants and hostelries, cases of liquor, many suitcases, and several steamer trunks (haven't seen those in recent travel documentaries!) for those doing the grand stay at the very aptly named Grand Hotel. All that was missing was a bit of livestock…a sheep or goat, perhaps a few chickens, to make the scene postcard perfect.

Once on the island, we headed down Main Street for a bit of sustenance and then booked space on one of the island's horse-drawn tour wagons (carriage would be a bit charitable). Being a "horse guy" myself, I was intrigued by the selection of horses and their harnessing. I found out there are over 600 horses on the island, mostly draft breeds such as Belgians, Percherons and Clydesdales (yes, they don't all pull beer wagons and play football!). For the rides through town and out to the National Park, the island drivers use a two-horse hitch. At the park itself, they switch to a larger wagon and a three-horse hitch reminiscent of Dr. Zhivago and his troika. This is all designed to minimize the impact on the ecosystem. It was a very cool, bright day and for me, riding on or behind horses is always a great way to spend time. Having done the full equestrian tour, we stopped at the Grand Hotel for its justly-renowned afternoon High Tea.

Sandra and I have been fortunate to have taken High Tea in Bath (home of the famed Bath buns), London, Edinburgh, and even in St. Louis. This tea, however, ranks at or near the top of the list. High Tea anywhere is an experience to be savored, but especially so in a setting like that of the Grand Hotel. The place simply oozes charm, old money, long-forgotten secrets, love affairs begun and ended, and the mystique of a world of privilege no longer to be seen. Tea begins with Champagne (or sparkling juice in our case) and moves slowly and gracefully on to silver trays – big ones – filled with artistically-arranged finger sandwiches and rich desserts; recipes from a time when butter was a delicacy to be enjoyed in quantity and meals were worked off with a nap. Of course, this high tea had the *de riguer* dish of clotted cream with which to generously slather the fresh scones.

The bright, expansive tea-taking room is elegantly furnished with antiques and original oil paintings and carpeted with the expected floral orientals. One takes tea reclining on a settee before a beautifully polished, dark mahogany coffee table. Everyone dining has a view of the famous front porch of the hotel, some 600 feet long, filled with classic rocking chairs and overlooking the waters between the island and the Upper Peninsula. One can also take tea on the porch itself, but this appears to require a degree of knee/armchair balance which I lack, so we dined in and savored the scenery and the ambiance of our setting.

Replete with wonderful goodies and some glorious tea, we sauntered hand in hand back to the ferry dock, there to re-board our excursion steamer. Once safely arrived back on the mainland, we trundled the RV to a quiet corner of the huge parking lot and settled in to plan the next - the Canadian - phase of our continuing odyssey.

CHAPTER 3

Issues

From Mackinac, we drove northward to Sault Ste. Marie (the Soo, as it is called), stopping first on the U.S. side for one evening, then crossing over to Canadian soil, our first border crossing. Here we took the opportunity, on a very chilly June afternoon, to ride a tour boat through the locks that allow big-ship navigation between Lakes Huron and Superior. Although I lived for many years near the lock system of the Mississippi River at St. Louis, I had never actually ridden through the locking process, so this was a real treat. The boat's captain does a good explanation over the loudspeaker of what we were seeing and of how the process of dropping some thirty feet works. It brought back memories for Sandra of her boating years and of how she had planned to take her diminutive 35-foot Ericson sloop through the Panama Canal in the midst of 900-foot freighters and tankers.

Because it was getting late after our lock excursion, we settled in a big parking lot in Canadian Soo, where we encountered our first mechanical difficulties of the journey. Suddenly, and with no prior warning, we were beset by generator issues. The diesel genset that supplied evening power when no shore hookups were available just wouldn't start. Period. I read the entire generator section of the RV manual, then got out the more complex guide provided by the manufacturer. Nothing I read seemed to match our issues so we spent a restless (and low powered) night wondering what to do.

Up early the next morning, I crawled under Regina Victoria to see if I could ascertain any reason why the generator wouldn't turn over. This is a vaguely intimidating process, as everything on the coach is super sized and you really get a sense of just how much weight is hanging over you when you crawl under. More manual reading and several more forays under the rig failed to resolve the problem. Clearly we needed professional help, so our next step was to begin searching for a repair center, not an easy task in a big rig even with the tow car removed. We got strange looks and stranger recommendations.

"Take it to the farm machinery place on the big highway….they must know about this sort of thing." or "Take it to Canada Tire – they have a big service bay." We did and they do, but they do *not* mess about with big diesel equipment. Just as I was entering a state of numb resignation, the Canada Tire manager made a phone call to a possible repair place. "No," came the answer. "I only work on the heads of diesel engines," but this "king of head wrenches" did know that Eagle Engine Repair, just outside town, might be able to help. I thanked everyone profusely and called Eagle whose manager told me to "bring her right out" and they would take a look.

This was the first of a number of experiences where a much-needed repair facility would emerge from the blue to handle a fix issue. It was also the beginning of a new realization that a diesel RV cannot simply be driven to the nearest friendly dealer for repairs, mainly because there is no single dealer. Chassis, engine, brakes, transmission were handled separately (and often by separate garages) from problems with the coach and its interior. The facility that could fix the big engine wouldn't touch a problem with, say, the slider for the living room. That involved another shop, often not even in the same town.

Once we drove out to Eagle, there came another important lesson: watch, listen and ask questions. I learned this from Sandra who is so good at questioning that she should have been a district attorney. An RV with a large engine, king sized generator and loads of subsystems really can't be fully documented even in a large manual, no matter how carefully it is prepared. So, at Eagle, we asked our assigned tech, John, how things were wired, how much oil the engine took (7 gallons!), where was the plug for this or the vent for that, and how to check the fluid of that six-speed tranny. John, bless him, was a very patient man and we learned more about our rig in that one day than I had figured out on my own in days of manual-studying. I also learned that there are limits to what you can do on your own.

A power plant requiring seven gallons of oil and a filter the size of Rhode Island was not suitable for a shade-tree oil change! As a plus, we also learned that diesels are very rugged and fairly forgiving of owner eccentricities. The generator, the root cause for our stopping in the first place, turned out to be wired to the house batteries, and the house batteries were old (probably originals) and pretty well shot. The search began for four deep-cycle six-volt batteries, a size typically found only in RVs and golf carts. We offered to go pick them up if the garage owner could even locate any, but he had the situation well in hand, and after a few phone calls and a brief wait, four shiny, very heavy new batteries appeared.

The remainder of the afternoon was spent installing them in the almost-inaccessible battery compartment. The process required the flexi-bility of an Olympic gymnast and the brute strength of a lowland gorilla, but our tech and his colleagues finally had everything in its proper place and tested. At several hundred dollars each, the new batteries made for an expensive afternoon, but we now had enough wattage aboard to light up Times Square! By late that day, we were once again on our way, this time up and around the Northern rim of Lake Superior.

Our first long stop in Canada was at Panhandle Provincial Park and there we discovered an interesting bit of Canadiana. Some provincial parks are not really designed to accommodate large American motor homes. Some could, of course, but differentiating them from the sparse info available was always a challenge. Panhandle Park proved difficult to maneuver in and we spent a good deal of time figuring out an approach to a prime site overlooking the lake. I actually took out a notebook, pen and a big tape measure to see if it was physically possible to enter our chosen leafy bower. Convinced that, at least theoretically, it could be done, we decided to chance it. I was mindful of how expensive an RV paint job can be, so I walked around and around the rig as Sandra crept slowly, inch by inch, into our spot. This actually was our first parking challenge, as we had been in relatively open areas until then.

Panhandle turned out to be a very pretty park and, surprisingly, uncrowded. We took time to explore the hiking trails and spent hours strolling the lake shore with its rocky beach. For the first time, Smokey got to run off his lead and near the water. He seemed to enjoy it immensely, even though our canoe experience on our first date weekend had made him very wary of large bodies of water, especially cold water! The little dog is a constant source of joy in our lives. He is loving, entertaining, and full of enthusiasm for whatever the day brings. Not bad qualities for us to emulate as well.

Our next stop was Lake Superior Provincial Park and the camping here was a much bigger challenge. The campsites are beautifully wooded and appear deceptively easy to get into. In fact, trees have grown up strategically (and I think deliberately) to block easy access, as though mocking anyone foolish enough to bring a motorhome to *their* park. Our first attempt at what we thought was a pull-through site quickly turned white knuckle. We scratched the side of the RV on a marker post which we then proceeded to flatten as we backed up. Deciding to abort, we found that the site's normal forward exit clogged with trees so close together we couldn't figure a way out. But fear not…my resourceful new wife to the rescue.

Sandra has an uncanny sense of the space around her. On this day, that instinct helped us back and fill, back and fill. Rearwards she would go, six inches at most. "Watch the tree by my right mirror!" she would shout. I would trot around to that side, assess our wiggle room and trot back over to report. "OK, you've got about two inches over there, but there's a big rock just by the right tire. Watch that." Over and over we repeated this game until at long last she could back the rig onto the service road. Our second attempt – this time at a different site – resulted in a broken rear-marker light, but at least we were finally in a space! Then we noticed that the site was very much tilted to one side, more so than it had looked as we first approached it. With the RV's built-in hydraulic jacks working overtime, I scurried about finding rocks and limbs to prop under them. I thought about this later and realized that in any prior life I would either have just let the rig tilt or simply given up and crashed through to another site…another "I can do this" moment and a bit of quiet pride.

We finally achieved at least a degree of "levelhood" which would make both us and the testy fridge happy. And, because rain threatened, I had to do something about the smashed marker light, which hung on a thin stalk of wire 12 feet in the air above me. Duct tape to the rescue! I am not good with ladders (or heights, for that matter), but here was another chance to demonstrate something important to myself.

First, I had to find the three-foot extension that had to be hung on the bottom of the fixed ladder (a system designed apparently to keep passing trolls from stealing the 500-pound air conditioners off the roof). Finding the extender required removing the contents of one cavernous underbelly compartment. Of course, the ladder was at the bottom of the pile, and at the very back of the compartment. Once I had it up and all the gear re-stowed, I was able to climb to where I was level with the damaged light. Leaning uncomfortably far to my left, grasping the ladder in my right hand with a death grip, I worked left-handed to slap a patch of tape over the light fixture and hoped that it would hold in the coming rain. A new item to put on the next repair list, I thought, but it was okay for now and I felt a sense of achievement as I retreated gratefully back down the ladder.

Perhaps because of the real challenges in setting up, Superior Park actually became one of our favorites. As a reward for all our efforts, we had a treed site with views of the sparkling lake just a few yards away. Lake Superior is so big that it has weather and waves rivaling an ocean. We had a perfect ringside seat for a major summer blow on the big lake. As the wind picked up, the waves built until they were crashing onto the slippery gray granite rocks just feet in front of our coach. Occasionally, spray flung high would hit our windshield.

One idyllic afternoon we spent hours sitting side by side on a large piece of driftwood skipping rocks into the lake. We discovered the musical possibilities of different sized pebbles and rocks and spent time achieving what Sandra called, "the pebble harp effect". Since we are both keenly interested in music, we had a lovely time that afternoon creating our own musical effects from just rocks and water.

We also found that we were beginning to truly revel in the solitude that surrounded us. To Americans used to a longer summer with earlier school endings, the park appeared almost deserted. We shared over a hundred spaces with perhaps a dozen other campers. The solitude, the quiet is something that often struck me about Canadian parks and about

Canada itself. There aren't a lot of Canadians and they live in a small zone in the south of the country. I already knew this intellectually, but the emotional impact of it is surprising to an urban American.

I came to love the Canadian experience, especially in the provincial parks that are not on the favored tourist routes. That, and being early in the summer season (schools let out in late June), meant that more often than not, we had most of entire parks to ourselves. It proved to be a very special way to experience the emptiness of Canada; that feeling of endless "elbow room" proved to be a highlight of this early part of our travels.

In the U.S., as in Europe where Sandra and I had often travelled before we had met, there are tracts of empty space. Certainly, the great American national and state parks systems offer solitude and the chance to see large areas of relatively unspoiled wilderness. But in Canada, the vastness is, in some hard-to-define way, a very part of life. Canada's unique emptiness is not something set apart, fenced off and quantified with statistics about so much land in this park or that preserve. In Canada, the sense of vast space is part of the fabric of daily life. We were amazed at how few people live in this huge space; the wilderness comes right up to your door. As we stayed longer, we discovered that it was usually just a short walk out of the park into large areas that were just like the park only without "parking spaces".

The idea that one can drive for hundreds of miles, even in the populated lower belt of Canada, without finding cities, or even big towns, was a very eye-opening experience. I commented to Sandra that during our courtship, I had driven back and forth across the state of Missouri, certainly not an overpopulated area for the most part, but I had always had another fair-sized town just a few miles away as I drove the 290 miles from St. Louis to Northwest Arkansas. In Canada, that same distance might net three small (*really* small) towns, a hamlet (yes, they are still called that), a truck stop with a small grocery, and a weed-choked motor court of the sort I remember from family trips in the late 1940s across the U.S.

West of Toronto, towns had the friendly, more intimate feel of many U.S. municipalities 50 or so years ago. Even Winnipeg, boasting several hundred thousand residents, came across as less intimidating than an equivalent U.S. city today. There seems to be a closer connection with the territory surrounding a town, a sense of the town *belonging* in that space, not intruding, but rather serving as a focal point for humans in a very large wilderness.

One of the delights of this early part of our trip was running hour after hour alongside the Canadian Pacific Railroad. Sandra and I were both fascinated by the sheer size of Canadian trains, usually with three (or sometimes many more) diesel locomotives pulling and another locomotive or two trailing at the very end, pushing away for all they were worth. It was also enlightening to contemplate the huge variety of goods being shipped on that straight steel highway...containers from China, Japan, Korea, Germany, Italy, England, Holland, Denmark and many other countries. We always tried to guess what might be in them...Danish cheese, Italian Vespas, Chinese computers, etc.

We were probably infrequently right, but it brought to mind previous travels in our "before-we-met" lives, and it was a good opportunity to share more about each other. When we saw a Swiss container, it reminded Sandra of her months in Geneva during her student days and led to a string of very funny stories about her experiences there many years ago, including my favorite.

She happened to be sitting in a small café in Old Geneva, frequented by left-wingers, students and other bohemian types she loved. It was about 6:00 p.m. on a major holiday, Swiss National Day. All of a sudden, some of them stood up and lit off a massive amount of fireworks which they had aimed directly across the small plaza and into the second floor open windows of the police station. The policemen all came running out the front door looking like characters in a Charlie Chaplin movie. Sandra nipped out of the café and jumped into the driver's seat of a car her girlfriend had earlier parked there. A policeman came up and told her to move on but she explained she didn't have keys to the car. He opened her door and started to drag her out of the car at which point she stood up and slapped him to the resounding cheers and applause of all the café habitués.

The officer arrested her and she was thrown into a jail cell with nothing but a cement slab to lie on.Sandra being Sandra, demanded to make her permitted phone call and was told, "No calls…in Switzerland, we follow Napoleonic law and you're guilty until proven innocent." So she just lay down on the slab and went to sleep, thanks to having had several glasses of wine earlier.

Many hours later, she was awakened by another officer who whispered, "You're in big trouble…that was the Chief of Police you slapped. Better come up with a plan or you'll rot here forever."

Her immediate resource was to call for the Chief and when he came to her cell, she started crying pathetically, apologizing and asking his forgiveness, saying in perfect French that she had simply been fiercely afraid when he pulled her out of the car. At that point, he said he would release her but it was after midnight and not safe for her to walk home alone. He would be happy to escort her. On the way home, she was trying to figure out how to keep him out of her bedroom and when they arrived at her door, she said she would love to invite him in but her landlord, who also lived in the house, did not allow her any guests. She quickly scrambled up the steps, unlocked the door, ran inside and locked the door.

Similarly, a Danish container reminded me of my more recent visit to that wonderful country. I had gone with my sister a few years previously and we had both been struck by how physically attractive the Danes were. Men and women alike simply radiated good health and physicality and their friendliness in the English language was unexpected and very welcome. My efforts at Danish were so bad that most Danes immediately switched to English in sheer self-defense. The degree of linguistic sophistication on the part of many Danes was quite remarkable.

I told Sandra about a morning at our hotel, a wonderful converted warehouse over 500 years old, when the desk clerk had us in stitches with his very droll comments contrasting Danish and American tourists. (The Admiral Hotel in Copenhagen should be a definite if you are travelling to that "Saucy Old Queen of the Sea".) American tourists, the desk clerk said, can always be spotted by their white socks, shorts and sneakers, while Danish tourists all wear baggy shorts, long black socks and dress shoes. It takes a fair degree of language skills to make that funny early in the morning, but the Admiral's desk clerk could do it.

Our journey around Lake Superior had, as a highlight, the Neys Provincial Park where we stayed for a number of days. Neys is on the northern rim of Superior and the campgrounds are dispersed at the very edge of the lake — wonderful in summer and undeniably brutal in mid-winter gale season. We also at this juncture began to get much more interested in the local wildlife and in trying to identify the plants and trees we were seeing. Canada was beginning to look "different" and we welcomed not only the new vistas, but also the new birds and animals we could see, usually first-spottings for both of us.

It is very hard to forget your first moose, grazing peacefully just off the roadway. Ours was a large bull and paid us no heed as we slowed to a crawl to savor this experience. Up close, his sheer size was amazing. Probably topping half a ton, with an antler spread of more than six feet, he was a mature bull. We watched him for as long as traffic allowed; finally, he ambled slowly and majestically back into the woods. And then he just vanished! That an animal that large could so quickly disappear into the forest was startling.

Neys Provincial Park was a wonderful refuge from travel stresses. We were able to park Regina Victoria facing the waters of Lake Superior and then just sit back and marvel at the scenery. Lake Superior, that great claimer of ships, has all the qualities of a true inland sea. Weather, wind and waves all combine to produce an oceanic effect and we sat for days enchanted by changing vistas, from dead-calm to energetic wind-foamed whitecaps.

CHAPTER 4

We Ride the Purple Sage

After enjoying the scenery of Lake Superior, it was time to move on westward, out of the gorgeous mountainous terrain. At first, the land as we headed west was similar to what we had been seeing, but by the time we reached Saskatchewan the terrain was beginning to flatten and stretch out. It was as if the land itself needed a bit of a rest…a change from the craggy, boulder strewn drama of the Lake Superior area. Here we were travelling into an area where the sky, rather than the land, provided much of the daily drama.

The celestial bowl over this portion of Southern Canada is as dramatic as any I have ever seen. Huge white clouds in highly fanciful arrangements would be our companions during long sun-filled days of prairie travel. At sunrise and sunset, the clouds were shot through with bolts of red, red-brown, gold and sometimes a hint, a *soupcon*, of violet. Occasionally, of course, it rained - often gently but sometimes with a passion that cleaned Regina Victoria better than a truck wash. These were the elemental storms of the northern prairies, the storms that made you quickly realize the power of weather in a vast open area with no sustaining, sheltering human structures in sight. Storms like these had greeted our ancestors as they slowly advanced from the eastern tree line into the Great Plains… storms that had, fundamentally, both nourished and ruined farmers for generations.

As an historian who had once taught about the migrations of Hispanics and Anglos to the Great Plains of the American West, I felt a vivid sense of connection as we rolled westward. There was also a feeling of being in a area that I have always loved because it reminded me of childhood readings and of my father, a great fan of western author Zane Grey. I could visualize the Riders of the Purple Sage, one of Grey's classics and a book I had devoured soon after acquiring the magical skill of reading. My father, a practical, no nonsense electrical engineer, loved the romance of these novels and I think he read and re-read them many times. I remember him sitting in his favorite chair, smoking his pipe, and occasionally reading a few lines from Zane Grey aloud to me as I sat at the dining room table working on some long-forgotten school project. Dad seemed to gather some inner strength or affirmation as he read these novels of the Early West. And here Sandra and I were on very similar plains with many of Zane Grey's characters awaiting discovery.

As we slowed and stopped for food or fuel, we got to meet the locals who were, indeed, Zane Grey's cattlemen and farmers…big straw cowboy hats, worn boots, elaborate belt buckles, deep suntans. These were men and women who were frontier people, possessed of a hardiness that short, intense summers and cold winters had etched into their features. They were always helpful and courteous as I had found such men and women to be in other parts of the world as well. I remember one young fellow pumping diesel into the RV and also cheerfully cleaning the windshield. Considering the sheer acreage of glass involved, we were highly impressed at this ancient ritual, "Fill it up, sir? Would you like your windshield done?" from my boyhood and long since forgotten elsewhere. Service with a smile was alive and well on the Canadian grasslands.

We made an important decision while driving the prairies. We had seen an endless caravan of cattle trucks pulled by lumbering over-the-road tractors, nearly all filled to capacity. Sandra finally exclaimed, "I can't stand it anymore to see those pink little noses of the cows poking out of the side-vent holes of the trucks, sniffing the air desperately for freedom."

So we gave up juicy, delicious beef. For me, the guy who would cheerfully eat a hamburger every day, this was a HUGE deal. We did, however, allow ourselves one special cow-based meal every month, a ritual we usually celebrated at the best steak or prime rib venue we could find.

Arriving at Winnipeg, deep into the Canadian Great Plains, helped me overcome some of my cravings for bovine-related delicacies. We stayed at the local Big Box and savored how international and cosmopolitan Winnipeg is. We saw a wider variety of ethnic types than we had seen for quite some miles and marveled at the vast range of culinary experiences available. The Walmart parking lot where we stayed was interesting in its own right. The lot is huge, with acres of blacktop available to park every manner of RV. We saw everything from pop-up campers filled to overflowing with young families, to fifth-wheels, travel trailers, and every imaginable brand of larger motorhome. It was an orderly mob of relaxed campers, and by evening, many of us were wandering through the lot chatting with other campers and listening to a young guitarist/singer who was perched on the hood of his tow car playing old Pete Seeger stuff. And for safety, the Big Box rent-a-cops were out patrolling the lot without in any way hassling the many campers there.

We detached Julietta Jeep (pronounced the Spanish way) and went exploring in Winnipeg, finding it a very charming (albeit very flat) city with some surprisingly handsome architecture and a smorgasbord of restaurants. As we hadn't had any Thai food for a while, we used our trusty GPS to locate a Thai restaurant in the heart of Winnipeg. Sandra and I both love to explore new cities, so we left ourselves plenty of time after a delightful dinner to wander about aimlessly, knowing the GPS would lead us back to our parking site no matter how lost we got in the depths of this jewel of a city.

Past Winnipeg, the Prairie begins in earnest and continues for seemingly endless miles all the way out to Calgary in Alberta. We travelled slowly and gently through the Prairie provinces, often stopping to photograph the spectacular sky and cloud patterns or to try to get a shot that would typify that incredible sense of space and endless horizon that this land exhibited. I don't know if either Sandra or I succeeded, but the fun was in the trying. If some of our shots at least remind us personally of that vast sweep of sky and land, then we did well.

We also tried to capture something of the farms and ranches we drove past. Horses and cows were there in abundance and we marveled at fields of golden canola, a crop that neither of us had seen growing before. Canola plants are beautiful, short and sturdy, and their golden sheen could be seen for endless miles. Then there were the luxuriant fields of flax, vibrantly green and spring-like even well into the summer growing season. And always I wondered to myself what this land looked like in the grip of winter with howling north winds, driving snow and plunging temperatures.

No wonder that everyone we met or saw seemed intent on milking all they could from the pretty summer weather. Pickups with campers towing fishing boats were everywhere and the provincial parks were finally full of campers and picnickers. These Plains Canadians seem less frenetic in their search for summer sun than people I had seen elsewhere. In Northern Europe, for instance, Germans, Danes and Swedes and all of their cousins seemed obsessed with capturing every last photon before the long days gave way to longer nights. But it may have been, too, that I saw mainly city folk in Europe, not workers close to the land and sky as these Canadian sun seekers were. Canadians in this area were not fussy about their travel rigs. Older trucks were the norm and camping gear was minimalist. Boats were often flat john-boats or simple aluminum fishing skiffs with old outboards on older trailers. Canadians appeared to think that you could catch just about as many fish their way as you could using a candy-apple-red bass boat with a duel-axle trailer.

Canada tends to teach an American some new perspectives on what is important and what works. I began to see as we drove that I was learning a few new life lessons. If these were lessons I had learned earlier in my life, then at least travelling in Canada was bringing them to my forebrain once again, a salutary experience and one that I became more conscious of as we rolled westward. Slowly, I was beginning to relax, to let the journey go on without my constant direction, without making myself responsible for every event of every mile of travel. I was beginning to allow what I saw as a more relaxed Canadian perspective get inside my head. To a Canadian, especially one from a big city, this may sound like quaint nonsense, but I really do think that Canadian life moves at a different pace from that in the U.S. , perhaps not slower necessarily, but rather less focused on some of the more individualistic goals that we Americans tend to see as our top priority.

One of the things that gradually began to sink in during this portion of our trip was that we weren't seeing litter. I don't know if Canadians are born genetically cleaner, but it occurred to both Sandra and me that our northern neighbors had, perhaps, a greater respect for the natural scenery or even a greater respect for each other than we had experienced before in our many prior travel adventures. Scandinavia came closest to this sort of attitude of respect for others, but I had never seen it manifested quite as clearly as it was in Canada. Or perhaps it isn't that at all…

maybe young Canadian children are threatened with terrible perdition if they accidentally drop a gum wrapper. Maybe they are threatened with exile in the U.S. if they stray. Whatever the truth, it makes for some very clean highways.

Just past Winnipeg, we came to a decision point: go north on Highway 16 to Saskatoon, or stay south on Canadian Highway 1, the Trans-Canadian Highway through the lower reaches of heartland Canada. We opted for the more southerly route and set off through Portage La Prairie on our way west following Highway 1. We also wanted to see the extent of the massive flooding that we had heard about over near the Saskatchewan-Manitoba border. Media reports indicated that the Trans-Canadian highway was closed in that area, but reports seemed conflicting so we pressed on anyway.

We did become more conscious of the degree of flooding as we drove onward. Trains seemed to be unusually long and some appeared side-tracked as if waiting for a distant stretch of track to reopen. This was, in fact, the case, since there really is only one East-West track system and it had been devastated by powerful flood waters to the west. We also saw many tractor-trailer rigs with flatbeds and lowboys moving heavy road-building equipment westward. That gave us pause as we thought about just how damaged the road might be, but CBC reports indicated an improving situation.

We motored slowly as we were in no hurry to wait in long detour lines. Proceeding cautiously, we continued to enjoy the drama of flatland and vast sky. I really like that kind of landscape. Sandra did too, up to a point, but she is a tree person, a born tree hugger who grew up near California's giant and majestic redwoods. She loves trees not only because of all the shade and comfort they offer, but as she says, because of how they put her life into true perspective and "I see how small I really am." I am a bit more claustrophobic about dense woods so the prairie lands gave me a chance to catch that vision of vast distances that I always long for after being too long in towns (or, yes, even in trees).

I love the late-night sunsets on the Plains as the sun dips down in dramatic glowing colors, often with a grain elevator in silhouette. These "cathedrals of the Prairies" were to be seen in such abundance that we came to understand why this area was Canada's and, indeed, the world's breadbasket. Wheat, first brought from the Ukraine by farmers who understood dry-land cultivation, was everywhere. It stretched beyond the horizon and we imagined wheat berries ripening as we stared at the neatly plowed fields, so long and warm and glorious were these days of deep summer.

By the time we reached our next major destination, Moose Jaw, it was problem time again for poor Regina Victoria. This time, the fault lay entirely with her human occupants. Prior to arriving in Moose Jaw, we had come upon a Visitor's Information Center off the highway and down a short gravel road. The posted road sign said "Open", but it appeared quite shut up. However, we did see another RV and a car in the lot. As we got much closer, we saw a picnic table across part of the entry road. By that point, of course, it was too late turn around, so in we went, narrowly skirting the picnic table. So far, so good, until we turned into the parking lot and immediately and dramatically discovered that our RV would not move forward. No budging...not another inch, she wailed!

We got out to look and realized that we were stuck fast in thick, gooey, great-for-farming mud. We tried rocking back and forth with gear changes. Nothing. Then we tried the little 2X4 pieces of wood that we used under our leveling jacks. The result of trying to build a ramp for a 34,000-pound vehicle with little boards was simply to bury the boards. End of exercise (minus our jack boards, of course ...we were not going to try to dig those out!). Then Sandra, thinking in a crisis as only someone who had sailed alone might do, suggested we use our little entry rug in front of the left rear tires, the easiest to reach.

I laid our sacrificial rug down carefully, tucking it under the dualies as much as I could. I stood back and signaled Sandra to "go for it". She revved the big Cummins and slowly the RV crept along the rug and into shallower mud. Sandra is a genius at these matters and just kept going, gaining momentum and getting the RV unstuck, followed explosively by the towed Jeep. She then headed out of the quagmire lot along an obscure dirt trail (that only she could see, perched high in the RV), through a field and back to the main entry road. As I watched her pilot the big rig through the last of the muck and up the dirt road, I heaved a huge sigh of relief and gratitude that my partner was the capable woman she has so often proven to be.

That incident was another of the many life lessons to be learned on this road trip: trust your partner's capabilities and learn to laugh (which we were able to do) when everything just begins to look bizarrely hopeless. It is hard not to laugh, albeit with just an edge of hysteria creeping in, when you stand back and look at a 17-ton vehicle mired in what appeared to be a solid parking lot. I also learned that my wife is quick on her feet when it comes to finding practical solutions to unusual travel problems and I acquired a bit of insight: it's okay for me not to be the one to find a ready solution to a that pressing problem. Sometimes it's reassuring to say "*we* can do this" rather than just "I can do this." From the ill-named "Welcome Center", we proceeded onwards towards Moose Jaw.

I'm not sure why exactly but Moose Jaw has always been a place I wanted to see. It could be that I mistakenly identified it with some long-ago radio show I had heard as a child. Actually, I had believed that Moose Jaw was where Sgt. Preston of the Yukon hung out, not realizing that Moose Jaw is several thousand kilometers south of the Yukon, the location of Sgt. Preston's many adventures. Moose Jaw turned out to be a rather delightful little town smack in the midst of a lot of very flat land. It is just off the Trans-Can Highway and the big box parking lot there was a welcome sight. We decided to stay there for the night and try to get a few repairs done on the RV the next day.

Our recent adventure at the Welcome Center had ripped the tow bar's electrical connections off the receiver hitch on the RV. This actually needed to be welded back on and I had also discovered the source of a mysterious rattle that we had been living with for the latter part of the trip. By accident, while putting supports under the motor home's leveling jacks, I had bumped the side of the RV just below the driver's side window. In so doing I had created the mysterious, highly annoying sound that we had been hearing while driving. It appeared that the side panel had lost a rivet (or several) and needed attention.

Settled in Moose Jaw, I detached the Jeep and went in search of a repair facility. It was too late that evening to find much open, but once again I was struck by Canadians' friendliness and willingness to help a stranger. I had been (mis)directed to a big- bay facility near where we were camped for the evening, and so I drove over and went inside. Two ladies, the only occupants of the rather cavernous interior of the building, explained that this had indeed once been an RV repair facility but that they and their hubbies had just bought the property and were turning it into a truck line terminal. They were very sorry that they couldn't be of help, but they knew of at least one repair facility a few miles out of town and even looked up the telephone number for me. I jumped in the Jeep and went charging back up the highway in the direction from which we had just come. I was trying frantically to get to the truck and tractor repair place before they closed in a few minutes. I made it – just!

In the front office was a very laconic young man just cleaning up after having his hands and arms deep in the innards of a huge John Deer tractor sitting right out in front. I quickly explained what I needed done and he mumbled (I think) that he could take a look at it (maybe) sometime the next day if he wasn't too busy. I explained that we were travelling and needed to get going but the terms of (possible) service didn't change, so I answered that we would either be back really early in the morning with the big rig or else we would just mosey along unfixed. That seemed wholly acceptable to the young fellow, so I disconsolately retraced the path to Moose Jaw.

I soon discovered that I couldn't remember which highway exit was the one I needed in order to find Sandra, Smokey and the RV. As a result, I took the wrong turn (of course) and wound up in the southern part of Moose Jaw. This actually proved to be an interesting and worthwhile detour, as this is the historically more significant part of the town. Al Capone and several other notorious bootleggers hung out in this very area in order to avoid the increasingly long arm of Eliot Ness and the then newly created brainchild of J.Edgar Hoover, the FBI. There was even a full size 1920's-era black sedan mounted on a pole outside a local motel and eatery, advertising that "Scarface Stayed Here."

Just past this tribute to prohibition I discovered a street whose name I remembered seeing when we had first driven into the town earlier in the afternoon. I made a right turn, and wound my way easily back to the parking lot where my bride was waiting. Since it was dinner time, we decided to eat out in Moose Jaw. We retraced the path I had just taken to get back and found a very nice Chinese restaurant on the main drag through town. After a pleasant dinner we decided that we really ought to attend a 12-step meeting.

We had obtained an address on-line, and asked our waitress where it might be. English not being her strong suit and both Sandra and me being deficient in Mandarin, we finally puzzled out that the meeting was actually quite near, in the basement (as usual) of a church. We hurried over to be on time, and discovered that it was another type of 12-step meeting. We were good-naturedly welcomed, but we wanted to find an appropriate meeting and several people took the time to give us good directions to where the meeting we wanted was being held. We jumped back in the car and sped to the other end of town, arriving just in time for the start of the meeting. How good it was to see those friendly faces!

Afterwards, we stood around chatting with the local members, recounting some of our travel adventures. We also mentioned some of our repair needs. It happened that one young man worked as a welder for a local big-truck repair facility and other members agreed that his employer was doubtless the best place to have our work done. A gentleman then jumped into his pickup and beckoned for us to follow him in our car, explaining that he would actually take us to the repair shop we had been talking about. That way, he said, we would know just where to go in the morning as the facility was quite large, with a number of buildings and service bays. We set off after him and in about two miles came to an enormous parking lot full of tractor/trailer rigs and several long buildings with garage doors that seemed tall enough to accommodate the Goodyear blimp.

We hoped that at least one of those might be available in the morning for our RV. Our guide suggested that we really ought to consider bringing the RV there very early (as in 6:00 a.m. early!). We gulped, but agreed that this was a very smart idea and promised to be back bright and early with our rig the next day. After bidding our guide goodnight, we wandered around Moose Jaw a bit more, just soaking up the ambiance and enjoying an ice cream at the local sundae shop. One of the delights of the trip across Canada was how much later in the evening we had daylight. It didn't feel as though we were that much farther north, but indeed the distance up from the Midwest was enough to make a significant difference.

I set the alarm for 5:00 a.m. to give us plenty of time to get going, as neither Sandra nor I is a morning person, and the dog absolutely refuses to get up and out from under the covers at uncivilized hours. Fortified with some VERY strong coffee, we made it to the truck repair facility with time to spare (the German in me hates to be late, even at 6:00 in the morning!). We checked in at the service center office, explained what we needed to have done and mentioned that their facility came highly recommended by locals we had met. The service manager agreed to have his tech look at our problems and told us which bay to put the big RV in. Sandra rolled the motor coach onto the huge, open grease pit, straddling it dead center as though she had been driving big rigs all her life. Even the tech looked impressed!

John, our contact at the shop, got right to work on our problems. I just loved being in a big truck repair facility. I got to see Kenworths, Macs, and Peterbilts up close and personal. It was also entertaining and instructive to watch the mechanics labor over these behemoths. Most of their tools were on a gargantuan scale to match the sheer size of their charges. I don't think I had ever seen wrenches that big before, not to mention the huge screwdrivers and other more arcane bits and pieces. The service techs also commanded a vast array of pneumatic tools, all hammering, wrenching, and chiseling away at truly awesome decibel levels. Many of the trucks they were working on had a million or more miles on them, while others were essentially brand new. It did give me some hope for the longevity of our motor home when I realized that it shared a number of components with its beefy, workhorse cousins, including the Cummins diesel engine and the faithful Allyson 6-speed transmission.

These big truck repair guys are, in my view, some of the best in the business of working with machinery. And they all seemed to have a pretty fair sense of humor. There is an air of good-natured banter among the big truck workers and I must say that they treated us extremely well. I had never been close to so many huge trucks before. It was fun to watch the diesel mechanics climbing all over them. My favorite image is of a young mechanic filling the crankcase of a huge Kenworth with gallons and gallons of oil, perched literally on top of the engine, holding a five-gallon can of oil and the biggest funnel I have ever seen. That, I thought, now explained the advertising sign in front of the shop, "Oil Change Special $179.99". You don't see that often at your local Jiffylube.

Once the major repairs were done, I thought of several smaller things that needed doing as well, and the shop foreman was perfectly willing to accommodate these extra jobs. One that I really wanted done was to replace one of the rear marker lights (located some 12 feet up at the top rear of the coach). We had wiped out that lens while trying to back out of one of Canada's provincial parks, and I felt a whole lot better with a shiny new glass in place and my improvised duct tape repair consigned to the waste barrel.

So efficient was the crew working on our RV that we were done and out by early afternoon, rolling westward through the vast prairies of Saskatchewan province. This is the countryside of Mom and Pop gas stations, with little diners and groceries attached. We always try to patronize these kinds of businesses whenever we can, and they were unreservedly friendly and welcoming. In fact, it was at one of these local diners just off the Trans-Can highway that we discovered one of Canada's great culinary treats, *poutine*. This concoction of French fries (often hand-cut and fried while you looked on) and cheese curds covered with thick brown gravy became a favorite of mine as an afternoon treat, a reward for hours behind the wheel, or while waiting in line to fill the big diesel tank. I suspect this is not cardiologically good food for two travelling Seniors, but it is absolutely delicious . . . Canadian comfort food at its homemade best.

One similarity to driving on the Great Plains of the U.S. was the absolute profusion of insects that flung themselves suicidally into the path of Regina Victoria. Within miles of refueling and cleaning the big wind-shield, we would find ourselves looking through a film of dead insects, a miasma which would grow thicker and more impenetrable until we finally resorted to the washer/wiper combo. This usually proved ineffective, but we felt we were at least trying. Generally, it produced a slightly cleaner stripe at approximately eye level and lots of smeared insect parts over the rest of the windscreen. Eventually, we would blast so much solvent on that the view would improve a bit. Fortunately, Regina Victoria had a solvent tank that could double as a swimming pool for a party of garden gnomes, so we never ran out of bug-blaster.

One of my concerns was that the insect fluids would prove corrosive to the large expanse of paneling that makes up the RV's front end. This proved unfounded, as our coach is largely fiberglass (a fact that I didn't know, for some inexplicable reason, at that time). So, damage repair consisted of copious amounts of cleaning solution and LOTS of elbow grease. Sandra and I went through many an old rag in the evenings trying to keep ahead of the day's insect pileups. I was surprised (pleasantly) at how well the motor home's paint withstood insect road rage. A pile of rags, old sponges, mild detergent, and two determined cleaners generally got the paint looking shiny again by the time we left off for the night. And it was good exercise for us, since we spent too much time sitting either at the wheel or as a passenger in the big, leather armchair on the starboard side of the rig.

CHAPTER 5

Westward Ho

From Moose Jaw, our next major stop was at Medicine Hat. At this point in the trip along the Trans Canadian, we had some reservations about how to proceed. We were now in the locale where Canadian Broadcasting stations had reported road-out conditions along the Trans-Can due to severe rain-induced flooding. We stopped in Medicine Hat for the night and talked to as many locals as we could, to try to get a feel for what we faced ahead and just how bad the washouts were. Reassuringly, the consensus appeared to be that only one fairly short section of road was still under water and that an acceptable detour was being built around it to keep traffic flowing.

Armed with this local knowledge, we decided to stay in Medicine Hat for a couple of days, camping at an old Sam's Club parking lot (the entire facility seemed to be for sale) along with more than twenty other RVs and big over-the-road semis. There was plenty of room to maneuver and we chose an area towards the far end of the lot, which allowed us to walk Smokey in grass along the edge. Well, grass is perhaps a generous term for the vegetation growing right there, but it did have to compete (seriously) with the local prairie dog population, which had built a sizeable city right off the parking lot.

Smokey never tired of the game of "Find the Prairie Dog" and would cheerfully have spent every waking hour wandering from hole to hole waiting for one of the little rodents to pop out so he could give chase. Unfortunately for Smokey, they were extremely well organized and never appeared anywhere near where he was. But Smokey never seemed to mind – he has that wonderful quality that says, "The fun is in the trying." This rest stop made for a very happy Chihuahua, especially as he got to run about off-lead, something we normally couldn't do in the parks where we usually set up camp. It was great fun to see our little companion having such a grand time, with new smells and experiences to add to his trip memories.

Since it was July 1 (Canada Day), our new friends in the local 12-step group directed us to a spot high on a hillside where we could sit comfortably and watch a spectacular display of fireworks. We had our 4th of July fireworks, only three days early and in a different country, but the feeling was definitely the same. We had come to admire the politics and culture of our northern neighbors, so we felt right at home oohing and aahing over their independence-day fireworks!

Restocked and refreshed (both physically and spiritually), we pinned the Jeep back onto the RV and pulled out of Medicine Hat heading towards the setting sun. In a few hours we came to the detour section, which amounted to a hastily constructed dirt and gravel roadbed that wound around flooded low-lying fields and a very swollen small river (probably a creek in drier times). I just watched where the big rigs went and followed in their tire tracks, arriving safely back on Canada 1 in fairly short order.

Once past the worst of the flooding, we decided that it would be fun to try another of Canada's many provincial parks, this one a really rather quirky but delightful park aptly named (this is the prairie, after all) Buffalo Pound Provincial Park. I really liked the image of once-vast herds of large, shaggy bison pounding through the low hills and rolling grasslands that characterized this part of Canada. As always, the Canadian Parks personnel were friendly and very helpful, assisting us in finding a camping spot that would accommodate our rather larger-than-Canadian-size rig.

Locating a suitable site on the check-in station wall map, we got directions on how best to find it (and, more importantly, how to get into it). The getting to it part, however, turned out to be something of a challenge, as much of the miles-long approach road was hilly, very muddy, and full of tire-devouring potholes. Rainfall had been far heavier than usual, and the road had really taken a terrific beating, with many washouts and deep gullies. Crews had been diligently at work with some very heavy grading equipment, but the road was definitely a work in progress. At dead slow speed (diesels are very good at this) and with very careful steering, we managed to avoid the worst of the really deep holes and arrived with only a new undercoating of thick, gooey mud to mark our passage.

Arriving at our assigned campsite, entering it became the next obstacle. This was the only park thus far encountered in our voyage where the vagaries of topography dictated that we had to pull off the road to the left and park parallel to the service road in our assigned space. We pulled the RV up to the assigned site and surveyed the prospects. Parallel parking required a bit of thought, but we discovered that we could do it without removing the tow car if we went around the loop again and then very carefully pulled into the site while letting the Jeep hang out into the roadway just a bit.

We fervently hoped that no one would attempt to pass by us on the road driving an even bigger rig than ours, but in several very idyllic days we never saw that bigger rig! The parking finally accomplished, we both heaved a big sigh of relief. The site we had selected turned out to be delightful, with clean modern showers within easy walking distance. We were also very close to a shimmering, cool lake where we could watch children swimming and fisherman out in canoes and John boats looking for perch and lake trout. Buffalo Pound Provincial Park is really much lovelier than we had anticipated. Entering it, you are still driving through essentially flat prairie land, with little hint that the park itself will be full of different terrain. But once inside the confines of the park itself, a whole new series of vistas unfolds.

After parking, letting out the sliders, and hooking up, we let Mr. Doggers out and decided to stroll around exploring our new surroundings. The lake itself was considerably bigger than I would have anticipated given the Great Plains kind of country side that we had been driving through for days on end. What a pleasant change of scenery and what a delight to the eye to see gorgeously clean, clear water with just a hint of wind-ruffled whitecaps beginning to break as evening approached.

Towards the end of the afternoon, I decided to take a solo hike up one of the many lovely round hills in our immediate area. These little hills were something of a stroll-back in time as far as I was concerned. It was easy, as I reached the top of my chosen promontory, to imagine the 19th century herds of buffalo coming to drink at the beautiful lake that traverses the heart of today's park. And closing my eyes a bit, I could see the First Nations people who depended upon those magnificent animals camping right here in these very hills. I kept an eye out for arrowheads and spear points, convinced that I was probably right in the very heart of a major hunting encampment.

Standing in the warm late afternoon sunshine, I was surrounded by gently waving stem grasses and many varieties of wild flowers. I shot photos in all directions, but especially northward across the lake towards a low range of soft hills similar to the one on which I was standing. With the campground several hundred feet below me, I could hear the wind in the grasses and make out distant bird calls.

This was the essence of peace and silence, heavenly after days in the big rumbling coach. Sandra and I both love parks and less improved areas of Canada where we could just turn off the big diesel engine and hear... nothing! The value of silence, or at least of quiet, was growing within me. I hadn't realized, before I had met my new bride and begun these travels, how much background noise I thought I required. Sports going on two or three TVs at my house or classical music on several stereo systems, the need to be in crowds at the mall, or the familiar pattern of listening to many simultaneous conversations in my office...all of this had served as a needed, familiar backdrop to my everyday activities.

I hadn't realized how much I had filled my life with random noise, often operating only at a background level, but still with never a chance for real silence. Perhaps, I reflected that day on the hillside in Canada, I had not been entirely comfortable with myself, with my train of thoughts, with the committees in my head that fought for dominance. Now, on this long motor trip, I was beginning to strip away that need for sound. I was gradually coming to appreciate the grandeur of nature's silence and her softer, more intimate sounds, like the bird calls I had heard earlier

My first real adult experience with profound quiet had happened many years before when, as a young graduate student, I had driven the old highway 66 (and some then-new parts of the fledgling interstate system) to California, passing, of course, through New Mexico and Arizona. I had decided to stop at the Painted Desert as a very welcome break from shepherding my new (graduation gift) VW Beetle along that ribbon of road joining St. Louis to the fabled West Coast. Once inside the National Park that protects the desert's fragility, I had turned off the little bug's 4-cylinder air-cooled engine, stepped out and begun walking as far away as I could, stopping finally when the tell-tale tic-tic-tic of the engine cooling no longer echoed in the clean desert air. Once completely out of earshot of the car, I suddenly encountered the most profound silence I had ever (not) heard in my young life. It was a quiet as vast as the landscape, a silence that completely negated the importance of all the sounds that might so much as dare to intrude.

Standing on that hill in the afternoon at Buffalo Pound, I once again felt that overwhelming sense of calm and quiet. As evening came and the light gradually failed for my photography, I slowly made my way back down my "private" hill and recounted the adventure of that late afternoon to Sandra, who listened with the understanding of someone who spent years alone in a small sail boat on a very large and unforgiving ocean.

After lovely days at Buffalo Pound, we awoke one morning and both of us had the feeling that it was time to move on. We had no particular schedule, but this was a phenomenon that Sandra had told me about from her sailing days. You just wake up one day and decide it's definitely time to ramble along, either out to sea or down the asphalt. It didn't take us long to ready Regina Victoria and we were soon off and out of the park. We rejoined the Tran-Canadian Highway just south of Buffalo Pound and continued westward towards Calgary. We debated long and hard over whether or not we actually wanted to be in Calgary for the famous Stampede, one of the world's premier rodeos and all-around Western event.

In the end, we decided it was simply going to be too much hassle with the rig and tow car, given that Calgary's population increases by some insane factor during Stampede time. It was interesting that, at the time we were passing through, there was quite a debate being waged in the local papers and on the internet as to whether the famous "Chuck Wagon Races" should be allowed to continue. Even though I count myself as a "horse person", having learned to ride in my middle forties and having served as Executive Vice President of the St. Louis National Charity Horse Show, I had never before heard of this type of equestrian event. Apparently the races are hell-for-leather driving contests involving multi-horse teams hooked to "chuck wagons", circling a closed circuit.

The probability of mayhem and injury to both horses and people is quite high. In fact, there had been fatalities to horses in recent years and a number of fairly vocal citizens wanted the races stopped. As a horse lover, horse owner, and horse show organizer, I had a real sympathy with that position and almost decided to stop for the Stampede just to find out in person how the issue was resolved, but my wife's saner counsels prevailed and we pressed on through Calgary.

Driving out of Calgary turned out to be one of the most visually interesting experiences of our whole trip. Rolling stolidly through a plains landscape that was, at most, gently rolling, we suddenly topped a hill and there – startlingly, unexpectedly – were the Rocky Mountains. No gentle windup, no long-distance preview for hours and hours in advance. Nothing like Eastern Colorado, where the American Rockies seems to grow slowly and inexorably out of the sage and mesquite ranch land of their eastern neighbors. Here in Canada, on that highway out of Calgary, the full majesty of the Rockies revealed itself in literally the blink of an eye.

The mountains were huge, real, and appeared incredibly close. I had never seen anything involving mountains like this before, and I commented to Sandra that it was a bit like the first time I had seen Chartres Cathedral rising out of the flat plains of central France. I had been driving around a curve in a small rental Peugeot. Suddenly, as the road straightened, there was the full magnificence of Chartres, famed Rose Window and all.

Sandra and I were both moved by the rugged grandeur of these mountains and were delighted that we had chosen this pathway to and through them. From a roadstead busy with summer traffic, we suddenly saw this amazing vista of snow-capped peaks and very rugged lower slopes.

The journey to Banff, set in the very heart of the Canadian Rockies, was, as they say, well worth the price of admission. We drove through some of Canada's most drop-dead gorgeous scenery on our way to the famed old resort town. Finally we reached Banff itself and paid our entrance fee into the local provincial park. We drove slowly into town, hoping to find a pleasant private RV campground or Canadian park where we could stay. Unfortunately, we had arrived mid-afternoon of the last day of the Canada Day festive weekend.

Banff was jammed, stuffed, surfeited with Canadians and visitors from what appeared to be almost every identifiable nation on earth. Opening the driver's side window of Regina Victoria produced a cheerful cacophony of languages that would have done a UN cocktail party proud. And here we were, in the exact center of this press of humanity flowing from sidewalk to street, inching the motor coach slowly forward with the faithful Jeep trundling respectfully along two paces to the rear.

This clearly was no time to be in a hurry! Carried along by the press of traffic and the sea of humanity, we made our cautious way through town. At what appeared to be the end of the main drag, we decided to turn left (from the wrong lane) and followed a long string of huge tour buses just in front of us. The road led us up a hill and deposited us at the very entrance to the famous Banff Hotel, a Victorian railroad hotel from the Age of Opulence. I was a bit unnerved at this point, because I wasn't at all sure that I could turn our nearly 60 feet in the tight circle in front of the hotel without having to buy them a very nice new decorative fountain to replace the one that had just loomed suddenly in front of me.

With succinct directions from Sandra peering out her side of the coach, we delicately maneuvered around the traffic circle and headed back into the urban fray. Just down the hill from the hotel we encountered our first Rocky Mountain wildlife – a young elk serenely munching grass at the roadside, oblivious to the hordes of tourists who suddenly jumped from their tour buses to have a go at him with their Nikons. This had a slightly surreal feel and reminded me of a year before, in Denmark, when so many Japanese tourists were trying to photograph the iconic Little Mermaid that they began pushing each other into the water of Copenhagen Harbor

We proceeded back through town and onto the highway to Lake Louise, where we knew from our guide books that a large campground existed. We decided to stay there for a number of days, reveling in the beauty of the scenery surrounding us. We like mountains nearly as much as we like coastal areas so we were in a kind of scenery paradise. After a bit of research on our laptop, we found a recovery group meeting on Sunday night, this time at the Banff general hospital. Our fellow sojourners were most hospitable and shared local news and weather info for the days ahead.

Always on the lookout for good (or at least unusual) eateries, we queried our new friends and were directed to the Post Hotel in Lake Louise, actually quite near our campsite. The next night we treated ourselves to a gastronomically delightful dinner at the Post, in their very elegant dining room. We were greeted by a dignified maitre d' and fussed over by a stellar waiter who took his calling seriously in the tradition of many European waiters Sandra and I had encountered. Our "gentleman of the white napkin" even found a special candle for our table when Sandra told him that we were on our honeymoon. With our waiter's prompting, we decided to sample the local wild game dishes, opting for the bison and caribou roasts, both done up in excellent sauces. These were gourmet cuts of meat at their best, and I began to understand how caribou, in particular, had become such an important (and delectable) part of the Far North diet. Camping at Lake Louise was very special – spiritual in fact – because everywhere we looked from our campsite we could see mountains, glaciers, and sparkling lakes. Each morning we would have our coffee at our picnic table while enjoying incredible alpine scenery.

After working on our several writing projects, we would tour the large campground with Smokey leading the way, his little button nose close to the ground as he followed the scent of small furry mammals. The campground was also convenient to the little town of Lake Louise, where we could buy the obligatory postcards, stamps, groceries, and even some warmer clothing for me. It turns out that I had brought far too many preppy short-sleeved sport shirts when what I needed were sweatshirts, long sleeved shirts, and even a heavier jacket. I found everything I needed in several very well stocked clothing stores right on the main plaza. There was also nearby a little grocery store (narrow aisles, tall shelves) that had some very high quality fresh produce, which made Sandra happy indeed, as she appears to have an inexhaustible supply of vegetable recipes to draw from.

What was interesting was finding fresh produce in an area that was so remote from farmland, but the Canadian transportation system gets the job done! We also took several opportunities to visit the famed Lake Louise itself and the Victoria glacier which, even in the height of summer, hangs towering just above the frigid waters of the lake. At Lake Louise, the famous old hotel and its grounds are manicured and the lake itself is accessible by paved walkways with many interpretive signs scattered around the walking trail. The view of the Victoria Glacier is far more magnificent in real life than in any photo one might have seen previously. It is simply one of those jaw-dropping experiences that only occurs occasionally in a lifetime. A sense of merciless, ageless cold is pervasive. Despite the warm July sunshine, we could very clearly senses the presence of the deep, bitingly cold lake and the massive glacier poised just above it that feeds a continuous supply of icy runoff. The lake water is filled with the "rock flow" that we were to see here for the first time in our journey. This is the fine powder that results from the massive face of the glacier grinding rock to a very fine flour. Lake Louise doesn't thaw until well into May and then begins the refreezing cycle in September, just about the time the heat is starting to ease up a trifle back home in the Midwest. A sudden awareness of just how long and hard the winter is here at Lake Louise made us all the more appreciative of the long, golden days of mid-summer. We felt very fortunate to be seeing the lake and the glacier under such good viewing conditions.

We also made an evening journey to view neighboring Lake Moraine, just a few kilometers from Lake Louise. Personally, I rather enjoyed Lake Moraine more than I did Lake Louise, if only because there were far fewer tourists. The road to Moraine, though paved, is undulating with sharp changes in altitude – not easy to drive and worse if you suffer from any degree of vertigo (a malady to which both Sandra and I seem immune). The vistas of the lake are grand, and the challenging road to it provides mountain scenery "snapshots" that are the stuff of any landscape photographer's dreams. The lake itself is not large (neither is Lake Louise, for that matter), but the ten peaks (all named by the First Nations peoples who lived here) that surround it combine to create a Hollywood-perfect Alpine set, just right for Nelson Eddy as the dashing Canadian Mountie when he serenades Jeanette MacDonald. (Okay, I said I was a Senior.)

An added bonus to visiting Moraine is that, if you climb a marginally maintained trail at one end of the lake, you can get to the top of a rock outcropping that presents exactly the view portrayed on Canada's $20 bill. I climbed, puffed, rested, took out a twenty, and lo and behold! it was the same scene exactly. More than that, the view was one of the loveliest I have ever seen, certainly one of the grandest, and largely still untamed except for the small lodge/restaurant and parking lot off to the side and well out of the viewing line. This was wonderful scenery, made even lovelier by the evening sun glancing off the tall, snow-capped peaks and sending gorgeous reflections into the still waters of the lake below. One thing that I began to really appreciate here in Canada was how much more daylight we were getting as we travelled north. High summer meant that we could enjoy lakes and mountains at 10:00 in the evening and still have enough light to navigate back to our RV tucked into its snug little campsite.

There is about this part of the Canadian wilderness a ruggedness that bespeaks recent mountain building. I had brought along my (long out-of-date) college Geology 101 text, well thumbed. I discovered the obvious – that these Canadian Rockies were relative newcomers and most interesting in their geological complexity. My wife's B&B lay in the heart of Arkansas' Ozark Mountains, and the contrast between those very, very old mountains and the young Canadian Rockies is sharp indeed.

The Boston Mountains (of which the Ozarks are part) are ancient and worn. Shaped by wind and water incredible eons ago, they are the roots of once much bigger and grander mountains. The rolling, weathered appearance of the Ozarks suggests to me that they have been here so long that they witnessed the birth of most of today's great mountain ranges around the world. They appear nearly timeless, relaxed, gentle even, with space for trees, the occasional grazing horse or cow, and even a bit of room here and there for those upstart humans. The Canadian Rockies, in contrast, are young, assertive, upthrust - pugnacious in the intensity of their jagged peaks and tumbling, sheer slopes. They are stark mountains –nothing gentle or rolling in these latitudes! These are mountains inhabited by survivors – Big Horn sheep, and the charming and elusive mountain goats, creatures evolved to tackle tough slopes and mighty crags.

On a warm, sunny afternoon, we decided to treat ourselves to a good lunch and a ride on the funicular that climbs the mountains overlooking Lake Louise. Enjoying a delicious sandwich at the lodge restaurant near the foot of the mountain, we decided to see what would happen with the ubiquitous big black ravens if we left some edible bits and scraps on our plates. Other diners had told us that the birds would quickly appear. Sure enough, as soon as we backed away, several of the ravens descended, to size up the best pieces.

We were charmed to see the ravens actually take pieces off our plates (we had retreated a short distance to take photos of this good-natured thievery). The ravens were magnificent birds and we spent time admiring them and trying to coax them just a bit closer for photos. When they realized that no more treats would be forthcoming, they flew off with a final, mildly irritated squawk and we decided to hike over to the chair lift area. We took an open chair (no enclosed gondolas for Sandra) up to the highest point that we could attain.

This became another "I can do this" moment for me. I am not keen on heights, and the idea of the big gondola (all nicely enclosed) was very appealing to me. But Sandra encouraged me to try the chair lift and I was surprised that I took to it quite comfortably once my initial tinge of terror subsided. From up in that lift chair, the Canadian Rockies were spread out around us. The view was one of the grandest I had ever witnessed and we spent a very pleasant hour at the top, drinking hot chocolate from the little concession stand and taking photos in all directions. The view of Lake Louise in the distance, surrounded by those incredibly rugged mountains was one I suspect I will never forget until I die. I can still recall it in exquisite detail and it was one of the best panoramas I have seen in a moderately long lifetime.

Knowing that we still had many klicks to go before reaching Alaska, we decided to pull up stakes at Lake Louise and head north on the Ice Fields Parkway, where travelers can actually get off the roadway and take a walking tour of an active glacier. The drive through the Rockies at this point is just a geological miracle. As we moved northwards and came closer to Jasper, the land began to change. The Rockies give way to lower, less dramatic mountains, and the landscape becomes a good deal drier.

Following the road out of Jasper, we came to a very nice private RV campground, and decided to spend the night catching up on our emails (they had wifi!) and cleaning up the RV's interior because we knew that now we would be back to more open road driving again. In the morning we took the highway east from Jasper and headed towards Dawson Creek, the legendary beginning point of the Al-Can highway. Not a large town, and not especially alluring, Dawson Creek encouraged a stop only for the obligatory snapshot photo of the Mile One marker post denoting the start of the Al-Can highway. We did, however, "diesel up" as we knew we were entering stretches of highway that had few towns along the way and even fewer diesel stations. Looking at our growing collection of maps, we realized that we were now entering a phase of our journey that could safely be called "Into the Wilds".

CHAPTER 6

Wilder Roads

As we headed first towards Fort St. John, we found that the Al-Can quickly became a good deal drier (alternating with being a lot muddier after rains) and that traffic was more sparse than we had anticipated. Many reference works on the subject of driving the Al-Can suggested that we would see an army of RVs, trailers, cars and pickups with boats in tow, and even the occasional elderly VW camper painted in daring colors. Instead of all these fellow sojourners, we found ourselves practically alone most of the time. I really don't know why this was so – maybe a bad economy, a rainy summer, or high fuel prices but whatever the reason we never found ourselves stuck behind the predicted long lines of lumbering vacation vehicles. In fact, as we headed northwest, we began to feel a (welcome) sense of greater isolation. Towns became smaller and less frequent as we wandered through this more northerly part of British Columbia. Again, I was struck by how very few Canadians live in the northern part of any of the provinces.

One of our favorite places along this stretch of Canada 97 was Liard Hot Springs. This delightful spot is about half way between Fort Nelson and Watson Lake and possesses a small but attractive provincial park. Unfortunately, by the time we arrived late in the afternoon, the park appeared to be full. There was only one remaining big-rig site still open, and the chap in front of us (in an even bigger motorhome) would get it if it could actually be determined to be available. The lady at the check-in kiosk proceeded to have a very loud, heated walky- talky conversation with someone in the depths of the park who was supposed to be checking availability. It transpired that there was, indeed, one site remaining, and Mr. Huge Rig in front roared off at once to get it.

This left us climbing back into our RV, to ponder how, exactly, we were going to get it turned around behind the entrance office. Well, I hadn't had a good driving challenge for some days, and it appeared that the only way out was to drive forwards, into the tight parking area for day-users located just behind the check-in station. I proceeded slowly and with some trepidation into that little lot and then, by bouncing both the RV and the tow Jeep off a few curbs, managed to extricate us and head back out of the park. No space for the night…but luck was with us!

At the end of the 1/4 mile road out of the park, we spotted a truck pullout (a very *big* truck pullout) that we had missed before when trying to find the well-concealed park entrance. This was a truly primo version of a truck pullout, with vault toilets, no less! We made a beeline for the far side and found an excellent space where we would have room to extend our sliders and even run the generator. Since several trucks were already in place as our neighbors, Sandra and I made sure that it was okay with them for us to run the genset. They were all friendly and one knight of the highway went so far as to ask us if it was OK if he ran his truck's big diesel, as it could get "mighty cold" in his sleeper at night. He was sure that his truck engine would prove a good deal louder than our generator, but we immediately agreed that he should do whatever it took to stay warm. Reassured that everyone in our little circled wagon train was happy, we set up camp for the afternoon, knowing night might bring a chorus of diesel basso rumblings but we would all sleep comfortably.

We decided that there was plenty of time to change into our swimming suits and head back across the road to the provincial park and find the trail to the hot springs. We walked along a lovely boardwalk through oddly luxuriant vegetation (made possible by the hot springs' micro climate) along with a variety of biting insects (the ants come with the picnic, I suppose). The springs themselves are accessed via two separate swimming areas, partly natural rock formation and partly man-made walks and surrounds. The first and more developed pool was wading depth, with a sandy bottom and interesting stone boulders set into the pool so bathers could literally sit and "take the waters" as the Victorians used to say.

The pool was divided into several distinct areas depending on temperature, with really hot water coming directly from the rock wall at the head of the pool. We opted for the more moderate temperatures in the middle and had a terrific time splashing and soaking. It was even deep enough to swim a few strokes and we both proceeded to bounce around the perimeter like a couple of teenagers freed for summer recess. Before long we began to feel the effects of the hot water and decided to get back out and walk over to the other pool to see how it was configured.

We strolled hand in hand for several hundred yards, going up and down with the rock formations until we found the other pool, this one much deeper and a constant even warm temperature. There was even a diving board at one side, but we slipped in more sedately and enjoyed another ½ hour or so of leisurely swimming and floating. At the end of this second session we were thoroughly relaxed (read, feeling like wet noodles), so we got out and simply sat in the fading sunlight, drying in the gentle breeze and chatting softly so as not to break the tranquil mood of this very special place.

The next day we departed the hot springs area and continued north on 97 to Watson Lake, a town of very high gas/diesel prices and a certain small town sameness about its few stores and motels. It did, however, possess a rather nice main street area where we could grab a decent restaurant meal. At Watson Lake we turned onto Highway 1 and headed into the Yukon, one of our major goals since first entering Canada. What excited us about Highway 1 was that it was slowly but surely taking us further and further away from "civilization, and deeper into territory that we had only dreamed of visiting when we had first thought about this honeymoon odyssey. Soon we would be entering the legendary home territory of "Sergeant Preston of the Yukon", one of my early boyhood radio adventure heroes.

Preston and his wonderful dog, King, roamed this vast land, keeping law and order. I remember that I had even prevailed upon my long-suf-fering mother to buy the cereal that sponsored the good Sergeant so that I could collect box tops and send off for my very own "secret decoder." At the end of each day's episode, Sergeant Preston would give another secret letter or number which, when decoded, would gradually reveal a message about the storyline or about an upcoming episode. Of course, I knew that the message came directly from the courageous and intrepid sergeant himself! I think that this was the only secret decoder I ever wrote away for, but that time in front of the radio in the afternoon was a very long time ago.

It's funny that this late in my life I can remember the sounds of that radio show, which often featured a great deal of howling snow noise, the barking of King as he helped the Sergeant apprehend assorted evil doers, and the frequent slamming of heavy cabin doors, representing succor from the fierce storms of this trackless wilderness.

My beloved had a special interest in the Yukon, herself. As a young international adventuress, she had fended off a seducer who had tried to bed her with the unusual tactic of showing off deep, angry scars on his back which he claimed he had gotten in a major fracas with a grizzly bear somewhere deep in the Yukon Territory. Ever since that odd encounter, Sandra has wanted to see this fabled wilderness for herself. And now we were here – just married, on our honeymoon, and more than a bit amazed that we had actually made it to this storied part of the world. But our goal was even farther north, so after hugging each other at the "Welcome to the Yukon" sign, we swung back aboard Regina Victoria and roared onward. (Roared is a relative term when applied to large diesel pushers. The decibel value is there, thanks to an exhaust pipe about the size of the Lincoln Tunnel, but forward progress is sedate, even modest).

On this next leg of our journey we stopped at our very first Good Sam park, this one in Dawson Peaks. The RV park was clean, modern, and – for once – large enough to accommodate our RV and tow car without requiring odd pretzel movements. It also had a lovely lake within a few feet of the campgrounds and Smokey jumped from the RV the moment we stopped, so eager was he to run and play along the shore of that beautiful alpine body of water. There were low mountains on the other side of the lake, which added to the majesty as the sun finally, late in the evening, sank behind them and set the lake shimmering with auburn hues. This was worth every penny spent on diesel fuel and repairs. Here was a view that insisted I keep my camera firing as the sun slowly sank.

We enjoyed this campsite enough that we remained several days, eating in the rather charming café attached to the campground office and even buying a couple of souvenir tee shirts that I still wear regularly. Sandra and I remember and joke about this campground at Dawson Peaks because, on the second morning there, she ordered the super deluxe breakfast with the extra bacon and never got the extra. But we remember most the wonderful bird life that we saw along the lake, including blue herons and a variety of Canadian ducks and bustards. We dutifully noted them in our little Audubon bird book, and realized that we were seeing species that we could never have seen elsewhere.

Feeling considerably rested and refreshed, we decamped on the third morning and headed towards our next major stopping point – Whitehorse, deep in the Yukon Territory. Whitehorse was another of those names from childhood and a place that both Sandra and I had wanted to see for a long time. We thought we would probably have to stay in a commercial campground, as provincial parks were becoming extremely scarce, due, I suspect, to the paucity of travelers in this remote area. What we were to discover later in in our journey was that most travelers simply pulled off the road alongside a river or into an old gravel pit and spent time communing with nature, free of any restrictions. However, once arrived in Whitehorse, we thought we would try the pretty little city park first as a camping place, as it had been recommended by other travelers (driving much smaller rigs, I later remembered).

The park did, indeed, have lovely camping facilities, but not for a rig our size. We discovered that with forceful clarity as soon as we drove in and saw there was no way to turn around. We tried turning left in order to make a U-turn, but that proved impossible and we were embarrassingly stuck with the tow car at such an angle that we could not remove it. Somewhat sheepishly, I explained our predicament to the young lady who was the park attendant. She immediately summoned several of her young, t-shirted, and obviously muscular male friends and they all converged on our rig. Finally, the only solution was to actually uncouple the tow car at the receiver hitch, something I had never tried before.

With lots of young muscle power it could be done, and we donkeyed the tow car loose. I got in and backed it away, while Sandra managed to get the RV turned around in a really tight space and got us heading outwards again. Then the same young men helped hook us back up and wouldn't take any payment for their troubles, which I thought was rather touching. Sadder and wiser, we headed for the commercial campground with the big sign that we had seen driving into town an hour before.

Our chosen campground in Whitehorse was a typical commercial one with big rigs packed in cheek-by-jowl. But it did have good internet (so we could sit in the sun with our laptops and catch up on our many emails), really nice hot showers, pleasant places to walk Mr. Woofmore, and a big laundry where we could wash a boatload of dirty clothes. The RV has its own little Italian-made washer/dryer which I love to use, but it requires that we be hooked to a sewer facility and have 50-amp electrical service available, as well as the 30 or so spare gallons of water that it requires for each load. And it is very slow.

We thoroughly enjoyed our time in Whitehorse as the campground was ideally located just on the edge of town and we could disconnect our Jeep and go exploring all over the Whitehorse area. We also decided that if we were even to consider tackling the (greatly feared) Dempster Highway all the way to the Arctic Ocean, we would need a new spare tire for the Jeep. A visit to the Canada Tire store resulted in a shiny new tire for the Jeep's spare tire carrier (the old spare looked at bit like a cartoon balloon tire). It was our sincere hope that the really big RV tires were in better shape than the Jeep's spare had proven to be.

We also decided that, for a variety of reasons (both aesthetic and practical), the two vehicles needed a thorough washing. I knew it was time to take action when I saw my bride writing "Just Married" in the grime on the rear window of the Grand Cherokee. Well, that, and having to change clothes every time I had to approach the RV at all closely! Getting the Jeep done was easy – regular car wash, big vacuum, some elbow grease and our tow looked presentable again. What was a bit sad was to see the damage that had been inflicted by the towing process.

The headlights had been scratched and the lower driving lights were completely gone, the victim of large stones along the Al-Can. The front of the hood was pitted from stone damage and the side louvered vents were filled with small stones and debris. But, the Jeep was still running well and had survived a grueling tow along the famous WWII highway.

Regina Victoria was a bit trickier proposition because of her sheer size. After lots of inquiries, we discovered that there was a truck wash of sorts right in the center of Whitehorse. We drove there and found a big truck repair facility and an enormous parking lot behind it. We took Smokey out for a walk around the lot and a gentleman appeared and asked if he could help us. We explained what we were after and it turned out that he actually owned the whole facility and that his truck wash operation could easily handle our RV. He invited us into the office and we spent quite some time chatting with him about our adventures thus far. He was very helpful and gave us some sound travel advice along with some very strong coffee. We love to visit with whichever locals will talk with us, and this kind gentleman proved a mine of good information. He also convinced us that the Dempster highway, while a bit "hairy", was certainly doable by a couple of graying Seniors.

As we chatted, his very willing crew blasted and scrubbed to get the road grime off our RV. Once cleaned up, our girl even seemed to run better (but then I always think clean vehicles run better). It was also a considerable boost to our spirits to see our beloved vehicles cleaned and (almost) shiny. It did occur to both of us that if we were ever to do this trip again, we would probably do it in a smaller, cheaper rig, as we had seen so many others doing. After surveying the damage to our vehicles, we understood why!

We spent a good deal of time in Whitehorse enjoying the surprisingly varied local cuisine. In fact, one of our favorite restaurants was a Chinese eatery where we dined several times and always had excellent dinners or lunches. They featured terrific egg rolls, tasty egg foo yung, and chicken dishes that were surprisingly sophisticated. We also found a couple of good Italian bistros, and a number of restaurants with fresh fish dinners. We got to sample more bison and other more exotic game dishes while making the culinary circuit. One evening we dined on the main drag where we had seafood chowder followed by Caribou Stroganoff. That was a meal to remember, especially as it came with delicious homemade rolls and loads of fresh butter and honey.

But the heart of our Whitehorse stay was "The Eagles". We had gone to a Sunday night recovery meeting and had hung around afterwards, as we always did, chatting with our new friends. Several of them mentioned "The Eagles" and our antennae went up as we were constantly looking for new (to us) wildlife (birds especially) along our route. It turned out that just a few hundred feet closer to town than our ill-fated adventure at the city park, there was a small turnout along the main road into Whitehorse. We had seen the turnout on the way to the meeting and had seen some cars parked there, but had driven by too quickly to make much of it.

Our friends explained that the turnout was the home of a pair of Bald Eagles, high up in a nest where they were very publicly raising their young chicks. The whole town, it seemed, had adopted these eagles and everyone made a grand social occasion of going out to view them and the chicks and see how they were getting on. This pair of eagles had been nesting here for several years and the local community rallied to save their nesting site when their old tree had collapsed during a storm the year before. To encourage them to come back, the local power company had erected a camouflaged dark green utility pole hidden in a pine tree and had even fashioned a sturdy platform for the big birds so that they would nest there again. The trick had worked and the eagles were happily ensconced some fifty feet up on their huge open platform.

Usually one parent was on or near the nest while the other was out searching for food to feed the insatiable appetites of the two fledglings. What we loved about this story was that, everywhere you went in Whitehorse, people were talking about the eagles, charting the progress of the young chicks, and even taking bets on when they would first fly from the nest. Anytime, day or night, that we drove past the nesting site we would see people walking by, stopping their cars for a look, whipping out binoculars or cameras, or riding their bicycles around the area. We even saw a wiry professional photographer from New York taking photos with about four cameras slung about her neck and one of the biggest telephoto lenses I had ever seen. That evening she was in luck, because both parents arrived separately with fish just scooped from the nearby Yukon River.

By this time in the summer the chicks were nearly the size of their parents, so feeding them required *a lot* of fishing! Sandra and I took many photos ourselves and one of her best was taken later that same evening, towards full dusk, as both eaglettes stood in full view in the nest.One was at the very edge, flapping its wings enthusiastically and uttering loud cries. That young bird was going to fly in the very near future, possibly even the next day. Unfortunately we were unable to stay in Whitehorse long enough to find out if both soloed as predicted.

The image of the eagles and of the city that went out of its way to support them is a cameo that has remained fresh in our minds as we travel onwards. If people ask me "what is Whitehorse like" or "Is it worth going that far to see", the answer is, it's a city of warm-hearted people, and yes, drive a bit and visit it. Who knows, the eagles will probably be raising another brood if you arrive in the summer!

After cleaning the vehicles, eating exceptionally well, catching up on e-mails and world affairs, and feeling clean and rested, we set off to stock up on supplies for our continuing push northwards towards the

Land of the Midnight Sun. The Walmart in Whitehorse deserves mention in its own right. Small as such stores typically went, it had one of the biggest parking lots we had thus far encountered. And the RV community had adopted that store and its parking lot. Rarely had we seen so many camping rigs on one lot at the same time, some even with "For Sale" signs prominently displayed. A number of the bigger rigs had their sail-size awnings extended and little BBQ grills set up under the acres of canvas. One older gentleman had his big ladder out and was industriously cleaning the topsides of his 40 footer.

I am pretty sure that the local RV campgrounds can't have been happy about Bentonville's largesse, but since they were mostly full themselves, they appear to have adopted a laissez-faire attitude about the free camping facility. We marveled at this scene before buying the necessary supplies inside. Walking across the lot to a Starbucks (yay! strong black Café Americano once again), I ordered the biggest cup they had of that wonderful elixir and then we were ready to hook everything back up and head north.

Our first stop was at Talkeena Hot Springs, a location highly recommended in several books. This was not to prove the fun experience that Liard Hot Springs had been. For starters, the spring is located in a private campground and the source of the hot water itself is kept hidden from view in a brick shed. You actually access the restorative waters via a standard swimming pool divided by roping into hotter and cooler sections. This didn't seem very appealing, but since we were already there, we decided to check into the campground for a few days. I gulped at the high cost of a night's camping, but dutifully got out my credit card and signed up for a couple of evenings. That done, I was given a map of the campground and told how to find our site. The directions were, actually, quite awful. As a result, we found ourselves on a narrow, uphill road with almost no maneuvering room. Sandra was driving and did her best to keep within the narrow roadway that appeared to be leading nowhere. The way became so narrow and twisting that we had to literally drag the Jeep around as its tires were at their maximum angle of sideways travel.

Suddenly, we heard a loud pop. Thinking that we had just hit a tree branch, we quickly stopped in order to have a better look. What we saw was disheartening and left me a bit angry with the camp ownership. The faithful Jeep had blown its left rear tire – how we didn't know, but probably by contact with a large, sharp tree root in our path. The biggest problem was getting the Jeep to some level spot where I could begin to figure out what to do. That meant, again, dragging the car around by brute force, this time with a very flat bit of rubber at the back. Sandra managed it skillfully and we finally descended to a flat spot near the roadway where we had just come in. I "got out and got under" and was relieved that it was only a flat tire and not damage to a structural member. That said, tire changing is not one of my strong suits. But, here again, a little voice in my head kept saying, "Okay, I can do this."

Providentially, while in White Horse we had bought an electric scissors jack that ran off the car's battery. I had never had it out of the box, but now was certainly the time to press it into service. Unwrapping it, I read the instructions and decided that this might actually work. My first attempt did not go well. I had the jack under the wrong part of the Jeep and nearly punched it through the floorboard! My second effort was much better, as I found the actual jack pads built into the car's frame. With my fingers crossed, I hit the remote control button and, slowly and majestically, Julietta Jeep began to rise. Now came a moment of truth – silver haired Senior vs. 12 year old lug nuts!

I applied my brand new, shiny tire iron and after some serious grunting, got the first nut to begin turning. Oh happiness, oh joy! The others were just as tough, but after the first one I knew I would prevail. Then came the messy job of grasping the tire in a Full Nelson and wrestling it off the axle. That done, I had to – carefully – open the trunk (should have done that first) and remove my new spare with the paste-on labels still in place. I hoisted it out, rolled it to the side, and prayed I had enough upper body strength to get it on the wheel. I did – barely - and then proceeded to re-install the lug bolts. I even tightened them in the pattern that my Dad had taught me many years before when flat tires were a good deal more common. While I was engaged in all of this auto-craft, Sandra was quietly taking pictures of me changing my first tire in nearly half a century!

Finally I reversed the jack and pulled it out, stowed the paraphernalia and followed Sandra to the site where we were originally instructed to go. Oddly, although it did not have water or sewer facilities, this expensive little bit of real estate did have 50-amp service, one of the very few times we were to find that luxury in Canada.

The shredded tire made us re-think our preparations for the Dempster Highway. This was a road we had been talking about travelling for weeks now. The Dempster stretches over 400 miles from just east of Dawson City, Yukon, to Inuvik at the Beaufort Sea in the Northwest Territories. From what we had read, the Dempster is mostly gravel and dirt, with whole sections of the road often closed. The Dempster also sports two river-crossing ferries and one gas station/hotel squarely in the middle. This road has a reputation for eating tires because it is often paved with flint-hard pointy bits of shale. That said, it was also reputedly one of the world's most scenic and less-travelled highways, and the only one in this part of Canada to reach inside the Arctic Circle. We definitely thought we ought to give this fabled pathway a shot, but we had to decide what other preparations we needed to make in order to be safe and actually enjoy the experience.

We decided that we would only take the Jeep up the Dempster. Everything we had heard and read indicated that the road was simply impassible for a big RV. So if we were to rely on the Jeep, it had to be better shod. All of the Jeep's tires had in excess of 30,000 miles on them and two had been somewhat damaged when I had failed to get the transmission properly sorted out prior to our first attempt at towing. We had simply dragged the Jeep, without realizing it, until a passing motorist had made frantic motions for us to look at the tow car. Then I discovered my error (ah hah, the key has to be in the second "on" position) and had quickly corrected the situation. Now, I was worried about those two scarred tires. Finally, we decided to drive back to Whitehorse and get more tires or neither of us would feel secure on the Dempster. Back we went to the friendly Canada Tire store again. They could not help us that afternoon, but I was to return at 7:00 the next morning and they would "work me in". Everyone, it seemed, needed lots of new tires that week!

The next morning I was back bright and early and left the Jeep to the friendly ministrations of the Canada Tire techs. I wandered over to the adjoining Wamart and had breakfast at the McDonald's there. I then decided to take my laptop over to the nearby Starbucks, ordered a coffee and settled in to catch up on emails, only to discover that this coffee house (possibly alone of all the world's Starbucks) had no WiFi connection. My charming *barrista* also wasn't at all sure where I might find WiFi in town. Somewhat coffee logged and a bit disconsolate, I wandered back to the tire store, only to discover that they had excellent internet connectivity – right there in the customer waiting room! I quickly set up my laptop and got to work, so by the time the tires were on, I had accomplished quite a lot.

With the new tire paperwork done, I gave the manager my Visa card in order to pay my bill. Oops – card rejected. OK, let's try the Master Card. Hmmm, same result. By now the manager is looking at me oddly and probably thinking that he is going to have to un-mount the new tires, maybe even call in the Mounties to cart me away for Tire Theft (Grand).

I suspected that the issue was travel-related, so I got on the phone to the credit card company and tried to explain the situation.

After the usual security checks (the Pentagon isn't this hard to get into) I outlined my problem. Yes, I was still travelling. Yes, I was still in Canada. No, I wasn't sure how long I would be here, etc., etc. I thought the matter resolved and gave the manager my cards again. Same results! Back to the phone, same annoying questions, only this time I was also lectured that all of this rigamarole was for my own protection! Finally they agreed that I was who I said I was and that I was indeed in Canada... please, could I spend a large of amount of money on my new tires? They finally – albeit reluctantly – agreed, and I was able to complete my purchase and drive off on my shiny new Dunlops.

Back in Talkeena we decided to take one last advantage of the pool, at least, and had a nice swim. Talkeena was one of the few travel disappointments along our way. Overpriced, with difficult internal roads, RVers even ended up paying extra to use the dump station. On the plus side, the blown tire had made us think about our upcoming travels and had led to better (we hoped) preparation.

CHAPTER 7

The Dempster

From Talkeena, we motored north and west to Dawson City, a town that – over time – became one of our favorite travel memories. We arrived in Dawson City late in the day, tired from hours on the road and eager to find an RV park as we planned to stay awhile. By the time we found a suitable park we were both feeling a bit grumpy and I suddenly realized that today was Sandra's recovery "birthday", her sobriety date. This is a day that anyone in recovery remembers with vivid clarity and to which we all attach real importance. I rather lamely (and late) wished her a happy birthday and she unloaded on me, reminding me that she had presented me with a lovely oil painting of herself (done without any clothes blocking the view!) for *my* recovery birthday and that I had not so much as mentioned hers until this late in the day. This was a bad mistake on my part and one that I wasn't at all sure how to remedy. Sandra was in full cry at this point and recounted to me exactly how much that painting had cost. That was highly unusual for her who regarded mention of money as somehow *nouveau riche* and therefore highly suspect. It dawned on me that I might be better off remaining quiet, hoping that this really tense moment would pass in the need to focus on getting settled for the night. At the same time, I also became aware that I needed to pay more attention to my wife's emotional needs.

After we had found our park and settled in we talked about what had just transpired. Birthdays and holidays in general are not terribly important to Sandra. In her world view, most of them were created by and for the benefit of commercial interests. Her family had made little of Christmas or birthdays, so Sandra was not a woman who began preparing for "The "Holidays" months in advance. But her recovery program had saved her life and her sobriety birthday was one day on the calendar that she took very seriously.

Fortunately, we looked online for a 12-Step meeting in Dawson City and found there was one near us and starting in a few minutes. We jumped in the jeep and headed for where the meeting was supposed to be. We got lost several times (which I found amusing after we had driven thousands of long miles without really losing our way to this point), but eventually discovered a group of people standing in front of a building. Ah hah, we thought, that looks just like a typical Step meeting. We made inquiry and discovered that this was, indeed, exactly that, but the person with the key to open the meeting site was nowhere to be found. After further waiting and chatting, Sandra finally suggested that we all go back to our RV, which was parked in a very nice campground just two blocks away. Everyone agreed, so we trooped back to our coach and had a delightful 12-step meeting in our living room, big coffee pot working overtime, with all the chairs swiveled to face each other.

The Dawson City folks in recovery are now numbered among some of our dearest friends in our program and we always remember them with great fondness. These were truly 12-Step friends and we have remained in contact with them ever since. One friend is a musician, an excellent guitarist and harmonica man whose CD we still love to play while on the open road. Another was a public health worker. Several members of the local group were fairly new to recovery and we tried to share how we had made it thus far in our own recoveries. And of course, there was the local "character in recovery", a classic northerner, working as a trapper, fisherman, gold prospector and even sometimes, ironically, as a bartender. (I have always believed that recovering drunks make great bartenders - they never drink up the profits).

Having a meeting in our RV with people we had just met turned out to be a very moving experience. We didn't have all the literature that a meeting would normally follow, but we did quite well by memory (some of us had quite a long time in the fellowship). After this wonderful impromptu meeting, our new friends invited us to join them for dinner at the local Chinese eatery. We all sat around a long table and enjoyed a great meal and some very wonderful personal stories. This was the Yukon up close and really personal! We all got to share our various stories of both recovery and our travels, lingering long over excellent green tea. We also learned a lot about the history of the little town and about the climate (as low as 60 degrees below zero in mid-winter). We were told that travelling actually gets easier in the winter, as the frozen roads are less hazardous than the same roads in summer when permafrost heaving makes them hard on springs and spines.

At this initial dinner we also learned that the Dempster highway is only intermittently open and our idea of several spare tires was one of our better ones! Our new friends pointed out all the touristy things to see and do in town; we absolutely had to get out and see Gold Mining Dredge #4, restored to all its huge splendor and with a good guided tour to illustrate the fine points of gold dredging. It was interesting to learn about this dredge, as we had seen whacking great piles of tailings all over the outskirts of Dawson when we had driven in earlier. It was comforting to know that they were made by a dredge and not by a huge and demented gopher! Dredge #4 resembles nothing so much as an old time cartoon steam shovel, but one enlarged on an exponential scale.. The machine is gargantuan, with an interior the size of a modest cathedral.

Surprisingly, it can be operated by a very small crew despite its overwhelming bulk. I was fascinated by how mechanized gold extraction became after the great initial 1898 rush of pick-and-shovel miners. These early gold miners were a rugged breed, desperate to stake a claim and become rich. So desperate, in fact, that the Mounties finally insisted that each and every miner coming into the gold fields around Dawson carry a long list of requisite survival gear and supplies, especially as there were mountains to be crossed first and I suspect the Mounties had become tired of Alpine rescues!

We had assumed that the huge piles of tailing to be found throughout the area were the result of some kind of mining operation, but I hadn't realized that it was the result of gold mining practiced on a scale I had never dreamed of. Interestingly, gold mining on a more intimate scale is still widely practiced in Dawson and amounts to a very healthy cottage industry. One can still stake a claim in the Dawson area, and many of the locals have done just that, working their claims in between other jobs.

The town of Dawson City is a charming example of a gold rush (ca. 1898) town in its heyday. Unlike many touristy places, however, many buildings here actually do date from the very early 20th century and are, in fact," the real deal". During the past century, the few remaining citizens who still lived in Dawson City petitioned Parks Canada to restore the town as a full-fledged tourist attraction. I don't know the full story of why Parks Canada agreed to do this, but my hat is off to them for their foresight and sense of history. The town as it appears today is much as it would have looked a century ago. My favorite feature is the highly practical wooden sidewalks that run everywhere in town in front of all the businesses. These are the necessary walkways of a region that suffers monumental frost heaving each and every year.

Dawson City is built on permafrost and the result of seasonal changes is clearly evident both in the poor state of the streets and the structural "oddness" of the older buildings. One such edifice has been left standing and unrepaired as a visual lesson on what permafrost can do over time. The result is not pretty! This was a small two-story structure that suffered from a massive confusion of angles and planes, leaning drunkenly at odd angles in disquietingly unexpected directions!

Crossing the Yukon river is a very old but serviceable ferry that can take even large vehicles across to the other side if one wants to begin the tortuous road to Alaska. A charmingly restored old paddle wheeler dominates the attractive berm at the side of the main street on the Yukon River. This street, which is probably the best paved in the entire area (if not the entire territory), always elicits the same story from the locals. It seems that a provincial legislator got the idea (probably very late at night in a bar) that Dawson's main streets should be attractively paved instead of just being the traditional gravel used throughout the Yukon (for good reason, considering the permafrost). This legislator got approval for a special road paving material that supposedly could handle the permafrost.

The new surface product was imported from France and had to be shipped in specially designed containers to keep it warm in transit. It was supposed to be a lovely, transparent material that would complement the beauty of the Yukon River. Unfortunately, it ended up costing about $1 million per foot and as soon as cars and trucks drove on it they turned it a shade of grey very close, in fact, to that of gravel. The material ended up paving part of Main Street at the river's edge and the government gave it up as a really bad investment.

Having explored Dawson City thoroughly, we were now eager to get on with the adventure of the Dempster Highway. Alas, the fabled highway was closed. At the RV park where we were staying we would check the bulletin board at the office to see if there were any updated faxes as to whether (or when) the Dempster would re-open.. A summer of heavy rains had swollen the local rivers and streams that paralleled or, in some cases actually ran across the Dempster, resulting in an unending series of washouts, mudslides, and rock falls. This made for very dangerous going, and the Canadian transport people were very careful about how and when they opened the highway. If I didn't like what I saw at the RV park office, I would walk down to the big tourist center near the river, to see if they had news I would like better. Invariably, the results were the same – no traffic, or traffic permitted only on certain sections.

We thought that it would surely be open by the next Sunday, and got the Jeep all ready, with water, doggie bed, Smokey's food, extra clothes, emergency rations, etc. etc. We had removed our multispeed, shiny (and rarely used) bikes from the Jeep and had prepared small duffle bags. We even put in big quilts and pillows in case we ended up having to sleep in the Jeep. Older travelers can be very prepared! But the summer rains seemed to be conspiring against us.

Sunday morning was leaden and dripping, and the Dempster was still closed. Since we were in no rush, and really wanted to make the journey, the day was spent in relaxed but watchful mode. We had long since figured out that the highway could reopen as suddenly as it closed.

Surprisingly, the next day found us staring at the fax we had waited to see for many days – the Dempster was open! What miracles of road building the Canadian highway department had achieved overnight was mind boggling, but we were ready. The campground owners agreed to keep an eye on our big baby, so we grabbed a quick cup of coffee and a stale donut and got moving. Smokey was particularly happy to be on the road again. He loves new sights and smells and had been in the campground long enough to have marked every bush within his short reach several times over. He needed new territory to explore and lots more bushes to mark.

We drove the few miles to the beginning of the Dempster and decided to fill up the Jeep there. The gas prices were, of course, outrageous, but that came as no surprise, considering this was the only gas station before actually starting up the highway. The next gas would be over 200 miles away, so I also filled up an auxiliary can I had brought along, just in case. We were, I thought, about as ready as we could be for this new road warrior's adventure!

Fully fueled, and with better donuts in hand, we began the journey that we had talked about for over a month. Sandra and I were beginning an unforgettable 800-plus-mile odyssey to Inuvik at the Beaufort Sea and back. The scenery all over the Yukon is beautiful – the scenery along the Dempster is beyond beautiful. It is awe inspiring in its total isolation, in the barren splendor of the mountains, in the variety of tundra and meadows, black spruce forests, taiga, wildflowers in profusion, and animals and birds that we had not seen before and probably would not see again.

After a few introductory miles of pavement, the road reverts to its natural state – dirt and gravel for the most part. It is not a road that you can tear along quickly and it is a very tiring road to drive. I have the greatest respect for the professional truckers who drive it day in and day out to deliver supplies to the small, widely scattered First Nations communities that line the Dempster, many of them miles off the highway down much worse dirt tracks. The trucks are critical suppliers of the sheer necessities of life, including fuel, medicines, and critical tools.

Having talked with several of the highway pros at unofficial rest areas along the highway (read: simple pullovers), I learned that their job actually gets easier in some ways in the dead of winter, as the snows fill in the deep ruts and washouts, making for a smoother roadbed. The winter's freezing temperatures also turn the two major rivers that bisect the Dempster, the Peel and the McKenzie, into navigable roadways.

The Dempster offers unrivalled views over huge tracts of unspoiled, untamed wilderness on a scale that is simply staggering. In the Yukon, where the Dempster begins, live only about 33,000 hardy souls, most of them gathered closely around Whitehorse, the Yukon's biggest town (23,000 people). There are reportedly far more bears than people in this huge territory. And the Northwest Territories, where the Dempster ends, counts only slightly more humans in an even larger geographical area. Needless to say, human presence is not especially intrusive along this remote highway.

To be driving this remote road, the most northerly in Canada, constituted a major "I can do this" moment. In none of my previous lives would I have had the courage to set off on a driving trip in a place so remote and so potentially hazardous. Only a sat-phone can reach help here and we didn't own one. If we broke down, we would have to wait for help and fellow travelers were few, indeed. At our age, changing a tire took significant effort. And yet, after driving the big rig for thousands of challenging miles, we both felt that the Dempster was definitely within our reach. I had discovered that I was actually enjoying these ever-changing situations. Getting " down and dirty" was no longer something reserved for gardening afternoons in St. Louis – it was a part of the fabric of remote RVing and I discovered that I was loving it!

As our first day on the Dempster wore on, we changed drivers frequently. The strain of navigating a heaving, twisting road and the fear of hitting one of the sharp pieces of shale was fatiguing, so we took one-hour shifts behind the big Jeep wheel. We also took time to pull off and rest while finding photo ops at every stop. In fact, we were driving so slowly that I often shot good, clear pictures out the side window. By the end of that long first day we were more than ready to find the Eagle Plains motel/fueling station/ restaurant/repair shop, the legendary half-way point on this remarkable highway.

Eagle Plains is the only service stop along the more than 400 miles of the Dempster, so it is well populated almost every day of the year. After parking the Jeep, I went inside to see if there was a room available (we were ready to sleep in the lobby if necessary). Once through the airlock door (a necessity in the High Arctic), I found the little reception desk and rang the old-fashioned desk bell to summon help. A lady appeared who looked harassed and in a pronounced German accent asked me "Vat is it you vant, please?" I replied that we were looking for dinner and a room for the night for two adults. She asked if we had any pets with us and I replied that our travelling companion was a middle-aged Chihuahua.

Looking me straight in the eye, she asked me, "Does he shed?"

"No", I replied. "Would you like him to?"

She laughed and apparently decided we could be allowed to stay, so she assigned us a room in the "pets" section, the only one she had left. We were grateful, and after filling out the requisite forms, got the key for our night's habitation. I checked out the room before going back out to retrieve Sandra and the Smokester. It was a very typical older style motel room – queen bed, faded spread, Formica covered desk with a small TV, stark white bathroom (but clean and serviceable). After a day on the road, it looked absolutely homey. Once settled in, we went in search of dinner.

We found the large bar/lounge/dining room and took a seat near the big (and thankfully working) fireplace along an inner wall. Our waitress soon appeared. She was, in fact, the desk clerk who had recently checked us in. She was also apparently the maître d', the barmaid, and possibly the cook, for all I could tell. We asked for a menu, but her answer was

"Ham, beef or turkey". Okay, we thought, Sandra ordered turkey, so I followed suit, not at all sure what we would get. What came for each of us was a large and very tasty turkey breast sandwich, complete with a side of excellent potato salad. We had coffee with the meal (deciding that probably nothing liquid could keep us awake for long this night). We even had homemade pie for dessert, a rare treat while travelling.

After dinner, it was time to look around the Eagle Plains complex. I spotted the fueling area nearby and took the Jeep over to fill it up for tomorrow's next half of the journey. Then we walked Smokey all around the perimeter of the compound, admiring the view in all directions. Eagle Plains sits high and offers a commanding view of the surrounding valley, with low mountains in the far distance. This is, indeed, a remote place. The gentleman who ran the gas station told me that during the worst of the winter months, packs of wolves regularly traversed the parking lot chasing the local caribou. Everyone kept their pets indoors then as the wolves regarded the odd poodle as a tasty *hors d'oeuvres*, to be gobbled up *en passant*. I explained this to Smokey who let me know he was not at all afraid of any smelly, ill-mannered wolf, thank you very much! He seemed to take especial joy in marking every spot he could reach, just to let those pesky wolves know that a Real Dog had been there.

The next morning, we were up early and ready for the second half of the Dempster. After a substantial breakfast we loaded up and headed northbound again. A highlight of the morning was to arrive at the fabled, if imaginary, Arctic Circle, located at 66 degrees, 33 minutes north latitude. This is the boundary for the Midnight Sun. North of this location, the sun never sets on the longest day of the year. The Canadian government has erected an attractive and informative display at a rest stop marking the Circle's location. We decided to break out our coffee thermos and have a celebratory cup along with one of our remaining donuts to commemorate our arrival at a place we had both dreamed of seeing once in our lives.

While we were sitting at the picnic table, several other tourists appeared. This was a surprise all by itself, as we had seen so few other travelers on the Dempster, but these tourists were returning from farther north. A bit later, a young man from Austria stopped , heading in the same direction as us. He had rented a small RV and was exploring the Canadian wilderness for the summer. We had a very nice chat with him (his English was excellent) and all promised to keep an eye out for each other if we should see the other one stuck somewhere along the roadside. (We did see him again, indeed, by the side of the road, but this time in the company of a charming young lady driving an elderly, mud bedecked VW camper. Clearly he was in no need of succor at that point.)

Later in the day, we had to rub our eyes as we encountered an exact duplicate of a strange vehicle we had first seen in the Dawson City campground where we were staying. A German couple with two small children had brought over a huge truck-like RV that sported truly gigantic tires. This Teutonic motorhome was a steel monster, with ladders everywhere and a living area that began a good 5 feet off the tarmac. The German High Command, Afrika Korps, would have been proud to have had this rig as their mobile command center. One expected to see Erwin Rommel himself climb down the big steel ladder from the command deck, brandishing his swagger stick. I was struck by the fact that shipping these huge vehicles over from Europe must have made for a very expensive holiday.

Slowly following the Dempster north, we left the Yukon and entered the fabled Northwest Territories, a landmass so vast and so underpopulated by humans as to beggar description. This was very clearly the home of the First Nations, the original transients who crossed the Bering Straits tens of thousands of years ago as the first human migrations to North

America began. More signs began to appear with tribal names, pointing down dirt back roads to small fishing and hunting settlements hidden from sight. Land usage, hunting and fishing are controlled by the various tribal councils and subsistence hunting and fishing was a way of life here.

We saw numerous roadside billboards encouraging hunters to shoot Caribou in vital spots and to take only as many as were needed. If we pulled off the Dempster (very carefully) and stopped for a sip of our coffee or a snack, we could sometimes smell the smoke of wood fires wafting from afar in the distance over which fish and game were being smoked and cured, ready to help sustain First Nations families through the harsh northern winter.

Sandra and I were now in an area that we had both hoped to see for many years, the north of my childhood hero, Sergeant Preston. Here the First Nations people hold sway. They understand this land and the complex interrelationship of man, bird, and animal. No one here is a trophy hunter. To kill game is to feed the family through the long dark winter. Any surplus is traded for necessary supplies, a process involving long journeys in battered cars and trucks to Inuvik or to one of several tiny settlements along, but always hidden, miles off, the Dempster.

As we motored north along the highway, the scenery began to change. The land flattened, leaving rugged mountains in the rear view mirrors. More and more the land opened to tundra, taiga, and marsh, with small creeks running randomly throughout the area, each working its way steadily toward the McKenzie River delta and the opening to the Beaufort Sea not far from the end of this, Canada's most northerly highway. By late afternoon of the second day on the Dempster, we were eager to see Inuvik, the most northerly town reachable by road in Canada and second only to Alaska's Prudhoe Bay for being closest to the North Pole.

As we approached our final destination, Inuvik, at the end of day 2, we hoped we would be able to find a pleasant and comfortable motel to break our long journey and give us some needed rest. Driving even the flattest parts of the Dempster demanded constant attention and often some serious maneuvering, so we were both tired and ready for a brief respite. Age may have played a part, but I noticed that some of the regional truckers looked pretty beat by the time they got all the way to the end of the road, so we didn't feel too badly about our own driving performance.

We did, indeed, find a cheerful hotel where we spent the night in complete comfort: twin queen beds (we only needed one!), a mini-fridge, a gloriously modern bath, and light-darkening shades to block the Midnight Sun. We noticed as we drove around Inuvik that many houses and apartments had foil over the windows, probably to allow the inhabitants some needed sleep. After walking Smokey and setting up his food and water dishes, we decided to drive around Inuvik, see the sights, then have some dinner.

The town is built largely above ground because of the severe climatic changes which occur in this land of permafrost. All of the town's utilities run in a colorful grid of pipes mounted well above ground. Red, white, green, blue, brown -even purple- these pipes carry the water, electricity, and waste to and from each building in Inuvik. Painted in their cheerful primaries, these conduits offer a much-needed bright splash of color when the arctic night descends in winter. After taking in most of the sights (Inuvik is not a big town), we decided to find a place for dinner.

Strangely, a number of shops and restaurants were closed. This appeared odd to us, as we were here in summer which we think of as the tourist season. As one shopkeeper who was open explained, however, Inuvik doesn't really have a tourist season. To begin with, there are few tourists and this was the time of the year when whole families left town for their remote fishing and hunting camps in order to lay in protein for the winter ahead. School was out and nearly every family hunted and fished as part of their annual summer activities. Smoked game and fish were still very important components of the local diet and the process of acquiring meat and fish kept traditions alive for the next generation. As we had driven around outside of Inuvik, we had seen a number of these camps, usually with a drying/smoking shed and racks hung with fish and strips of meat being readied for winter storage.

For me, one of the entertaining highlights of that evening was our dinner stop. We were tired, hungry and many restaurants had already closed, so we decided on an Italian-sounding restaurant housed in a quaint clapboard building with a nice boardwalk in front and the obligatory airlock-style front door. The eatery offered Chinese cuisine, pizza, and Italian specialties. Now that's eclectic, I thought! Also,we were the only diners in the place.

We ordered something Chinese and I remarked to Sandra that our waiter didn't look at all like a native. He was quite tall and had a pronounced, interesting accent. After we finished eating, we went up to the main till to pay. While sorting out our credit card receipt, I asked the waiter where he was from. He replied that he and his brother, along with their father (who was the chef, I think), were originally from Palestine and had come to Inuvik by way of Edmonton. And we think the U.S. is a melting pot! After dinner, we drove around a bit more to locate a filling station (to no avail), then wandered slowly back to our hotel. The sun, of course, was still up.

The Midnight Sun was simply too glorious a phenomenon to sleep through. At the stroke of twelve, Sandra and I were outside the hotel, holding hands and laughing like kids as we read a newspaper in full light and snapped tons of photos. We had both always wanted to see the Midnight Sun, and to see it together on this special trip was a joy, indeed! I personally had always thought I would see the 24-hour day from somewhere in northern Europe, probably from far northern Finland or Norway. It had simply not occurred to me over the years that I would ever be in this incredible, remote area of my home continent with my new wife, driving our own car to the end of an unpaved highway ending in an Inuit town in Canada.

The next morning we were up and off exploring after a self-serve hotel breakfast. Off the main street through town we spotted a little indoor one-building mall we had seen the night before. We decided to stop just to see what they had inside. Serendipitously, there was a pharmacy at the far end of the building, and it happened that Sandra needed a medication refill. We knew that in Canada we would have to have a Canadian doctor countersign our American prescriptions. Sandra asked the very kindly pharmacist if he could give her enough of the med to last until we got to Alaska, our next major stop. He asked if she had her script with her, but, of course, we had left it in the RV back in Dawson City. However, Sandra said she had the actual pills with her. Could he look at those and identify the medicine? He agreed to try, so we raced out to the Jeep, dug furiously through our piles of "stuff", found the pills and returned to the bemused pharmacist. He had no trouble identifying the medication and agreed to give Sandra a two-week supply to tide her over.

She asked him how he could do that when no one else seemed willing or able to do the same thing in the more southerly Canadian provinces. His reply was an interesting take on the local politics. He explained that the Yukon and the Northwest Territories basically took their cues from British Columbia. That meant wide latitude in how they conducted affairs because of the remoteness of these territories, the tiny, highly dispersed population, and the enormous difficulty of travel in these far northern regions. A 40-below-zero mid-winter night was not a time to worry about the niceties of paperwork!

We stopped next to look at the famous Igloo Church, built of concrete and closely resembling the traditional igloos…the winter abode of High Arctic families while seal hunting. The church was closed, but the architecture was impressive and seemed to blend well with the town's setting. It reminded me that the reach of Christianity was long. I suspected that in this remote region, Christianity was still probably mixed, as it was in so much of Latin America, with indigenous beliefs, especially those involving the important totem animals critical to survival in this unforgiving land.

After lunch, we visited the Inuvik post office and mailed a large batch of post cards. We wanted the special Inuvik hand-cancel stamp to give the cards some added interest. The PO people were happy to accommodate this kind of request and we got everything mailed in a few minutes. Then it was time to reluctantly head back down the Dempster, retracing our path.

What proved interesting was that it was in no sense a boring repeat of the journey up. Viewed north to south, the land looked very different, and we began to see many details of geography that we had overlooked on the way north. Additionally, we had worries about whether or not the highway would actually be open for an appreciable length of time. Plus, we were concerned over the ferry system. Crossing the two major territorial rivers could only be done by ferry and they were frequently out of service at almost a moment's notice. Swiftly flowing high waters carrying a huge load of debris could clog the ferry cables or even damage the hulls of the boats, so we had our fingers crossed that we would somehow have good timing and good luck.

We were in no hurry, so we took time to stop and listen to the silence, watch falcons and eagles soaring above us, photograph the dramatic landscape, and talk quietly with each other about our feelings as we experienced this arctic wilderness. It is difficult not to feel very tiny in a land so empty. It also puts into perspective the struggles which had often dominated my life: status, recognition, advancement, wealth. Here, even without participating in the experience of year-round living in this wilderness, I felt I had to look closely at what mattered. In this environment, simple survival becomes what life is all about. Wealth and status are conferred only through the actual process of day to day living - being a successful hunter, feeding your family, making it through another day, another winter. This is a place where humans are truly stripped of all that is not necessary. My literary hero Hemingway would have appreciated this kind of brutal realism, this search for what matters inside each man or woman as it is revealed through every day's living.

One sight that afternoon that neither Sandra nor I will probably ever forget was our first glimpses of the vast Porcupine caribou herd. Numbering in the many thousands, this herd (which branches and divides into sub-herds) covers hundreds of miles in its peripatetic quest for forage. We were fortunate to get close to one of these many smaller herds, grazing so close to the Dempster that we could clearly identify individual animals, and even see the odd hump where the antlers bifurcate at the skull. As the herd moved slowly away from the roadway, we continued driving as quietly as we could beside them.

Finally, as they were approaching a distant hill, we froze. There, in hot pursuit of the herd's stragglers, was a really big grizzly, moving fast and with obvious determination. It was hard to believe that an animal that big could cover ground so quickly. The caribou, on the other hand, pretty much ignored the bear, simply picking up their pace a bit to keep in front of him (or her). It was intriguing to see how well-adapted both prey and predator were to the tundra environment, both seemingly unruffled by the odd springiness of the ground cover. We watched, fascinated as the drama continued to unfold, but soon both the herd and the bear were lost to sight around the curve of the hill. I wonder to this day if the bear got a meal or if the caribou simply egged it on until it was too tired to continue the chase.

As we drove south, we hoped the ferry issues we had heard about in Inuvik had been resolved by the time we reached the first one over the Peel River. This was the infamous cable ferry and certainly the more worrisome of the two. The ferry operates by being pulled back and forth across the river on a long cable. The problem is that debris in the water (and there was a vast amount of debris that summer) can clog the cable lines, snap the cable, or even poke holes in the ferry itself. Given the pace of the river's current, the latter didn't seem so improbable, even though the ferry is a very sturdy vessel. Fortunately, our timing was right. The ferry was in operation and we watched as she swung lazily across the river and slightly downstream to the little ramp on our side. We were the only vehicle waiting to cross to the south. Once over, we lumbered very carefully off the ferry, then following the advice of the boat keeper, gunned the Jeep up the steep south ramp and back onto the highway once more.

Our second ferry encounter occurred later that afternoon. The somewhat larger ferry crossing the MacKenzie River was reported to be *hors de combat* due to rapidly rising waters and more in-water debris (including some very hefty trees that would have brought a good price as major lumber in the lower 48). When we reached the problematical crossing, we slowed and then stopped behind a long line of parked vehicles. From the looks of things, everyone had been waiting for quite some time. Whole families were out of their cars and campers. Dogs were running about, one man was fishing from the bank, and several families had improvised picnic tables out of tree trunks and were lunching in high style!

This had the appearance of people settled in for the long haul, so I killed the Jeep and Sandra and I, along with Smokey, got out and shared some stories with fellow travelers. Suddenly, a signal came from the ferry that only those up close could make out, but it resulted in all of us slowly and methodically picking up our paraphernalia, collecting our dogs, and returning once more to our vehicles. Engines were cranked and out little convoy looked ready to roll. However, before we could proceed to board, a huge Cat tractor was called into service. The Cat operator's job, all day, every day, was to smooth the river bank and make a vehicle loading ramp out of whatever seemed readily at hand. After every ferry crossing, the clanking, diesel-belching D-9 is pressed into service to repair and heighten the berm, allowing access to the ferry's own huge steel ramp. With its work done for this crossing pass, the tractor retreated to one side in a sulphurous cloud of fumes

We then drove onto the ferry, which is quite a sizeable vessel, and proceeded across the MacKenzie under power to the other side. The trip across is slow but interesting as the ferry stops first at a very isolated First Nations community (no roads connect the little settlement to the outside world) and then continues some 400 yards farther downstream to the continuation of the Dempster Highway. Getting off had us sweating a bit, as the ramp looked none too car-friendly. The way out was quite steep and deeply potted, but we followed a huge 18-wheeler, letting its driver blaze a path for us. Once back on the Dempster, we felt very grateful, indeed, that we had avoided what could have been a very long delay, perhaps sending us back to Inuvik (if the road was open) or forcing us to camp in the back of the Jeep (not a cheering prospect for two Seniors, a dog, and several travel bags). As Sandra said, this was all part of the adventure.

I am coming to believe that the thrill of uncertainty is something I had been missing in my previous life.My path had been too secure, too certain, and (sometimes) too boring. I was actually enjoying the not-knowing-what-was-coming-next aspect of our lives on the road. This, to me, marked a new self-awareness, a realization that certainty and routine can be debilitating - mentally and emotionally. Once again, my bride put into words something that had been gnawing at the back of my consciousness for some time now – that I was growing through the process of the adventure, and that the journey really was more about lessons learned than about things seen.

From the south bank of the MacKenzie River we retraced our path to the Eagle Plains motel complex. Once again, although it was late in the evening, we were fortunate enough to score a room. The menu for dinner had not changed – Roast Beef, Ham, Turkey – with hearty German accent. This time we had the ham sandwiches (they were huge) and since we were now known to our waitress/desk clerk/barmaid, we were able to engage her in a bit of conversation. It turned out that her birth place was not far from where Sandra's father had grown up in Germany and, of course, Sandra got to try out some of her German on the kind lady. We even felt brave enough to try the desserts again, and the apple pie turned out to be an excellent choice, with some good strong coffee to wash it down.

After dinner we perused the lobby bulletin board where faxes from the Canadian highway department were posted, warning of bad travel conditions on the upcoming (southern) portion of the Dempster. This was not encouraging, as the highway was now closed at several kilometer markers south of our little complex. We could fully believe that the road was washed out as it had been raining a good deal that day. The weather had turned from damp and chilly to just plain cold, with rain and a strong wind.

We tried to make plans for the morrow, but without knowing the road conditions, we gave it up and went back to our rooms to rest and watch a bit of TV. I took poor old Smokers out for his late night walk, but the Eagle Plains parking lot had turned into a sea of mud, and it was very cold. I ended up bundling him into his little green sweater and carrying him to the highest ground I could find so he could complete his ablutions. I then carried him back to the hotel entrance, dried him as best I could and in the airlock-style entrance, took off my shoes as a large sign asked me to do. It appears that mud and snow are two constants on this part of the Dempster.

The next morning we awoke early and went to the dining room/bar for breakfast. Sandra overheard the head housekeeper talking with one of the wait staff, telling the younger woman not to let on to the guests that the Dempster might be open for an hour or two that day. "If you don't tell them, we can hopefully get another night's stay out of the same sheets," she had said.

Sandra is blessed with very good hearing (I had missed this conversation), so as soon as breakfast was over, we loaded the Jeep and I went in to pay our tab. The desk lady said that the road was closed and we would all have to stay another night. Somewhat forebodingly, she wouldn't even let me pay my bill, insisting that everyone was going to have to stay at the hotel until further notice. I went out to the Jeep to report this to Sandra, fully prepared to take the stuff out of the car and put it back into our room.

Sandra, however, had other ideas. "Jump in", she said, "We're going to go around those barricades over there and head on down the Dempster."

"What barricades?" I asked. And then I saw that during the night, the highway workers had erected barrel barricades at the end of the parking lot, blocking access to the highway. Sandra repeated the conversation she had just overheard, so I somewhat fearfully heeded her commands, jumped in, and off we went across the parking lot.

"Don't worry about the bill," she said. "They already have your credit card number."

Okay, I thought, this is going to get interesting fast, but Sandra, always up for a challenge, plotted a careful course around the barrels and back onto the Dempster. Her logic was that we would be first in line to get through the closed parts once they were reopened. I was a bit uncomfortable about crossing the barrier, based largely on my ingrained respect for signs in general, and my fear of being arrested by the RCMP in the person of someone very like Sergeant Preston. At this point, we were betting on the highway being open again that day. I was none too sure that this would be the case.

"Besides," said Sandra. "I remember studying about tundra in grammar school and could never figure out exactly what it was. Today, we can pull over, jump out and dance on the tundra. I can hardly wait!" She exuded her usual confidence and lack of worry, so I went with the moment and began to enjoy the adventure once again.

With Sandra driving very slowly, we had plenty of time to really see the surrounding landscape. Sandra had a good plan in mind – drive slowly, enjoy the beautiful scenery, and listen to one of her favorite CDs that we brought along. This one featured charming Hawaiian music per-formed by a very spiritual singer, Israel Kamakawiwoʻole, whom Sandra had met years before on her island travels. At a beautiful turnoff on the Dempster, we stopped, turned off the motor, and played that recording. No one was behind us, no one in front of us, so we opened the Jeep's sun roof and really let the music soar in the clear arctic air. And then we were treated to a very memorable experience, one neither of us will ever forget. A Peregrine falcon flew slowly overhead, then settled into a tree just feet from the Jeep. He stayed perched there, ears cocked and sharing that special musical moment with us. When the music ended, the beautiful bird took wing again, slowly rising and finally disappearing from our sight over the hills to the west. We remained wrapped in the serene silence for a long time afterwards, thinking of our solitary visitor and wishing him good hunting and a safe winter ahead.

When the CD ended, we jumped out and all three of us tangoed on the tundra. Very soon, we had to get on the move again, as two cars from Eagle Plains were suddenly passing us at breakneck speed, heading, it appeared, towards the first re-opened stretch of our highway.. Apparently, a fax had come to the hotel from the CanTran people indicating a new window of opportunity. We joined the procession, and I took over the driving for a while. This turned out to be quite exhilarating. I put the gas pedal down and really rocketed along the bumpy, curvy highway. I hadn't driven like this for many years, not since my sports car days of the 1960's. The Jeep was not the Austin Healey 3000 or the Jaguar XK150 of my more adventurous days, but considering the state of the roadbed, I was very glad for its high ground clearance, four-wheel drive and its generally forgiving nature. We quickly caught up with the other two cars in front of us, travelling on what was, fortunately, one of the smoother stretches of the Dempster. Soon we came to a place that I still think of as "The Great Washout."

Here we stopped behind the other two cars, turned off the car, and walked forward to see what the damage to the roadway looked like. One of the many local rivers had dramatically overflowed its banks, taking a huge chunk of highway downstream. The road looked a bit like those photos you see on the internet, captioned something like "Florida couple watches their home disappear into a giant sinkhole." One Northwest Territories denizen was out of his car and had climbed down the bank to where the river was making its way up to the road. Standing a bit upstream, he was using his tiny camper's shovel to methodically stack large rocks and mud into a small side channel of the river to help create a diversionary path. The rest of us decided to just cheer him on, as the day had turned quite cold and damp again.

After we had all been waiting and watching for a spell, a three-person road crew came up the hill leading to the washout. They had managed to get their (really) high ground clearance pickup truck across the washed out area by the seldom-advised trick of driving along the roadside at a 45 degree angle. The orange-clad trio was checking the most recent damage. Their boss, a short but very sturdy lady who ran the highway works in that part of the Territories, told us they had radioed for a big power shovel to come and fix the road. This was reassuring, although she immediately deflated my enthusiasm.

Coming up to Sandra, she snarled, "You illegally went around our barricades back at Eagle Plains and that maneuver rendered your auto insurance null and void."

I don't actually know if that was true or not, but considering we were already at the washout, I decided not to worry about it and instead, to concentrate on keeping warm and chatting up our fellow travelers. One young couple, missionaries on their way to Alaska for a religious meeting, had emigrated to Canada from Australia and were living far up the Dempster. They told us we had been wise not to attempt the Dempster with the RV since they had had a travel trailer when they first came to the area which had been pretty much eaten up by several trips down the famous highway.

After a 20-minute wait, an over-the-road tractor towing a low-boy trailer showed up on the other side of the washout. On the trailer was a huge power shovel which the truck driver quickly and expertly unloaded. After a consultation by radio with the boss lady, the driver fired up the shovel, lumbering forward on wide caterpillar treads to the edge of the washout. A few gulps with the gargantuan shovel produced a satisfactory temporary roadbed of rocks and dirt. A couple of taps with the back of the shovel and the road bed was ready for travel. All that remained was for the driver to back and turn in a tight circle, then load the big earth mover back onto the low-boy and huff clankingly to one side, anchor chains swinging loose, as he made temporary room for our convoy to get across.

Crossing this very temporary roadway was somewhat more an ordeal than expected, as up close the roadbed looked rather forbidding in its sheer cragginess. But the lady supervisor came to the rescue. She and her two workers jumped into their pickup and served as our pilot car, leading us safely across the new roadway which was barely the width of a car and which water was already beginning to cover again. I was in awe at seeing a road literally created right before our eyes in a matter of minutes.

Once over, we accelerated towards the next treacherous section of the Dempster only a few miles away and probably lacking another large earth mover to help us out. This time, the collapsed span was smaller, so the problem was less severe. However, the situation actually appeared more dangerous because the water flowing across the road was deeper and swifter than at the first disaster site. Once again a headline popped into my head, "St. Louis couple drowned in car while attempting to cross remote Canadian Highway". I didn't share that one with Sandra. Again, we were fortunate in that we were lead across by a pilot truck. This time, though, I had more of a death grip on the wheel as I could feel the Jeep, even in 4-wheel mode, slipping awkwardly and sliding sideways as we moved very slowly through the deep water.

"Whew, what a relief," I thought, as we finally gained solid road-way again. From this point on the going did get a bit easier, although we traversed seven of these washouts on the way back to the head of the Dempster.

Driving the Dempster highway was an adventure that was worth taking at many levels. The scenic beauty was without parallel. It is also one of the last great road adventures in North America. The Dempster is an

800-mile (round trip) odyssey into another time and place. The highway leads to solitude and a vast silence which has to be experienced to be fully appreciated. Driving this very remote highway provided a healthy dose of physical and mental challenge and the reward was commensurately wonderful. It's a trip that every road warrior, even a Senior one, should try at least once. It changed Sandra and me in ways that I haven't entirely sorted out yet, but that is what trips like this should do.

The time spent on the Dempster is forever with us. We see on our laptops the photos we took and they evoke strong memories of the wild beauty that surrounded us for those magical days. Part of it, I think, was just the act of rising to this challenge of a trip that was like nothing either of us had tried before, driving a road like that one hardly ever finds these days. This was a trip from the early days of motoring, where highways were non-existent, roads were trails, cars were primitive and prone to failure, tires could be counted on to collapse daily, and you carried your own tools. And, like the early days of motoring, while on the Dempster, you were largely out of contact with the rest of the world.

Cell phones are useless and pay phones pretty much no longer exist anywhere . Short of having a satellite phone, you don't call for help on the Dempster. If you break down, you improvise a repair. If you break down seriously, you flag down another Dempster driver and ask them to send help from either end or from Eagle Plains. And then, you wait and hope you can stay warm and not run out of water and energy bars! Even with good luck, driving the Dempster involves a very slow pace, looking out for potholes and massive frost heaving, and always – always! - watching out for the famous sharp, pointed rocks that eat tires and make carrying several spares a necessity

The Dempster also requires a certain willingness to sacrifice a bit of car paint to rocks and debris tossed up by passing trucks as they lumber back and forth in return, of course, for one of the grandest road adventures still available. This wonderful highway takes you back in time in another, more geological sense, as well. The highway transects the vast interior region that remained essentially glacier-free during the last Ice Age. As a result, today's adventurer is gazing at the very path the ancestors of First Nations people took as they walked the exposed land bridge from Siberia, through Alaska to the present Northwest Territories.

To stand today on the tundra where they camped, to visualize them preparing in the chill early morning mists for a hunt (perhaps against the dangerous Wooly Mammoth) is to journey along a time track that helps us understand the resilience and savvy of today's hunter/gatherer First Nations peoples. Plus, the wildlife you will encounter is like nothing you will see elsewhere except perhaps in game parks or zoos. For all of these reasons, Sandra and I were very tired – and very, very proud and happy – as we turned off the Dempster at its source and headed west to Dawson City – once again on pavement!

CHAPTER 8

A Special Festival

We spent the next several days in Dawson City, enjoying time with our 12-step friends, eating at all the restaurants we could find, cleaning up the Jeep and making plans for our next road adventure. Once back in the RV park, we discovered yet another fascinating vehicle whose likes we had never seen before in our many miles of travel. Parked across from us was a tour-bus-size red vehicle with awning and canopies sprouting from the sides, stoves and fires going outside and big cauldrons of food steaming away. Along the side were self-stowing stairs and gangplanks that led to little doors opening onto tiny sleeping compartments, a bit like the old upper and lower births on early 20th century trains, but with outside entrances.

We were intrigued by this vehicle because, looked at from a certain angle, it resembled a bright red mausoleum on fat tires. It turned out that this was a contraption rented by Far East tour groups and moved from site to site around this part of the world. The food smelled good, and the vehicle was certainly a marvel of Swiss-Army-Knife-style engineering, but it appeared to be a bit too much of a group experience for our tastes. For self-contained efficiency, however (it even had chairs and tables that folded out of the lower edges) it was pretty hard to top.

While ambling about in Dawson City one sunny morning, we heard about a festival that was to take place that weekend. We decided we simply had to attend. The festival is the biennial Moose Hide Gathering, so named for the easily recognizable outline (the result of a previous land slide) of a moose hide which is a natural feature of the mountain just north of Dawson City. The Gathering brings together any and all of the First Nations peoples who have lived in this part of Canada for uncounted generations. It is a three-day celebration of food, song, stories, crafts, and language, and – best of all - outsiders are hospitably welcomed.

Asking around town as to the best way of getting to the celebration encampment, we soon discovered that the site was about a mile down the Yukon River and reachable only by a flotilla of small watercraft powered by very noisy outboards. Every boat owner in the area appeared to have volunteered his or her boat as a water taxi, so there was never a long wait in order to get to or from the Moose Hide Gathering. Boating on the Yukon was an "I Can Do This" moment, as I had to force myself to climb *very* carefully into a 14-foot skiff bobbing vigorously well below dock level. Getting in was much scarier that actually riding in the little boat, as once in one just had to hang on and get caught up in the adventure of the ride on one of the most beautiful rivers I had ever seen. Bouncing along inches above the icy water, I briefly wondered what would happen if we capsized, but it was just too much fun to worry about.

We decided to go mid-afternoon to the Gathering, as we had heard that the dinner that night would be quite special, full of First Nations recipes, all prepared by tribe members. The Gathering place was a big clearing just above the river bank. The day was quite warm and by the time we negotiated the steps and paths up the hill, we were happy to shed our coats and enjoy High North summer in light shirts with sleeves rolled up. Because we have slightly quirky senses of humor, we each bought matching souvenir Moose Hide Gathering t-shirts, crafted in a lurid shade of pink with sides depicting the famous representations of the Moose Hide on the mountain. They are among our favorite souvenirs of our adventure, and we wear them proudly whenever the weather is warm enough. Besides the obviously "souvenir" goods on sale at the Gathering, there was some seriously fine artwork and jewelry on display as well.

I rarely treat myself to jewelry, but this occasion was an exception. Sandra, a connoisseuse of jewelry, helped me find a carved ring with the profile representation of a raven's head, the feathers and eye decorated with gold from the Yukon River. The ring itself was carved from a piece of caribou antler and I actually got to meet and shake hands with the artist himself, a young First Nations man. When I asked him about the source of the antler, he explained that the caribou lose their antlers every spring and that he simply walked about the tundra looking for discarded horn of the right color and texture. That ring and the little story about its creation have remained with me ever since and I can still see its creator smile as he described the search for just the right piece of antler and how he himself panned for the small amounts of decorative gold dust that he required for his craft work.

For the rest of the afternoon, Sandra and I wandered from table to table, looking at dolls, scarves, carvings, First Nations flutes and drums, and listening to the storytelling (which held several large audiences spellbound) in the native tongue of the Gathered. The storytellers were older men and women, animated as their stories unfolded, sometimes emphasizing a point with rhythmic flourishes upon a small drum. It was encouraging to see children and young people in the audience, absorbing at least some of a rich heritage that faces increasing competition from

Canadian (and yes, U.S.) values and ways of living. But at this Moose Hide Gathering, at least, the traditional ways were alive and well.

As the sun dropped a bit lower and our hunger increased, we heard the call to get in line for dinner. We patiently gathered at the rear of one of the several long lines now snaking across the clearing towards the big serving tables heaped high with exquisite food and baked goods. At this point, something quite remarkable happened. A native woman about our age walked up to us and said, "You two are elders. It is not right for you to wait back here in line. Please come to the head of the line with me and you will be served right away."

Since I was hungry and we didn't know if it would be polite not to accept this offer, we complied and soon found ourselves faced with agonizing culinary decisions: Moose stew or freshly-grilled salmon? Fried fish or a rich Muligitawny? Yams or white potatoes? In the end, we tried as much of everything as we could fit on our plates. I am a great fan of moose stew and this one was particularly savory, coming as it did with the added spice of eating it outdoors with very friendly and talkative First Nations people who welcomed us warmly and shared their culture with us. We found two empty spaces at a table already filled with Natives, who shoved together to give us a bit of eating room. We told them of our travels and mentioned we were newlyweds. That brought big smiles and many questions.

When we asked them the history of the Moose hide Gathering, an older women seated next to me replied that Moose Hide had been founded because the elders had not liked what they had seen of the then-new Dawson City and all that went with a wild frontier town from the Gold Rush era. To protect their traditional culture, they had decided to move the village about a mile away, to the present site where we were eating our evening feast. Gradually, the older generation died off and young people left the area for jobs in Dawson or elsewhere and to attend high school. As the village declined, the decision was made that there should be a gathering every two years of all the villagers who could come back, plus other First Nations peoples who shared this vast area. The gathering would keep alive the old traditions, languages, crafts, and cuisine. Late that evening, after listening to more stories and being entertained by local folk singers and even a low-key rock band, we climbed back into one of the waiting taxi boats and returned to Dawson City, the sun still above the horizon as the time neared midnight.

Feeling relaxed and energized after the wonderful afternoon and evening, we decided to drive to the top of what Dawsonians called The Dome, one of the numerous mountains surrounding the little town. The view from the top of The Dome is quite astonishing, as even this late at night the sun is still setting in the west and the moon just rising above the surrounding mountains to the east. The river valley and the meeting place of the two great rivers, the Yukon and the Klondike, were colored with a soft purplish light that gave Dawson City a wonderful glow. We both took pictures and walked all around the top of The Dome, finally sitting on a park bench located about 20 feet below the very top and offering 270-dgree views. This was the kind of scene where I devoutly wished I had the photographer's eye of Ansel Adams. But this scene really *had* to be done in color, so amazing was the palette that nature employed on this particular evening in late July.

The next morning we began to make plans to continue on to Alaska, so tantalizingly near, and yet so difficult to attain if the infamous Top of The World Highway were to be closed. Like the Dempster, the Top of the World had suffered from serious and prolonged rainfall that summer, and could be quite impassible in several places. To add to our foreboding, there were reports circulating among RVers that one motor home had tragically plunged off the mountain and fallen several thousand feet before coming to rest. It had not yet been recovered, so difficult was the terrain.

Sandra and I much preferred to go via the Top of the World; otherwise we would have to back track many hundreds of miles along the same dusty, rocky highways we had already navigated getting to Dawson City. The Top of the World begins just across the Yukon River from Dawson City, and goes directly into Alaska at the United States' most northerly border check point, Poker Creek, Alaska.

The Top of the World, much like the Dempster, is maintained in summer (which means pouring in tons of gravel and grading the potholes) and, somewhat ominously, is closed in winter (which is, in fact, most of the year). It is almost entirely lacking in guardrails, has very narrow switchbacks and has collected about itself quite a number of harrowing stories. The consensus in Dawson City was that it was tricky but doable and quite spectacular if we were lucky enough to attempt it on a clear day. If it was open but the weather misty or rainy, then it probably wasn't worth doing and would prove even more dangerous than usual.

We waited at the RV park in Dawson City during that second week in town, with me walking several times a day down to the RV office and then on to the Dawson Visitor's Center to see if the faxes from the department of highways all agreed concerning the Top of the World. They did…time after time. But finally, a fax came through that had me trotting back to Regina Victoria. The Top of the World could be open all the way into Alaska as early as Sunday, just one day away. Now we had a deadline and a window of opportunity. Would the weather continue to improve? Would we have a good day on Sunday to make the drive?

CHAPTER 9

On to Alaska

Sunday morning dawned bright and clear, the first such day in a week and, amazingly, the Top of the World Highway was expected to be open! This was great news and we decided we would give it our best shot, especially in the face of a laborious backtrack. Plus, the Top of the World is not nearly the length of the Dempster and connected two friendly countries in just a bit over a hundred miles. We quickly unhooked from our RV site, hitched up the Jeep, bundled Smokey into his warmest sweater, and headed for the little ferry to cross the Yukon River and begin the journey to Alaska.

"I feel really sad," said Sandra as she looked back towards The Dome.. "I loved it so much up here and I really don't want to go home."

"Me, either," I replied. "But we can always come back, right?"

I was amazed at my newfound positive attitude about possible future spontaneous adventures.On that beautiful Sunday, the scenery was all we could have hoped for, with spectacular views in every direction. The road climbs steadily until you suddenly realize you are driving from peak to peak along a series of seemingly unending ridge lines; travelling literally the "Top of the World". The views were constantly worth slowing down for, and the number of pixels consumed in my digital SLR was astounding as I snapped away right and left. We took turns changing drivers frequently because the Top of the World, while much shorter than the Dempster, is in some ways a much worse highway. The potholes and frost heaves are deeper and more pronounced, and the almost complete absence of guard rails made for a slow and sometimes nail-biting experience, especially as the curves around the many sheer cliffs made for tight going in our long rig. The road was also washed out in places, with water streaming across the path and mud forming a frequently formidable barrier to forward progress. We often even had to drive through streams.

There are a number of places where one can look over the side straight down for over 2,000 feet. Driving the highway on a bright, cheerful day took away some of the scariness. We used our engine braking system a lot and tried to save the air brakes as much as possible because we had been warned there would be some steep downgrades. One thing we had learned *not* to do in our travels thus far was to pick up speed heading downhill. Going down, the engine and tranny on the RV have a tendency to go into free-coasting mode. With the combined weight of loaded RV and tow car, it's possible to accelerate quickly downwards, often achieving quite uncomfortable speeds.

After many hours of exceedingly careful driving, we approached the U.S. border post into Alaska. There were the Canadian Maple Leaf and the American Stars and Stripes flying on either side of a shared administration building. Two American customs officers were visible in an unpretentious tiny shack, and one watched our approach to the gate with huge binoculars. I assumed this was a "just in case" precaution, as it was a really remote duty station and the approach had been made clear for at least a kilometer. Both gentlemen were very pleasant and one requested

I remove my sunglasses so he could compare me to my passport photo. He asked if our license plate, "OR-BUST", was a real plate and I assured him that it was. He then asked if he could see Smokey's papers which Sandra had ready. When we mentioned being from Missouri, his partner inside (he of the large binoculars) perked up and asked us what part of the state we were from. It turned out that he was originally from Springfield, Missouri, where Sandra had served as Director of the Springfield Regional Arts Council for some years, commuting occasionally back and forth to her B&B Inn in Eureka Springs when needed by the staff she had hired to run it in her absence. The officer's sister had recently performed a singing role in a local Springfield production of "Little Shop of Horrors". Sandra, during her tenure there, attended every cultural and arts event in town, and was pleased to tell the officer that she had actually seen the young lady in the performance. Once again the arts provided an instant connection over many thousands of miles

The custom's official smiled and said "Oh, you guys are just fine" and waved us on without even looking inside our RV. We passed several rental RVs that, curiously, appeared to have been pulled over, perhaps by the Canadians, and we watched several rather disconsolate drivers wandering aimlessly around the parking area. We drove around them cautiously and then made our way slowly downhill, realizing how lucky we had been not having to wait a long time at the border and how thrilled we were to be back U.S. on soil once more!

On the American side of the Top of the World, we discovered it was just as tough a drive as on the Canadian side. The Canadians explain this as being due to a specialized road treaty making the U.S. responsible for all of the road's maintenance. True or not, the highway was difficult, and the weather was starting to change to cloudy which meant rain soon. We pushed as much as we could, finally leaving the Top of the World Highway for a bit tamer road heading southwards toward the famous town of Chicken, Alaska. Every RVer we spoke with earlier in the month knew of Chicken, as it was the first town you actually come to after the border crossing. The name comes not from an excess of chickens in the area, but from the fact that the early settlers couldn't spell the name of the local chicken-like bird – the Ptarmigan. So, "Chicken" the town became.

As we drove around Chicken, we noticed more cabins and fishing camps than we had seen on the Canadian side. Sadly, we also began to notice more trash along the roadway, a point we noted every time we crossed from a Canadian province back into an American state. From Chicken, we headed toward Tok, staying along the Tok cut-off highway at a campground that had one pull-through site (pretty much a necessity as tired as we were that evening) and a mile-long nature trail we tackled in the morning. We walked …Smokey ran (with joyous abandon!). It's always such fun to see his enthusiasm for exploring new places (and new smells), tail curled up high above his back, running as fast as those little legs can take him from bush to bush. He will go as far from us as he can; then he suddenly realizes he is a bit too far and comes flying back, ears pinned down and covering ground like one of my old coursing hounds.

We were struck by the variety of plant life, and particularly by the wealth of ferns covering every available inch of ground not occupied by something more aggressive. I am a great lover of ferns and often ponder their role in the early formation and development of plant life on our verdant planet. They are the sharks and turtles of the plant world, living fossils from a time long ago. After we had walked and photographed ferns and a wide array of mushrooms (reminding us we needed a guide to mushrooms), we took off deeper into Alaska once again, heading towards Anchorage and then points south.

Along the way southwards, we stopped for two nights in one of the most charming locations we were to find anywhere in our travels. Alaska, like the Yukon and Northwest Territories, is very lenient about allowing a tired RVer to pull off and spend the night in one of the many turnouts along the roadways. South of Glen Allen we stayed two nights alongside the road overlooking a beautifully pristine mountain lake (complete with bush plane on floats) looking towards the second and third highest peaks in Alaska, Mounts Hood and Wrangle. This was perhaps the single most beautiful location in which we had ever stayed, for the sheer grandeur of the setting was unmatched. To add the cherry to the top of this visual sundae, we witnessed several huge rainbows, one of them a rarely-seen double. We enjoyed an evening walk along the perimeter of the lake, and in the morning, awoke to the lacy charm of morning frost on the surrounding hillsides. And this, in August!

When we finally made it to Anchorage, we decided to stay the night at a friendly Big Box. Although we had been in "the wilds" long enough not to relish the thought of city traffic, we unhooked the Jeep and decided to take a look up close at one of America's most northern cities. With the sunroof open and Smokey perched on Sandra's lap, " sniffigating" for all he was worth, we took a casual tour of Anchorage. The town has more and better freeways that I would have expected for its population and the late evening light at that latitude cast a translucent glow over what was otherwise fairly prosaic architecture. Everyone, it seemed, was out and about, many driving with their convertible tops down.

I could understand their desire to soak up the maximum number of rays possible during the short summer. I had seen the same phenomenon in Denmark where everyone was out until the last bit of sun disappeared. The bright green grass in Copenhagen's many parks was covered by families, couples in love, children, babies and aging seniors, all absorbing the sunshine that would have to last them through the many long, cold, dark months lying just ahead. As much as Sandra and I came to love Alaska – the friendly people, the stunning snow-capped mountains, the glaciers, the rushing roadside streams, the charming small towns – still

I cannot yet bring myself to consider visiting in the dead of winter to a land frozen and dark. Maybe someday, it is an adventure we'll have to attempt, just to know we could accept the challenge and come to see Alaska as only the hardy who live there year-round get to see it. But for now, it was warm and sunny and August…time to get a bit of rest and then head southwards to Valdez.

The next day, we turned south from Anchorage along the Cook Inlet, driving a gorgeous stretch of roadway with constant views of the water to the right and mountains to the left. It is inspiring scenery. But even where it is flat, the road winds constantly, so vehicles such as ours are compelled (by law) to allow no more than seven cars to pile up behind. When that occurred, we were supposed to pull over and let them by which we tried diligently to do. This was not always easy as pullouts are infrequent in some areas, but people trailing us seemed to take the situation with good humor and we always waved and thanked them for their courtesy when they passed us (finally!).

The problem of being big and slow was compounded in the more mountainous stretches, but the Alaska Highway Department seems to have thought of that and provided more turnoffs as compensation. Altogether, the trip south was one of the most beautiful parts of our journey, suffused with the glow of accomplishment that comes from nursing the big rig through difficult roads and being rewarded with constantly more spectacular scenery. Whoever was not driving was blazing away with all the cameras we had on board, interspersed with binocular sessions to identify the many birds we so wanted to add to our Life List, begun when we left St. Louis,

By late afternoon we reached Valdez and checked in at our campground. We had decided to stay at a commercial campground as there were no convenient state parks and the county park had no hookups. The Bear Paw campground had two sections: one right on the main road in town and just across from the marina, and another about a block away where we were fortunate to get a site on the boat channel that took the local fishing fleet out into Prince Edward Sound. We parked pull-in style, which meant I had to route the electrical cable as well as the water and sewer hoses under Regina Victoria to reach the hookup points. The effort was very much worth it as we had a commanding view of the whole harbor from our big front window. This turned out to be one of those campsites where we wished we could stay forever, just watching the highly varied marine traffic parade in and out of the harbor. We stayed over a week, enjoying the fishing boats ablaze with lights as they returned during the early morning hours with their catches to be processed at the seafood plant just across the inlet from our location.

During our first night on site, we heard one of the more mysterious noises that we had encountered in our travels. With help from a town resident, we were finally able to identify the sound as the great "whoosh" of steam escaping from the cooking vessels at the seafood processing plant. The noise occurred with such regularity that before long it became a soothing background noise, especially when we were going to sleep (always late, it seemed, because of the wonderfully long hours of daylight Alaska gave us).

We also found a number of delightful restaurants and downing huge amounts of the local seafood was a real treat after being in the meat-stew interior so long. No more moose and caribou…now we could revel in aquatic delicacies. One Sunday afternoon, in honor of Pioneer Days, the town sponsored a seafood cookout in the little town park with the catch donated by local fishermen. We got there late, which turned out to be a good thing, as we were plied with quantities of takeaway grilled salmon hot off the fire pits. (We ate grilled salmon, salmon patties, fried salmon, salmon as Lox. for many days).

The townspeople at the event were amazingly friendly and we struck up numerous conversations about our travels. We also learned a lot about the weather in Valdez and about the local economy, which, of course, is heavily dependent upon being the terminus of the Alaska pipeline. It is also closely tied to the local fisheries which are not doing as well as they used to. Many fishermen are idle and blaming everything from Washington to competing Canadian fishermen - the list is nearly endless and, in some cases, the complaints were justified..

One of the most interesting climate facts about Valdez is that it is the snowiest location in the U.S. The high pass over the mountains leading into the city receives something on the order of 50 feet of snow per winter. That's feet, not inches! The town of Valdez can get 100 inches per month some years. I was amazed that the highway crews could even begin to keep the road open, but we were told they do it with neatness and dispatch. Interestingly, there used to be a ski resort at the top of the nearby mountain, but now the only way for tourists to ski the area is by dropping from a helicopter.

We also, of course, found the local recovery meetings, and went to a number of them while in Valdez. They were always interesting and often deeply rewarding. It was here, I think, that I made the important discovery, long known to Sandra, that the sharing of my story in recovery could be of benefit to others in ways that might not be obvious to me at first. This is not to say I had spent my years in recovery without sharing effectively, but I think that in Valdez I made a kind of breakthrough in which I began to open up at a much more personal level. Perhaps, in the past, I had been too much the intellectual, too controlled, too impersonal. In Valdez I opened up in a new way which has been of great benefit to me ever since. I felt as though I had had a kind of growing spurt, and I needed to process what I had learned, but Alaska gave me the time to begin doing just that.

The Valdez meetings were also filled with interesting characters – hippies, intellectuals, general non-conformists, and my particular favorite: a very nice man who rescued raptors and usually brought one or two with him in the back of his pickup or on his bicycle. We loved the huge Snowy Owl and a Northern Harrier he was rehabilitating. We got some great pictures of each of us with the critters, and I'll never forget his stories about rescuing these sometimes abused birds. He was a great source of information about the local wildlife and directed us to several spots near town where we could watch spawning salmon, hunt for berries, and perhaps (although we weren't lucky) see a bear or two. And, of course, everyone at the meetings directed us to favorite restaurants, told us where to get the best cup of coffee, and argued vociferously over which restaurant had the very best pizza.

One highlight of our stay in Valdez was taking the day-long sight-seeing cruise into Prince Edward Sound. As one might expect, the scenery was awesome, worth braving the cold on deck, Bundled up in big sweaters and wind-cheaters, we took scores of pictures as we glided through the Sound. I found a young couple huddled up against the bulkhead leading back into the salon and struck up a conversation with them. It turns out they were on holiday from Barcelona, so we switched to Spanish and had fun teaching each other the names of what we were seeing as we putt-putted outbound. I didn't quite dare try Catalan on them as I have been told I have what amounts to a terrible Germanic accent in Catalan, even when I am in Barcelona long enough to begin to speak it a bit.

As we moved slowly down the Sound, we got to see fishing boats hard at work and were told the "real story" of the Exxon Valdez and that ship's terrible demise. One revealing factoid was that the huge oil spill has never really been fully cleaned up. According to the crew on board our tour vessel, if you dig down a few feet anywhere along the shoreline you're likely to find oily deposits. I did not put this to the test, but suspect that they are probably right if other oil spills provide any insight. The captain of the ill-starred tanker is also not so vilified here as he is elsewhere, and there is a good deal of local sympathy for the problems he faced in terms of navigation the day his vessel went aground. The professional captains we talked with gave him more credit for preventing a worse disaster than he was generally ever accorded by the world's assembled media.

One of the high points of the trip was seeing and hearing two major glaciers calving…an unforgettable sensory experience. Our captain took us in quite close to each glacier, holding us steady as we watched huge chunks of blue-green ice slide off the front of the glaciers. The resulting iceberg calves would make their way through the Sound and out into the open ocean towards the Aleutian Islands. In fact, navigating to the spot where we could observe the calving process required moving through quite a dense field of recently created icebergs. Getting close to the glaciers is a very careful, very circuitous process! There were numerous slightly breathless jokes about the Titanic from the passengers, but the crew took it in good-natured stride, having probably heard the same old chestnuts a hundred times before.

During the afternoon we had a special treat. On this rare day, the water was calm enough that our ship could get close to a sheer rock wall hosting hundreds of Puffin nesting sites. Sandra has loved the little round birds since her sailing days; she was ecstatic over finding so many this close at hand. Some of her best photos of the area are her Puffin shots, made as the boat bobbed up and down within yards of the rookery. It was wonderful to see my bride so enthused and working so hard to get just the right shot. It brought to mind what she must have been like in her reporter/photo-journalist life years before.

I enjoyed being on our particular boat because passengers were allowed easy access to the bridge, where Sandra and I hung out on the latter part of the return journey. We admired the skill of our captain as he delicately maneuvered the big vessel, and we observed the radar, depth sounder, and other instruments at work. This was the kind of close and personal experience we had hoped for, and the Stan Smith tour delivered on that score.

CHAPTER 10

The Denali

Finally, there came that day when we looked at each other and decided, without any great discussion, that it was time to move on. We had no set schedule, but we could usually sense the point at which both of us were ready for new sights and adventures. Unplugging Regina Victoria and hooking up the long-suffering Grand Cherokee once more, we turned back northwards up the Kenai Peninsula and headed towards Seward where we hoped to spend more time near the water. This turned out to be *not* one of our great choices.

Leaving Valdez and crossing that glorious (in summer!) high pass back into the interior, we began to experience more and more rain. By the time we got to Seward, the rain was steady and we discovered there really was no suitable state park, or even private campground, where we wanted to make camp. Add the big cruise ships steaming in and out regularly and it just didn't seem the place we wanted to stay for long. Evening, however, was fast approaching and I didn't want to press on further that day. Sandra has very keen vision and quickly spotted a miniscule sign that indicated camping down a gravel road. It appeared that this was a county park, something we hadn't found often before in the North Country. Tired, we decided to give it a try.

Once at the park's entrance we tried to figure out if (and who) you paid, and where a vacant campsite might be. We decided to explore the possibilities by driving around the large outer circle that began just inside the park gates. We both had an inkling, a premonition, that this might not be our wisest course. Too late! The road was very narrow and got worse within a few hundred feet. As well, it bent far more sharply than we had anticipated. I couldn't find a way to get the Jeep off because of the bad angle of the tow bar, so we had no choice now but to forge ahead and through, adding a few more battle scars to the RV and running a good scratch down the side of the Jeep.

Finally, we circumnavigated the camping area and were at a loss as to what we should do next when we spotted a big graveled area just about where we had first come in. The site looked like a maintenance staging area, with piles of gravel, rock, mulch, etc. strewn about, but it was big, open, and could easily accommodate our rig. Already hunkered down there was a sizeable travel trailer, so we decided we would pull as far to the edge of the gravel area as we could and call it quits for today. We hadn't seen a ranger or park employee, so we figured the worst that could happen was we might be asked to vacate this area since it wasn't really set up as a campsite. I started the generator, which didn't bother anyone as several other generators were humming along as well, forming an electrical chorus. Smokey liked the park, even if Sandra and I had our doubts. Give the little guy some new trees to mark and he is in doggy heaven!

After dinner the rain finally stopped and we took a hand-in-hand stroll about the park, finding the trees and shrubs that had blocked our path earlier in the evening. We have developed the attitude that we like to protect the RV and the tow as much as possible, but if we are to have adventures in our travels, then we have to be willing to accept some dings and scratches as part of the payment. By this time in our odyssey, I had stopped fussing about a scratch here or there. The Al-Can highway had pretty much cured me of that aesthetic nonsense; now I just wanted to make sure everything was good mechanically so we could keep motoring on. We spent a peaceful night but decided we had seen enough of Seward and it was time to continue the Alaska journey.

Looking at our maps, we decided to cross the Kenai Peninsula, then head down towards the sea again, this time to the little town of Homer. Once we arrived in this picturesque fishing community, we found an excellent campground with sites just above the tide line. We could park with full hookups and have a wonderful view of the Cook Inlet. Backing into our assigned site was a bit trickier than it appeared at first blush. I did my best to wiggle-waggle us into the space. However, I seemed to have developed some mental block that day and managed to keep getting myself into ever-tighter corners. Sandra was outside the rig, trying to help me get into the space with hand signals and coming up to the window with directions on how to get the job done. Having achieved a state of complete frustration, she finally gave up and told me, "Just get it in on your own. You're not following my signals and you're not listening to me, so do it your way!"

She flounced down to the beach (Sandra flounces with considerable style!) finally out of patience with me (one of the very few times that happened). On my own and in a bind, I got out, surveyed a possible course into the site, and began the exceedingly slow and careful process of backing in. Not quite careful enough, as it turned out. Swinging a bit too close on one side, I upended a large trash can and put a souvenir scratch in the RV. But finally, I got Regina Victoria in, hooked up, and went to stand with Sandra to enjoy the beauty of the ocean. All was again well between us, and I had learned yet more lessons.

We found the 12-step meetings in town and a fellow in attendance began talking with Sandra after a meeting. She asked him if he knew a single-handing sail boater she had met at a meeting in Mazatlan while she was sailing in the Pacific more than 20 years before who said he was from Homer. To her delight, our new acquaintance had known the sailor/ fisherman in question. Sandra learned that her past sailing acquaintance had eventually given up sailing somewhere in the southern hemisphere where he became something of a contraband pilot, flying back and forth to Australia. He died when he crashed his little plane into a mountain.

"How sad," said Sandra. "He was so nice, too. He had stopped cruising, rented an apartment in town, and always let me come over after meetings to take a hot shower. Ah, that was such a real treat…and he was always a perfect gentleman," she added with a wink at me to let me know there was never any hanky-panky involved. This was one of those amazingly small world coincidences that travel often reveals. Six degrees of separation may 'way overstate the case sometimes!

The Homer Spit is the core of Homer and the area where we liked best to spend leisurely days. We found several terrific seafood restaurants and gorged on crab and fresh fish. Crab is an important part of the local economy and Homer is the base of the Time Bandit, one of the several big crab fishing boats featured in the TV series, "Deadliest Catch". I even found the pile of crab "pots" that the Time Bandit had left sitting on the commercial fishing side of the Spit and had Sandra snap a few photos of me posed beside a heaping mound of well-used crab pots. I was so excited about the connection to the TV show that I even purchased a "Deadliest Catch" T-shirt at the little Time Bandit souvenir shop on the touristy side of Homer Spit. Under a silk screened image of several large crabs, there is a picture of the Time Bandit's captain with his tag line, "I want that crab count and I want it NOW!" Years later, in the middle of desert Arizona I would meet a gentleman in recovery who had actually been part of the crew filming the "Deadliest Catch"!

The Homer Spit was also a great place to walk near the ocean. It actually has a sand beach, something lacking in most parts of Alaska. We let Smokey run free. He dearly loves beaches in all latitudes and this long stretch of sand was no exception. Once off lead, he would race madly off in search of exciting new smells and (hopefully) stranded sea life that he could examine up close. Occasionally, he would decide he had to excavate the beach if he couldn't find anything interesting on top of the sand. We could see his little legs scooping at the damp sand, and soon he would have excavated deeply enough to roll in whatever he had unearthed. Back and forth he would roll, his face a happy grin with his little tongue sticking out one side. Soon covered in sand, he would bound off at full speed, shaking as he went until he found another spot to practice his excavating skills. Finally, tired and happy, he would charge back to the two of us, stopping in a small shower of sand as he applied his "four paw" brakes and slid to a stop at our feet. I often think his *joie de vivre* was contagious and he has helped me in so many ways to relax and have fun in the moment. Quite a big lesson to learn from such a tiny friend!

The other major attraction in Homer (for me, at least) was the huge Safeway store, a fairly recent addition to the town's commercial life. I mention this because it had a wonderful Starbuck's right inside (as so many of the Canadian Safeways did as well) and I was finally able to satisfy my thirst for a really good Café Americano, made with extra shots of espresso and served in the familiar cups with the little fiber aprons. The Safeway also enabled us to stock up on some fresh fruits and vegetables and to replenish our larder of donuts (one of my many weaknesses). Shopping here was also an object lesson in just how far this food had to come in order to sit on the shelves in a little Alaskan fishing town. The price of that long ride is clearly reflected in what Alaskans routinely pay in order to have bananas, peaches, or even a can of pork and beans.

Homer was a hard to town to leave. We kept extending our stay because we loved our RV location, with its views of the Sound and the not-so-distant snow-capped mountains ringing the area. We spent hours watching the tidal changes just below our campsite, plus the fresh seafood on the Spit made eating out often an easy decision even though Sandra is a wonderful chef and we could easily eat from the RV's supplies. But we gradually realized this was August and there was a good deal of Alaska we still wanted to see. Being late August would have had no consequences in the lower 48, but here we knew inclement weather could set in very early in what we of the Midwest still considered late summer to early fall.

As a result of thinking about the weather, we finally unhooked and set off northward once again, retracing part of our earlier path but this time with our eye on the vast Denali National Park area. There is some confusion over the name of North America's highest peak. It was known to old timers as Mt. Denali. When McKinley was president, the mountain was renamed in his honor, even though the man had never set foot in Alaska or seen the fabled peak. It was politics pure and simple, a desire to hopefully get something from the President in return for renaming the mountain in his honor. Now, once again, it is being referred to as Mount Denali and that was where we were heading.

After navigating a return trip through Anchorage, we reached Denali late in the afternoon and pulled into the South Park Overlook parking area. The lot was big enough and we decided to stay there over-night. We then sauntered out for our first clear look at Denali. What an incredible sight! The viewing was perfect, the huge mass of the mountain topped with its perpetual mantle of snow, glistening in the afternoon sunshine. We found out later we were extremely lucky, as Denali's peak (and indeed most of the rest of the mountain) had remained hidden for all but three days that summer, obscured by the heavy rains and fog we had encountered everywhere in the north that year. But on this day, Denali shone forth in full splendor, a monolithic testament to nature's creative powers. Denali is actually - base to tip – taller than Everest, but Everest pokes higher into the stratosphere because it sits on a higher footing.

Sandra and I stood arms around each other, entranced by the sheer beauty of the scene before us. There were a couple of tourists there as well, but the scene was so majestic that we were very quiet, all of us awestruck by what we were seeing. And then, as we let our eyes wander down the slope of the mountain, down to the little valley below, there appeared a mother grizzly and her cub, fishing for salmon in a rushing stream. To me, that completed this incredible picture of the Alaskan wilderness. Wanting an even better view of Denali, I opted to climb the many steps of the pathway that lead to the highest vantage point I could reach. There, with the sun beginning to set behind the mountain, I simply sat and stared at one of nature's truly grand vistas.

The next morning I set the alarm to get up at dawn to photograph Mt. Denali in the glow of sunrise. Not usually an early riser, I made the effort and was rewarded by an absolutely breathtaking scene as the sun came up above my shoulder and illuminated Denali in a gorgeous pale light. I snapped away with my SLR, changing positions to capture the mountain in as many "poses" as I could come up with. By the time I finished and the sun was fully up, Sandra had a wonderful breakfast ready and we ate at our little table in the RV, gazing out the big front window at Denali fully revealed in the light of the Alaskan summer sun.

We opted not to drive into Denali Park, itself. While we would have liked to see the wildlife presented on the various bus tours that roam through the vast natural reserve, we would have had to put up with the crowds of tourists, plus, leave the RV in a parking lot just inside the Reserve. We couldn't take Smokey with us, so he would have been alone for many hours. We had already been fortunate enough to see many of the park's resident mammals, including bear, elk, and bighorn sheep. Instead, we decided to undertake another Far North highway challenge – this time the Denali Highway, so named because it begins at Denali National Park. While shorter than the Dempster and a bit longer than the Top of the World highway, it was 130 rugged miles of gravel and dirt, known for some serious wash-boarding and potholes that could swallow a small tank! It was reputed to be one tough road. We thought Regina Victoria was up to it as we had been on relatively smooth highways for days with no sign of any mechanical issues, and of course, Julietta Jeep tagged along wherever Regina went, so we decided to go for it.

Once we turned on to the Denali, it became clear that this was truly a "road less travelled". We saw almost no signs of any other traffic, and the little we did see came in the form of a well-used pickup or an occasional ATV piloted by hunter types in camouflage gear, toting rifles or shotguns. I wasn't sure what could be in season in the high summer, but the North has different hunting seasons and traditions than the Lower 48. Or it could have been that deeply ingrained Alaskan desire to be fully armed when out in the wide open spaces, a concept I could appreciate somewhat after spending time in isolated areas.

The scenery was lovely as we drove eastward, and as long as we kept our speed low and drove defensively, we did well. The biggest challenge was anticipating the wash-boarding, which would cause the RV to undulate quite alarmingly if we took it too fast. My greatest fear was that we would damage the tow bar, our critical link between RV and Jeep. I had unpleasant visions of it snapping as the RV went north and the Jeep went rapidly south. But that bar is built of sturdier stuff than I had imagined and it seemed to shrug off the road surface with disdain.

Regina Victoria, on the other hand, let us know she was not unduly pleased with the road bed. We could hear the frequent sounds of shifting dishes, pots and pans, and other, less identifiable, cargo going in unintended directions as we crept slowly forward. The Denali is a tiring road and by evening we were ready to take a break and make camp. Fortuitously, around a curve appeared a Bureau of Land Management campground off to our left. This looked like a great spot to haul in for the evening and we turned into the entrance.

In the distance down a hill a man was signaling for us to come to where he was. This seemed like a good idea as we could see other campers on the lower ground. I should have taken note that these were *much* smaller units than our 38-footer (60' if you include the Jeep), but we were tired and ready to settle in for the night. At the bottom of the hill, I jumped out to chat with the gentleman who turned out to be the camp host. I'm not sure he had realized how big our vehicle was when he first saw us above. He looked at me, looked at the rig, scratched his head and opined that we were not in a good spot. He told us we should have stopped at the top of the hill where there was a large parking area suitable for our size motorhome but without any hookups. That would have been fine if the spot had been visible from the driveway (it was not). Somehow, we had to turn the coach and Jeep around and go back up to the dry camping area, but that presented a challenge. We couldn't safely get the jeep off because we were on an incline. We couldn't back up, so the only way out was forward, around a distant clump of trees in a very tight circle back to where we were now.

Sandra took the wheel of the RV and I went ahead to spot a path and clear branches out of the way. We got to the clump of trees, and by dint of careful maneuvering, she managed to get us three-quarters around the tight circle. Then we discovered that a rock was squarely in the path of the coach's right front tire. It was way too big to go over so the camp host and I literally dug it out with a pry bar and some sweat. We finally managed to roll it aside and Sandra was able to get the coach fully turned around and heading back to the upper lot.

Finally settled in, we took Smokey for a long walk down the utterly deserted Denali highway, crossing a bridge where we could see trout lurking in a small stream. We continued our walk, moving slowly through an adjoining meadow until light began to fade and we considered it prudent to head back to the rig. This being bear country, we always tried to use caution at twilight.

After a peaceful night, we got on the road again early in order to enjoy the vistas of the Denali Highway which were growing more varied and colorful as we progressed east. By mid-morning we decided we needed to get out and stretch our legs. Pulling the coach to the side, we stepped down and discovered we were parked in the midst of a verdant patch of wild blueberries (or huckleberries as they are called in Montana where we would be Rving years later). Visions of blueberry pancakes and muffins suffused my hungry brain, so gathering a wild harvest became the order of the day. Equipped with plastic bags, we picked several quarts of the delectable little blue fruits. We only stopped when we realized we were going to have to go much farther afield to find more in the usable size range. What a treat to eat the berries right off the bushes as we foraged slowly around our parked RV! Having achieved a state of blue satiation, we climbed back aboard and headed down the Denali talking about all the recipes Sandra knew for using our "baby blues".

By afternoon, we had bounced and bumped along quite enough - it was time to set anchor, so to speak, and let Regina Victoria take a much needed overnight rest. A large gravel pit beckoned and we turned in to survey the area. These graveled areas to the sides of highways and roads occur frequently in Alaska and Canada and no one seems to mind if travelers decided to utilize them for overnight stays. This one was level, and showed signs of rock fire rings where previous campers had stayed and enjoyed an evening blaze to ward off the chill. Then Sandra suddenly came up with what sounded like a grand idea: why not pull through the gravel pit and up a slight hill so that we could park higher and have a commanding view of the huge river valley spreading out to our south? Plus, a storm was rapidly approaching and she thought atop the hillock would be a good spot to witness an Alaskan lightning display.

Suiting action to idea, we drove slowly across the gravel and up a slight incline. Without warning, things went very wrong. The RV simply stopped dead and then began to dig itself into the soft ground. This was seriously bad, and the only time so far that I had been really concerned about our situation. As we got out and looked at the predicament, I suddenly realized we did not own a shovel (a really stupid mistake). Somehow we were going to have to dig this 34,000-pound vehicle out with our soup ladle. Our first thought was to put some old rugs and blankets underneath the RV's tires that we had stored in the RV's cavernous underbelly. This technique failed and resulted in the coach digging itself in yet another few inches. By now, we had managed to bury the tow bar, so the Jeep couldn't be removed. That had to be fixed – quickly – as rain and fierce lightning was heading our way. In that country you can see a storm approaching for miles, which gives you more than enough time to become really worried about what happens when soft dirt turns to thick mud.

Digging frantically with a large stick I found, I managed to get the tow bar up to the light of day and quickly unhitched the Jeep, backing it far out of the way in case I figured out a way to get the RV reversed out of its present predicament. We then set about finding rocks and branches with which to build ramps under the big dual tires. We tried several groupings, with no more success than we had had with the rugs and blankets. And the storm was getting closer.

At this point, a miracle occurred. A pickup truck containing an older man, his adult son and two little granddaughters suddenly hove into sight in the gravel area. It is hard to imagine our relief just to realize we had a link with the world of succor should it be needed (cell phones are routinely useless in such areas). Better yet, they pitched in and helped us build better ramps. Even the little girls scampered about hunting for nice rocks and sticks. In the meantime, the coach had developed a pronounced list to the right. We decided to dump some of our suspension air, trying to leave just enough so that the coach would go into "drive" when the time came.

After trying (and once again failing) to move the big vehicle forward, we decided that reversing the process and building ramps to the rear would ultimately work better. Everyone worked to move the sticks and stones to the back side of the big dual rear tires. I jumped in, fired up Regina, and as delicately as I could, feathered the throttle and eased her carefully into reverse. Our strategy worked! Regina gathered momentum and we were able to heave her out of the sizeable hole that she had dug just a short time before. We were (and are) so grateful to that Alaskan family who came to our aid that day. I don't know their names, but they certainly embodied that spirit of helping one's neighbors that seems always to characterize frontier areas. They would accept no payment for their troubles and with a waved goodbye, explained they were late for a family get-together and wished us good luck in our travels. On another road trip a few years later, we were able to pay this favor forward by helping a young Mexican family stuck in a similar situation in the desert of the Baja.

We pulled the RV around so that it was parked facing the Denali, with a grand view of the valley out our large side windows. Then we assessed the damage. The tow bar was unbent, although heavily coated with mud and little stones. That was an easy fix. Because the coach had listed badly to the side, we had lost a lot of our potable water, but we could ration that if we decided to stay at this beautiful site. The biggest issue was the large stone guard that hangs down at the back of the rig. It has "Holiday Rambler" emblazoned across it in embossed letters on a metal plate fastened to a *very* heavy rubber backing panel, the whole unit suspended from a bar across the rear of the coach. The guard had been twisted and bent in the process of extricating the rig and it didn't look as though it was going to be road worthy anytime soon.

Here was another learning experience that I treasure now in retrospect. I am not mechanically inclined, but this was a problem to be solved here and now. Throwing on my oldest pair of dungarees, I "got out and got under" as the old motoring song would have it. Lying flat under the big engine, it was clear the guard would have to come off. There was no way it could be straightened by hand. It appeared there were at least three ways that it could be removed, but two of them involved removing very large, very rusty screws. If I had the arm strength, this might have been an option...removing two large ring bolts instead was the most feasible way of getting this monster loose.

I rummaged through my toolbox and found a very heavy screwdriver and several pairs of pliers that would serve the job. Equipped with my little arsenal, I crawled under again and very carefully twisted and pried until I had one fitting loose. Then I braced the heavy piece on a convenient rock (I wanted to end the day with all of my fingers!). From that point it was straightforward to unfasten the other end and let the whole piece drop to the ground. Pulling it out from under took just about all my arm strength, but I managed it and finally wrestled the guard into the back of the Jeep for transportation to anyone within a thousand or so miles having a hydraulic press of some sort. Feeling the sheer bulk of the thing made me realize it could not be repaired with any force at my disposal. But the rig could run fine without it and the Jeep already had so many stone nicks that a few more wouldn't even be noticeable.

We decided to stay in that spot for the night, figuratively nursing our wounds and taking stock of any other damage. Other than losing water and crumpling up the rock guard, we were in pretty good shape. The night was absolutely beautiful, as for once we had a full sky of stars (even if briefly). In fact, we stayed for four days and this turned out to be one of our very best camping adventures.

The area was completely bereft of any signs of civilization. Our companions were the ubiquitous Alaskan ravens and various unidentified animals who left tracks around the camp every night. We knew to be wary of bears, but we never saw any signs of them or any other mammals during the daytime. We worked diligently on our respective writing projects, took hikes away from the RV, and shot pictures in all directions. We were surrounded by distant mountains and a silence so vast that we could imagine ourselves as early settlers in the North American continent, declaring all of this to be "our" valley.

One of the beautiful aspects of staying there were the I-Max scale rainbows that appeared every day. These were huge, sky-wrapping, full technicolor rainbows displaying the visible spectrum from deepest red to eye-tearing violet. I had never seen rainbows so spectacular and was thrilled to be able to capture some of them on camera.

Each evening we built a fire in our little fire ring, using brush free for the gathering all over the area. The warmth and coziness of the fire was very welcome, as temperatures dropped into the 30's each night. The fires also made us feel a bit more at one with the First Nations peoples who had lived in similar areas of the North for many thousands of years and gathered around fires in the night.

The Denali highway turned out to be a highlight of our travels in Alaska. After four days of blissfully quiet camping, alone for hours on end, we were finally at a point where we should move on. We were low on water and didn't want to push our luck in terms of diesel fuel. The decision made, we fired up and trundled back on to the Denali, the Jeep obligingly bobbing along close behind. The Denali highway is, without doubt, a challenge, particularly for a large RV with a car in tow. The road is only open in the summer, from May to September, and it is so remote and requires such constant maintenance that it is never really in anything like good repair. Fixing the Denali is a task for the steadfastly optimistic. A vision of what it can be must hover in the minds of the stalwart road workers who keep tackling its potholes, washouts and deep dips.

We encountered quite a number of resolute Alaskan Highway Department workers. They were uniformly cheerful and we often chatted with them as we waited patiently behind their temporary stop signs for a load of gravel to be dumped or a big grader to level up a short section in front of us. They were always willing to talk with us, and we often shut down our engine because the waits could be long.

We would ask them questions about the highway like, "Would it ever be fully paved?"

"Probably not," came the reply with a big smile.

"How late in the year do you all work on it?".

"We're out of here by September 15."

"How do you reopen it?"

"Well, come late spring," explained our sunburned jolly flag-man, "We bring our biggest bulldozers up here and start on the snow. Sometimes we have to move 20 or more feet off before we can even get down to the roadbed."

With serious permafrost heaving and water washouts, the surface in the beginning of the driving season must surely be pretty awful. But this is one of those fabled "Last of their Kind" highways with beckoning appeal (like the Dempster) that captures your imagination and your soul. These same highway workers return to the Denali year after year, partly because they appreciate the sheer grandeur of their surroundings.

This highway presents views that are of "a time before people", when the cry of the raven is all the sound you hear. This is a land that treats First Nations people and Europeans with equal indifference, yielding little to the demands of civilization and keeping its ancient secrets locked frozen and impenetrable for much of the Northern year. The usual signs of life are lacking here – rare, indeed, is the songbird and most animals are seen only as fleeting glimpses far in the distance.

The silence along the Denali is as vast as the land itself, often a bit lonely, at times more comforting than lonely, at times more essential than anything else. The silence and the empty space characterized the very essence of the Denali. It's a road not to be missed and best appreciated when driven very slowly, with frequent stops to savor the quiet and the panorama. Driven hard, it is just a lonely road in the middle of nowhere. But driven with appreciation, it becomes a magical landscape.

The last 50 or so miles of the Denali were tough— partly because we were leaving a wonderful wilderness we might never see again, and partly because the road itself was in even worse repair. The last 20 miles of the Denali are paved (in a manner of speaking) which made the going easier but it also meant we were back in "civilization", with paved rest stops and trash cans and warning signs, and actual fellow humans in close proximity.

CHAPTER 11

And Bears... Oh, My!

O nce we exited the Denali, we were back on Alaska route 4 which runs south as far as Galkona Junction. The scenery along this route is what we came to call "typical Alaska" (if such a varied geographical entity has anything typical about it!). We drove through relatively flat valleys with high mountain peaks (some snow-capped in late August) keeping us company in the distance, always a picture postcard scene. This highway has a rural charm and is largely untraveled even in the height of the tourist season.

The vehicles we did see occasionally were interesting studies themselves. The majority were, of course, pickup trucks, well used, generally dirty. Some had still-older cab-over campers perched precariously atop the truck bed. We also saw a number of older trailers, in the styles popular in the 1970's, as well as converted school buses and a few (very few) motor homes about our size. All the vehicles were well scarred with rock nicks and many sported the same gargantuan steel bar front-end protectors observed on over-the-road trucks in many of the more remote parts of

Canada. All vehicles with Alaskan tags seemed to have the ever-present electrical plug sticking out from under the grille. These were for the engine block heaters and we did see quite a number of business and public spaces that had posts with heater plug-ins for the more severe winter days. In fact, at the Walmart in Anchorage we saw a number of heater posts designated for store employees. It would be tough to get off at midnight in 30 degrees below zero and try to start a very cold engine!

Pickup trucks abound in Alaska. They seem to represent the culture – frontier, no nonsense, self-reliant and a great place to keep guns! Some Alaskans must clearly enjoy shooting because we saw a truly staggering number of road identification signs, mile markers and directional arrows, riddled with bullet holes in a wide variety of calibers. I don't know if shooters get out and take aim (in which case they are very brave, considering the narrow roadways) or whether they fire *en passant* from moving vehicles (in which case they are very good shots, indeed!).The state highway workers deal with this so often that they have evolved a system of repair/repaint that keeps the signs legible in spite of the fusillades aimed at the signs. To someone from a city, this can be a bit unnerving, but at the same time, we saw less evidence of a conspicuous "gun culture" than in many parts of the Lower 48.

At Golkan Junction we turned north onto the Tok Cutoff, an inelegant name for quite a pretty stretch of road. We had been on this road earlier in our travels, and normally try to avoid using the same route twice but felt we ought to travel it again for several reasons. First, we wanted to get back into Canada and begin slowly heading south. Our experience on the Denali had shown that cold weather came much earlier here than expected. We had observed frost in the mornings and many of the low tundra scrub plants were already sporting autumn colors as were the aspen and larch we were beginning to see along this highway. Additionally, talking with locals at fuel stops or the occasional restaurant convinced us cold weather might be expected earlier than normal this year – even the Canada geese were packing their little suitcases and studying their maps to find the best flyway south!

We also decided that we *had* to reach the Hyder/Stewart area along the Canadian/U.S border in order to watch the grizzly bears scooping salmon from the streams. For these last months before the snow and real cold set in, the bears labor with almost manic concentration on fattening up for the long hibernation soon to come. We hadn't realized they lose up to 30% of their body weight during the long sleep, so feeding is critical at this time of the year. Also, we learned that the salmon probably stopped their spawning run by mid-September, so we wanted to get there before the last of the fish made their determined upstream climb.

Travelling Canadian and Alaskan highways in the reverse direction is still a terrifically interesting experience. Except for a few familiar landmarks, it's hard to believe you have been on the road before. Invariably, we found that the road run backwards appeared totally different from the road run forward. Mountain tops appeared at new angles, lakes, which had been empty before, now had flocks of ducks and even the rare moose (as in Two Moose Lake, which actually hosted two moose when we passed!). Distant valleys glowed with new colors under different light. Even the familiar frost heaves and potholes looked different (actually, they probably are different if it has been more than a few days since you last journeyed on a particular stretch of road). Driving the road back to Tok was just as beguiling as our initial adventure had been. There were a number of "Wow, look at that" moments, so the time to reach Tok passed quickly and pleasurably.

As soon as we reached the little town, we made a beeline for the biggest RV park we could find. We desperately needed to pump out and also as desperately, needed to fill our fresh water tank. Plus, it would be nice to plug into a 50-amp circuit and run our electrical appliances without generator noise or worry about battery drain. The RV experience can teach even a grey-haired Senior a number of lessons, and one of the most important was how wasteful most of us are concerning water. Before marrying Sandra and embarking on this Grand Adventure, I watered my lawn with almost religious fervor, took long showers just to relax in the steamy water and ran the washing machine or the dishwasher half full. Urbanites living with abundant water tend not to think about how much of the precious stuff is used and misused every day.

The Denali adventure forced us to be very careful about our water usage, and we were surprised at how little water we could get by with if forced to do so. Sandra was much more familiar with conservation of water than I was as this had been a sometimes life-and-death requirement during her years of solitary sailing in the Pacific. I grasped the concept quickly and enjoyed learning to use alternate means of cleaning (dishes cleaned in sand look quite nice if you don't manage to rub the finish off!). I figured a family from Trans-Saharan Africa would have no trouble adopting to RV life on tankage.

RVing has taught me what Sandra already knew: take very fast showers if at all, rinse economically (bodies, pots and pans), flush the commode watchfully, and scrutinize gauges and meters with healthy skepticism. Never entirely trust a meter showing either full or empty. And that is another lesson this trip has provided: to look at how we use all resources, both our own and the planet's.

We are both environmentally concerned, but being in the "Great Northern Wilds" opened our eyes to a number of issues. Seeing the Alaska pipeline strung along the landscape for some 800 mile was as eye-popping as it was eye-opening. The sheer size of it – some four feet in diameter and supported by special Teflon structures engineered to allow it to flex with permafrost or even earthquakes— made our excessive oil usage in the Lower 48 dramatically real. The volume of oil flowing through something you can see a few feet off the road is staggering – millions of barrels per day, every day. The oil flows north to south endlessly, accelerated at points by pumping stations with engines big enough to power a sizable freighter. Such a volume of oil speaks of a dependence on petroleum which is almost beyond comprehension.

At Valdez we had seen the southern terminus of this huge oil flow... the "black gold" stored in vast above-ground oil tanks just across the Sound from where we had been camping in our RV. Parenthetically, Alaska appears to have no refineries, so the oil from Alaska is shipped to the west coast, refined, and then shipped back to Alaska as high-cost gasoline and diesel fuel. (This, I might add, does not make Alaskans happy.)

Talking about oil (or the Exxon Valdez disaster) is not easy to do with natives. I remember our sightseeing captain on Prince Edward Sound saying the Exxon Valdez was a "learning experience" and how the only remaining traces of the vast oil spill could be found four feet below the shore sands. I remember finding this hard to digest, but everyone tries to put Big Oil in the best possible light since it is a critical part of the Alaskan economy.

Our trip up to this point had also taught us that rivers and wildlife were natural resources which, even in this vast, under-populated land, took more husbanding and thought than I had realized before coming here. I've always been a member of Green Peace, the Sierra Club and NRDC, but to read their brochures or emails while sitting on my suburban deck watching a chipmunk devour my petunias was very different, indeed, from watching moose graze from a distance of 50 yards and realizing the environment for these big creatures was actually very fragile. Best of all was seeing the difference in the various habitats up close. Wandering through the State Park System of the Midwestern U.S. does not really prepare one for the Far North's vast variety of environments. That was one advantage of travelling in our big rig – we were going slowly and so we got to observe the gradual changes between taiga, tundra, alpine, tree-line and lower valley meadows and forests. Now, when we see black spruce trees, a bell goes off in our heads and we automatically think "permafrost environment" or "that little spruce over there could be a hundred years old" or "bad forest fire, but just think of all the spruce seeds that were opened and will now sprout".

The complexity of the north's interconnected, frequently fragile environments has to be seen to be really meaningful. I've always wanted to protect and save wolves and polar bears, but until I saw the wolves' environment first hand, saw the great distances they cover, heard and saw the sights and sounds they hear and see – not until then did I appreciate what saving them really means. Now there is a personal connection with them and with their environment that I didn't have before this trip.

The whole process of saving wildlife has taken on a greater sense of urgency. The little Picas, first seen on the high slopes around Banff, play a key role in the survival of the bigger carnivores of the northern food chain. I can close my eyes and see the scree and shale environment where the appealing little rodents were sunning themselves in June, awake and brimming with energy for the three months of the year when they are not deeply asleep. Global-warming is forcing them higher and higher up their home mountains, thus removing them as a protein source for the carnivores that have, until now, relied on them as an essential dietary element. And I have a much better idea of what a moose's home turf looks like. I have seen it and can recall the scenes in my mind, where before, my picture of "moose-at-home" took the form of an idealized lake somewhere in Maine, probably part of an L.L.Bean catalog cover. It's sometimes quite surprising to see the great creatures of the north in odd settings – a herd of bison in the midst of a forest, or several moose in a little pond surrounded by acres upon acres of open tundra.

Our stay in Tok (at the aptly named Tok RV Park – people in the north don't seem preoccupied with cute names for places) gave us time to relax and refit. We took on water, diesel fuel (once again at a highly inflated price) and double-checked the engine and transmission fluids. I also spotted a very dilapidated building across the highway sporting a faded sign announcing a wide variety of mechanical services. Late on our first afternoon in Tok, I wandered over and found a very nice young mechanic (and various members of his extended family) in the front office. He said he could do an oil change on the Jeep and would be happy to service the big rig's diesel generator.

Once again, it was a delight to visit and chat with skilled, low-key local service people who appeared always to take great pride in the variety of things they knew how to do. I love being able to walk through the office and into the service area, with no "Keep Out – Insurance Forbids" signs warning me off. One traverses piles of old tires, mysterious large hunks of metal, usually finding the owner somewhere towards the rear of the shop, his head buried in the innards of an elderly truck. With our RV, I can bend over and put my head right in there, too, and explain what I think needs to be done and even guesstimate at how soon it might be done. These are people we trust with Regina Victoria because they are honest about what they can and can't do.

After some consultation, it was agreed they could do the Jeep yet that afternoon, but it would be tomorrow or so before they could get to the RV's generator. "Have to get the filter up the road a ways, you know" seemed to explain the delay. That timing was fine, because there was a large hydraulic lift in the rear of the shop and perhaps, they could use it to straighten the RV's bent mudguard. We left the mudguard in the shop's custody in the hope it would emerge in better condition. After chatting a bit about the weather and about the swift approach of winter, the owner mentioned that is it was already below freezing in the mornings at his house just outside of town and he predicted snow would be coming soon.

The next day, the owner turned us over to his assistant as he had to go on a tow call in Chicken, some 95 miles away, to rescue an ailing RV. I must say in admiration that he had the largest collection of tow trucks parked all over his property that I had ever seen up close. Some, like the massive machine he had taken that morning, were new and shiny. Others were much older. They came in a wide variety of sizes and shapes, and sported paint jobs ranging from 70's psychedelic to natural rust. There was even a battered U.S. Army tow truck parked out front, a monument to the titanic effort that had gone into building the Al-Can highway in 1942.

Later in the day, the assistant said he had tried to straighten the mud guard using the hydraulic lift, to no avail. Number 2 Man said he would mention it when the owner returned from the Chicken tow. I was not terribly hopeful, but the next morning, as we drove the coach over to the repair shop, the owner produced the huge mud guard and, with a big grin, demonstrated it was straight again (well, mostly straight). I don't know what bit of alchemy he performed during the night on that unwieldy hunk of metal and rubber, but the result was dramatic. The mud guard was now ready to be re-hung. Since everyone was busy, the owner's son agreed to help me re-install the guard. It was soon in place. The owner had even taken the time to polish it up and it really did look quite handsome again. With that done and the Jeep and generator serviced, we were almost ready to roll.

Before we left, to refill the big propane tank, I drove the rig up the street to a service station right across from the RV Park. All the pumps were self-serve except for the shiny propane tank situated inside its guard fence. Calling the number on the station's padlocked door, it turned out the station and the RV park were owned by the same folks. The owner came across the street in short order and we talked while he was filling the RV's oversized propane tank. He and his wife had owned the station for years and had made a real success of it until a large oil company opened an ultra-modern station just up the block. The couple tried to keep going in the face of the new competition for several years, making their money in the summer to tide them over the harsh winter months. But they just couldn't keep it up anymore and closed the convenience store part of the operation. l found this quite sad as the owner was a very affable gentleman and so willing to trade stories with travelers He was also a great source of local road and weather information and I pumped him about how best to get back to British Columbia and what road conditions we might encounter. When we left, I knew I would be telling every traveler we met that they should definitely plan on stopping at his gas station.

During our travels in Alaska and Canada, we had often seen boarded up small local businesses that had gone under... the price of "progress". We felt the loss both in terms of personal service and in "personalities"...those colorful characters who were so often the proprietors and denizens of the small local businesses. Here in these emporia, we often found people willing to reveal parts of themselves and their lives to the traveler who is munching on one of their hamburgers or buying a few gallons of their gas. Often, we would buy some small souvenir of the area– a pretty handmade scarf for Sandra, a jar of local jam or jelly – just to hear more tales.

Finally, repairs completed and vehicle restocked, it was time to leave Tok and head for the Canadian border. We realized with a touch of sadness that we were leaving Alaska and might not see these sights again soon, so we did our best to capture these vistas in our memories. We talked about the impression Alaska had made on us and remembered the delightful people we had met in the small towns and in the 12-step program meetings we attended along the way.

If Alaska wasn't to become a blur of competing mountain views, we had to isolate the experiences that had been most meaningful for each of us and for the two of us as a couple. It was not easy because we had taken in so much. Alaska can leave one with a kind of sensory overload where all the glaciers become one enormous generalized flow of ice and all roads become windy and climbing, nearly touching the surrounding mountains.

We didn't want to just remember THE Alaskan Glacier or THE Alaskan Snowy Peak. So we tried to remember and record specific details. How had Mt. Denali looked in dawn's first morning light? What had most impressed Sandra about Valdez? To me, how had the fishing fleet looked at night, returning from Prince Edward Sound after a hard day in a rough sea? Hey, remember that glorious morning in Valdez when the rain stopped, the mists lifted, and there…everywhere…was that incredible ring of high mountains bathed in the light of early morning surrounding the charming little town? Remember Prince William Sound and our cruise there – getting up close to the Puffins in their rookery or hearing the extraordinarily sharp sound of a glacier calving, huge chunks of ice breaking away with deceptive speed and power to crash into the near-freezing sea? Interestingly, we often associated an area or a geological feature with a person…someone who had helped us, or told us interesting things, or who had become a new friend. Those close connections made the scenery spring to life in our memories, and that may be the best part of being a touring visitor.

As Sandra and I talked while driving out of Tok, we realized Alaska, like the Yukon and the Northwest Territories, had worked emotional magic on us. Banff and Lake Louise, and the Ice Road Parkway out of Banff…all had special significance and tremendous beauty in their own right. Banff and Lake Louise and the surrounding mountains were guilty of almost mesmerizing natural beauty… the beauty of dreams, the joy of being human among Earth's mightiest mountains. But all these treasures somehow appeared "managed", if not manicured. Gorgeous Tyrolean-style chalets and ski resorts complemented the natural wonders to create an artful, if not deliberate, aesthetic experience. Chair lifts carried you to dizzying heights and let you off to view a mountain range that looked as though it had just been created. This was a kind of Hollywood set on a truly DeMille size scale!

The border crossing from Alaska back into Canada is a relaxed procedure. The lady at the Canadian border asked us a couple of questions, admired our doggy, asked if his vaccinations were up to date, looked at our passports, and waved us cheerfully on through. We were back in the Yukon and immediately hit one of the worst stretches of highway we were to encounter on the whole trip. This is the infamous "hundred mile bad road" that we had heard tales of from RVers as far away as Michigan. We knew it was here, but after all the tough roads we had already maneuvered, we figured this one couldn't be that bad. Wrong! We did much of the road at a dead-slow pace and by evening, we were exhausted. This highway is an alarming series of potholes combined with frost-heaving the likes of which we had not seen even in the farthest reaches of the far north.

It is interesting that the U.S. has assumed responsibility for the maintenance of this "highway" because apparently, 85% of the traffic is U.S. citizenry or military. In spite of the combined efforts of U.S. highway engineers and hardy Canadian contractors, the road remains a nightmare of deep holes, ruts, frost-heave, vanishing shoulders, too-narrow lanes and steep grades. And the cause is, Mother Nature! This is simply *not* a place where there ought to be a road. Besides the ever-present permafrost heaving issues and the harsh climate, the very soil itself is completely unsuited to supporting a roadbed. So the year-round effort on this roadway is a constant battle against Nature and soil elasticity. Most of the time, climate and soil come out on top!

On the flip side, driving anywhere in the Yukon is fun. The views are incredibly diverse and fellow drivers are unfailingly courteous when it comes to passing on the narrow roads. They wait for safe places to pass, use their turn signals, and rarely cut in too close after getting by you. We did notice we were now driving in a slightly lower landscape. Behind us were the huge, jagged peaks of the Alaska Range. The Yukon mountains we were now seeing through our bug-spattered windshield were more likely to entertain us with interesting rock formations and twisted ruggedness rather than with sheer size and majestic grandeur. These were mountains that clearly showed the effects of two major land masses colliding and slowly continuing to push up the landscape through which we were driving.

At the end of our first day back in Canada we were really wrung out and ready for any suitable resting spot that would take us. The Universe gave us better than we could have hoped for. We found a beautiful big gravel turnout to the east of the highway overlooking the sparkling beauty of Lake Kuane, with snow-capped mountains in the distance. This was the perfect place to stop, so the big Cummins was finally silenced and we went for a stroll along the lake shore. Sandra then prepared one of her signature gourmet road feasts to celebrate the end of a successful (and safe) day. The evening was spent playing a favorite card game, catching up on journals, and taking a myriad of photos of the sunset over the lake. What made the evening even better was a cool breeze late in the evening, creating little whitecaps on the lake and pushing foamy waves onto the rocky beach just below our RV. What a way to go to sleep – waves breaking gently on the beach and cool mountain air blowing through the RV's open bedroom windows.

The next morning dawned crystal clear, with just a hint of clouds forming a band about half way up the nearby mountains, revealing the bottoms and tops of the surrounding hills with a weird strip of invisibility

in the middle. Naturally we had to shoot lots more digital bytes to capture this interesting effect. Once underway that morning, we continued
around Lake Kuane, trying our best but failing to spot the elusive Dall
sheep or mountain goat. They really are more elusive than I would have
believed, especially after all the wildlife we had already seen. Wonder why
the moose don't feel they have to hide way back off the road? Looking
for wildlife kept us aware of all the birds to be seen and we managed to
add several species to our life list of birds. And finally, the road began to
improve. Once again we felt the pleasure of a big motor home on a good
road. We also noted the land was definitely beginning to flatten out as we
approached Whitehorse once again, this time from a different direction.

CHAPTER 12

Slowly South

A fter Alaska, we found we were in "greenery deprivation mode" as the Yukon's terrain became not only flatter, but noticeably drier as well. The scenery was still dramatic, with mountain vistas to entertain us throughout the afternoon of driving. Interestingly, as I saw the gentler (or at least shorter) mountains, I felt again a desire to go climbing, which is strange as I had never been interested in climbing mountains (or even short hills) before this trip. Travelling in the Yukon and the Northwest Territories, I had developed an urge to jump out of the RV and go hiking up the smaller cliffs, perhaps a result of seeing mountains less colossal and therefore, more attainable than the giant peaks of Alaska. This visceral response intrigued me.

Several factors were at play here. First off, the RV life does not give one much chance for sustained exercise. It requires a force of will to be active every day, and in cold, rainy weather that can be a decided challenge. This is especially true if you are on the road for long hours at a time, day after day, which is pretty much what the topography of the

Great North demands. The distances are daunting, and time on the road is, of necessity, quite long.

The desire to go hiking up and down hills may have been my body saying, "Carl, you've sat here long enough behind this wheel…go out and DO something." Secondly, the mountains in this part of Canada seem hospitable, at least in comparison with the really huge peaks of Alaska or British Columbia where climbing conjures visions of Tibetan- style expeditions, complete with Sherpas, huge coils of rope, mountain tents, and all the esoterica of dangerous, highly technical climbing. These Yukon mountains look more like a "jeans-sweatshirt-and- hiking-staff" kind of climbing, more suited to exercise than world-class conquest.

A lesson learned here was that I had become far more adventurous. The challenge of this whole trip, driving a large motor home with car in tow, managing all the day-to-day issues of hydraulics and power systems…all had made this Senior into more of a risk-taker.

"Oh, I'd love to do that if I had the time. Maybe *someday* I'll…" was my usual response to something "daring". Once we had accepted the challenge of this very long road trip, new challenges were being met much more easily. As I said to Sandra on more than one occasion, I'm much better than I ever was at 'getting out and getting under'.

Coming back to Whitehorse was a homecoming of sorts. The roads around the town appeared comfortably familiar and we immediately went to check on the eagles' nest down by the river to see if the fledglings had departed the nest yet. We arrived at dusk, and there, sure enough, was at least one of the juveniles. Larger now by far and sitting on the very edge of the nest, he was flexing his wings and giving that unmistakable eagle screech which can be heard over vast distances. We wanted to see the smaller one but he was facing away from us. This was no problem for Sandra who has a way with birds. Her affection for feathery friends all began when, in one of her many careers, she served as director of the Women's Committee of The Academy of Natural Sciences in Philadelphia, a fund-raising branch of The Academy which sponsored many exhibitions. As director, two noteworthy exhibitions came "under her wing" each year: The Academy's acclaimed annual "Wildlife Art Expo" as well as its "Wildfowl Expo". Additionally, she prepared for publication, Robert McCracken Peck's book, A Celebration of Birds: The Life and Art of Louis Agassiz, published by The Academy in conjunction with its renowned exhibition, "A Celebration of Birds" which also came under her purview. After closing at The Academy, that exhibition began a two-year, 10-city national tour under the auspices of the Smithsonian Institution. Some time later, my bride met a reputed expert on sea birds who had just finished studying The Academy's ornithological collection for a paper on the molting patterns of sea birds. She then spent several months travelling with him to assist studying the collections of other Natural History museums including Chicago's Field Museum and the Museum of Natural History in NYC.

I loved listening to my beloved's tales, and this avian one was no exception. I was bent over with laughter when she told me, "You can't imagine what fun I had, walking around those restricted scientific areas closed to the public, carrying a huge stuffed Wandering Albatross with its 11-foot wingspan under one arm and a goofy-looking Pelican under the other."

Years before we met, she recounted when she was living aboard her sailboat in Moss Landing and all the pelicans were dying. "I'd find one or two dead alongside my boat in the slip every morning and no one seemed to know what was wrong with them or what to do. It was very upsetting."

She went on to tell me about the morning she woke up and saw a pelican leaning next to the dock gate that lead down to her boat and looking like he was about to fall over:

"I had had a dental root-canal done the day before and had some penicillin pills and thought one might help the bird. I walked slowly up to him, grabbed his long elegant beak with my hand and shoved two pills down his gullet. He didn't even flinch but he stared at me and his eyes seemed to be expressing gratitude. I went back to my boat and about two hours or maybe it was three hours later, I saw him merrily flying off."

During travels with the ornithologist, Sandra said she spent a lot of time bird-watching. He taught her how to make a soft susurating noise while hiding under a bush which would often attract a bird's attention as it tried to see who was new to its territory. As we stood watching the eaglet, Sandra began this ritual cooing, and sure enough, the young eagle was soon eyeing us speculatively as she continued the soft sounds. Shortly, we heard the call of a distant eagle, the full-throated cry of an adult, answered immediately by the juvenile on the nest. And then the adult dove in for a landing on the nest, right in front of us! What a perfect "welcome back"! We were so happy to see at least one of the young eagles upon our return to Whitehorse after so many weeks away in the north. We drove off, wishing the eagle family the best of luck and hoping that if we return to the Yukon we will again see that big nest occupied by eagles, perhaps the same breeding pair that have been raising chicks there for years.

The next morning we made Regina Victoria ready for further travels. With water and diesel tanks full, we pointed our little entourage of vehicles down the highway towards Watson Lake. Our idea was to take the Cassier/Stewart Highway southbound from Canada 16, in the direction of Stewart, B.C. and Hyder, Alaska, two towns that hug the border between Alaska and Canada. The Stewart/Cassier marks another of Canada's remarkable road odysseys. The scenery is not as grand as that of, say, the Dempster, but it has its own beauty, nonetheless, with forests and gorgeous streams and rivers wandering right beside the road, to the delight of fisherman from all over the world who come to catch trout and arctic char in these pristine waters.

On our second day on the highway, we were camped beside a bright little river, running full force just below our windows. The scene was breathtaking in its purity and sense of solitude. Then, as we were going about our morning chores, we saw a man in a station wagon pull up in front of us, get out and unload a very expensive looking, pro-grade video camera, complete with mike, sound gear, and a large sturdy tripod. Intrigued, we watched as he lugged these over to the riverbank, set them up, then returned to his car for his fishing equipment. Once he had his fly-casting rod and reel ready, he activated the recording gear, refocused on a spot just downstream, then stepped into the scene. He let off some really beautiful casts, working carefully with the current and dropping his fly into one small eddy after another. He appeared to be a serious fly fisherman.

I didn't quite "get" the camera equipment, however, and overcome with curiosity, I waited until he took a break, then stepped out of the RV to offer him a cup of coffee. He was most appreciative and as we stood drinking some of Sandra's best Kona, he related he was a filmmaker and singer/songwriter from Seattle. Just finishing a Canadian family vacation, he had decided on the video production to show his friends back home that, indeed, on these rivers you really could catch a big fish with every cast, just as he had bragged for years. Unfortunately, because of the recent heavy rains, the rivers were swollen, and the fish just weren't biting, so his idea wasn't working out. Nevertheless, he seemed to be having a grand time just casting. His friends would remain unconvinced, at least for another year, until he could make the trip again, but he had some good footage of his casting technique!

We chatted a bit more and then before he left, he thanked us for the coffee and the conversation with a CD of his own songs performed with a variety of Seattle musicians. He also invited us to tour Seattle with him if we got that far in our journey. We thanked him and wished him a safe trip with many more fishing adventures to come. It's a fun part of travelling in this part of the world to reach out to strangers. They always seem to reach back with a hand of friendship, a smile, a small gift. This was our second unsolicited CD of the trip, and made a welcome addition to our music library.

As we continued southwards on the Cassier, we had one of the more surreal experiences of the trip.... driving through a just-controlled forest fire in the midst of this vast emptiness. Driving onwards, we could smell the aftermath of the fire, a smell like a recently extinguished campfire. More disturbing, we could see areas very close to the road that were still smoldering. We thought to call the local fire authorities, but then discovered, once again, we had no cell phone coverage. This gave us pause as we contemplated what to do if the fire suddenly blazed up again. For the next 30 or so miles we drove very attuned to smoke and to where we could turn almost 60 feet of vehicle around in a hurry if we had to make a run in the reverse direction. Fortunately, our fears proved groundless and we proceeded steadily, albeit sadly, through the burned out areas.

We had heard earlier reports that the Cassier had frequently been closed due to forest fires, but to drive through one in process of burning itself out was an unusual experience. It did point out to us that in the vast forested reaches of the Canadian north, a "live and let burn" philosophy made a good deal of sense, especially because such species as the iconic Black Spruce relied upon the heat of fires to burst open their cones and release the seeds needed to revitalize an old forest. So fires burned as they had for millenia and while we regretted the passing of all these beautiful older trees, we could, at the same time, celebrate the rebirth that would soon come as a result of these scourging flames.

The Cassier passes through beautiful mountain scenery so we shot tons of pictures as we rolled southwards. Often we took what we called road shots – pictures framed by the big windshield, bug corpses littering the foreground just to let us know later where we had been and what we had seen. At other times we stopped and tried for a more professional shot, paying stricter attention to composition, lighting, framing, good fore and middle grounds to accent the lovely mountains in the distance. To us older "film camera" people, who grew up with darkrooms, chemicals, dodging wands and burning plates, it is truly remarkable what can be accomplished with the menus in digital cameras.

I am not at all sure that I will ever discover all the permutations of things which my Canon SLR can do, but I am having a heck of a time figuring it all out! What fun to be part of the digital revolution at our age and to begin to really understand how these cameras work. At the same time, I must add that I brought along some real film, 35mm color as well as some black and white and I had in mind to purchase an older (as in Leica older) camera in which to use the film. I think perhaps I just miss the fun of darkroom work – developing one's own negatives and then printing a really good enlargement. Selecting the right paper, getting the enlarger adjusted correctly… these were all part of the creative process and something that I continue to miss with today's digital photography. On the other hand, I would have spent all of our trip money by this point if I had taken this many photos with a film camera!

Along all of our major routes as we travelled through the North Country, we tried to be creative with our photography. The Cassier was no exception, and as another of Canada's "roads less travelled", we were able to jump out frequently with cameras in hand, trying for that ultimate shot that would define the day, the moment, that particular piece of roadway, the feeling of what we were witnessing. If traffic and time permitted, we sometimes actually got it right. More often than not it was

Sandra who saw the perfect shot. She has a very keen eye and her years as a journalist doing her own photos give her great vision with a lens. I love her work and admire her artistic shots as some of the best I have ever seen. Period.

As we neared Stewart, B.C., we began to look for a place to spend the night. Once again, the hospitable Canadians provided us with a variety of delightful gravel pullouts, most with picture postcard views where we were free to camp. We chose one looking up at a series of mountain glaciers with a fast-flowing stream as foreground. The rushing water had the milky appearance we had learned represented suspended rock flour from glacier runoff.

Smokey and I went for our evening walk and decided to see just how cold these northern streams really were… that is to say, *I* decided. Smokey was none too enthusiastic about being anywhere near the water. After all, as he pointed out to me, a 10-pound Chihuahua does not have a lot of protective blubber. So, bravely I removed my deck shoe and sock and stuck a big toe firmly into the flowing stream. Yikes! It really was as cold as I thought it might be, maybe a degree or two above freezing. It was the coldest natural water I had ever felt and I quickly put sock and shoe back on. Returning quickly to the RV, I treated myself to a hot cup of Sandra's good coffee and, of course, got a treat out for Mr. Smokers. With a favorite goody inside him, he appeared to forgive me completely for getting him so close to water (which he continues to dislike in all its manifestations, except in his water bowl).

The next day found us driving through unexpectedly rugged terrain along the Stewart part of the Cassier/Stewart highway. Tall, craggy, often snow-capped mountains loomed close to the roadside, and everywhere there were glaciers, most with the slightly eerie blue-green tint that spoke of uncounted thousands of tons of compacted ice. Sandra had developed an excellent eye for this distinguishing color and we could now more readily differentiate summer snow pack from real glaciers as we cruised slowly along this breathtaking expanse of mountains. Because this was bear country, we kept looking for signs of Grizzly, but saw none. Our conclusion was they were all in Stewart/Hyder at the famous fishing areas there, probably gorging on an abundance of salmon. We assumed we would see plenty of bears at the special viewing areas in Hyder.

Serious error! As we neared the U.S./Canada border, it was raining much more heavily and the streams were flowing (no, rushing) much more swiftly, some at the very top of their banks and cascading violently from rock to rock, throwing spray in all directions. There were towering waterfalls coming down the sides of the adjoining mountains, waterfalls whose like we had not seen this whole summer. These were waterfalls that would easily finish second only to such giants as Niagara and Victoria Falls.

All of these factors taken together, we learned later, meant that fish were very hard to see (or catch) and the resident bears were certainly smart enough to know this. Once we found ourselves in town(s), we checked into the local RV park, unhitched the Jeep (now in driving rain) and headed into Stewart, B.C. Hyder and Stewart are indistinguishable but for an international border running down the center of the two towns. The architecture is identical, the accents are the same, and all merchants accept either U.S. or Canadian currency.

We drove from Stewart across the street into Hyder and tried to find the highly touted bear viewing area. This is where we hoped to see the big grizzlies and blacks making a meal of the spawning salmon. Unfortunately, the weather continued awful, meaning it varied from merely heavy rain to torrential downpours. Eventually, we did find the area and braved the rains in order to walk out on the wooden decks that were designed to provide a positive bear-watching experience. In spite of the weather, we hoped we might see a few brave or hungry bruins foraging for dinner. We had no such luck. The bears were clearly smarter than us. They were probably warm and dry at home, sipping hot chocolate and watching reruns of Yogi Bear cartoons, perhaps playing gin rummy or munching on goodies purloined from unwary tourists. But they certainly were not fishing.

Disgruntled, we drove back into Hyder and stopped at the rather quaint general store for a few supplies. In the back of the store was a flat-screen TV, set on top of the soda machine and showing a continuous DVD of bears doing all the exciting things bears do on good days! In the video, the sun was shining brightly and there were bears fishing, bears mock-fighting, bears with cubs, bears playing with logs, even bears yawning and seeming to mug for the camera. That was as close as we came in Stewart/Hyder to actually seeing bears do *anything*. For $24.95 we could buy that very DVD and have the whole bear experience at our fingertips whenever we wanted. Somehow that seemed like cheating, so we bought a few bear postcards instead and went back out into the rain.

We stopped for a pizza on the way back to the RV and I realized that watching CNN on the pizzeria's TV was the first live television we had seen in a long time. Oddly, we had not missed it as much as I would have thought a few months before, when this saga began. What news we had gotten had come from locals or from papers or from the internet (at very slow speed usually). I suddenly realized I had missed the entire NFL pre-season and had not minded that at all! How's that for some positive changes?

The next morning we awoke to the sound of rain pounding on the sliders of the RV, so we had a coffee conference and decided, time to move on. We were wet, we were cold, and the bears could (eventually) stuff themselves on fish without us watching. Slogging through the deep puddles of the campground, we reattached the Jeep, unhooked all the wet cables and hoses, and started the Cummins (what a blessing a dependable engine is!). We took the Stewart Spur out of town, essentially retracing our path back to the main highway system, then pointed southwards again through the lower part of British Columbia, heading for the more populated belt near Vancouver. As we drove onwards we admired the beauty of B.C., its mountains, glaciers, and dense forests, as well as its small, infrequent, always-welcoming towns where we could buy diesel, stock up on donuts and kibbitz with the locals while refueling man or machine.

As we drove south, we looked at our maps and decided it would be fun to take one of the ubiquitous B.C. ferries across from the mainland to Vancouver Island where we hoped to visit the "Veddy British" town of Victoria and recreate a bit of Sandra's past. But first, there was a major obstacle to be overcome just before Britannia, British Columbia – a 31-kilometer downhill grade that exceeded 13% in some areas. This is a tough grade in a car and can wear out brakes on the family SUV. In a big RV, it is truly punishing, but we were blissfully unaware of just how bad a grade like this would be. Not only is the road very steep, but it is filled with hairpin turns and a rather alarming lack of pullouts. What few turnouts existed were interspersed with escape ramps, many of which seemed scarcely big enough to stop a vehicle our size if it was out of control. I shuddered to think what would happen to any gargantuan Canadian road-train truck caught without effective braking.

None of our readings prepared us for just how steep this road was, nor for how much of it was downhill. This was a lonely, rural two-lane road, with little room to pass or maneuver. Almost from the moment we passed the last cautionary sign and headed downhill on this bit of insanity, we found our brakes being put to a severe test. Even with the exhaust braking system engaged, we still had to tap-tap-tap the air brakes. After a short time the brakes began to smell hot. Next, we saw wisps of smoke coming from the front wheel wells.

We stopped and I opened the side door and stood on the steps to see how the brakes on the rear dualies were surviving. It looked bad! Bigger puffs of smoke were pouring out of the rear wells. We continued on and as soon as we could, found a turnout and pulled off the road, hoping to let the brakes cool and praying that they were not fried. We walked around trying to enjoy the crisp mountain air and letting the overworked binders cool a bit. Thinking we had waited long enough and not seeing any more smoke, we pulled back onto the road and continued downwards. Shortly thereafter, things began to go very wrong.

Sandra was driving and exclaimed that she could see in the big outside mirrors a cloud of smoke somewhere near the back of the RV. Then, very shortly, we were unable to see anything behind us as the brakes were now putting out enough smoke to qualify as a Beijing smog hazard! At this point, I reached for the fire extinguisher, afraid the brakes might actually be on fire. This was a phenomenon I had witnessed more than once on Missouri highways as 18-wheelers navigated the Ozarks.

The brakes wouldn't last long at this rate, so again (very quickly this time) we sought the roadside, vowing to wait long enough to get the brakes fully cooled down before proceeding (if we had any brakes left!). Jumping out as soon as we had stopped, I had the fire extinguisher in hand, pin pulled and ready to start spraying. Fortunately, there were no signs of active fire, but we were enveloped in dense, acrid, asbestos-flavored smoke. This was very worrisome as we still had kilometers of downhill to negotiate and no indication that it was getting any less steep. It was really surprising how hot the brakes were and touching the hot tires made me fearful of blowouts at any moment. Blowouts in a 17-ton vehicle are not tackled with hand tools and a jack at roadside. The RV doesn't even carry a spare, since it would be too heavy to lift anyway!

Another concern was that we might have completely roasted the braking system. It was reasonable to assume that such a huge volume of smoke could only come from a large acreage of tortured brake drums, and air brake replacement could be a *very* costly undertaking. These were not happy thoughts, but we tried to cheer each other with the idea that if we let the brakes cool enough, we might be able to limp down to the nearest town and find a brake expert to assess our damage. We actually took time to brew coffee and make a snack, trying to ease our fears. The smoke gradually dissipated and the tires cooled to where we could touch them again.

Finally, we figured it was safe to go. Sandra eased the coach back onto the road and within a few minutes was shepherding the brakes again (an RV gathers speed with startling rapidity if it is pointed more or less straight down a mountain.) And so it continued. Tap-tap-tap, ease off, tap-tap-tap, ease off, all the way to the bottom. We stopped once more for a cool off, trying to prevent the overheating by stopping before we saw smoke. This time we were joined by a trucker, also cooling his brakes. With considerable relish, he related the story that just the past week, on this very same downhill, a motorhome had overheated its brakes with catastrophic results. The brakes had actually caught fire, igniting the undercarriage of the RV. The whole motorhome had gone up in flames, a total loss.

As we eased back onto the highway, we sensed the road was leveling a bit and we could now rely more on engine braking. For the first time that long afternoon, we breathed a sigh of real relief and even held hands for a moment in gratitude. Sandra had done a masterful job of husbanding the brakes and keeping our big rig on the road. With evening coming on and feeling exhausted, we limped into a pretty, green provincial park, only to find that our RV was too long for their regular campsites. Oh no, we thought... not another setback on top of all the problems this afternoon. But we needn't have worried! The cheerful, Scottish-accented lady in charge thought of a good solution and directed us to the park's large overflow lot, where we found plenty of room and even had a beautiful view of the fjord on which the park is situated. We had to be self-contained, which was fine with us and allowed us the freedom of picking what we thought was the best site in the whole place. With the brakes still giving off an unpleasant aroma, we unhooked the Jeep and drove into town to check out the ferry terminal (we like to be prepared for narrow entries, sharp corners and all the other problems that can come with boat load-ings). We also found a wonderful Greek restaurant and had a really tasty and very relaxing meal. We both adore Mediterranean cooking, and this was some of the best we had encountered in quite a while.

Once back at the RV, we let Smokey have a good run around the campground, and our little friend cut loose, charging full-tilt from one of us to the other. Watching his legs twinkling in the evening sun as he ran reminded me suddenly of a time at a summer music festival where I had been privileged to watch my favorite pianist, Orly Shaham, playing a difficult Scriabin work. Her fingers and hands had actually become a blur as she thundered through a particularly exciting passage. Seeing Smokey happy and running free provided a joyous end to what had been a very long and scary day.

CHAPTER 13

A Touch of Class

The bay on which we were camped turned out to be the most southerly fjord in North America, with Norwegian-style views of rugged rock cliffs and snow-capped mountains in the distance. The scene was so lovely that we decided to stay for several days. By the third day, Regina Victoria's brakes had become less olfactorily offensive and we decided to proceed on our journey. A short (and very confusing) trip took us in the general direction of the ferry terminal. Somehow, even though we had scoped out the route ahead of time, we still got lost getting to the ferry. Apparently things look different from the height of the RV because we missed the cutoff to the ferry and found ourselves back at our starting point in short order.

We rang up the ferry terminal, and a very pleasant lady directed us through the narrow streets of Britannia to the correct drive leading to the ferry docks. Since we had made an advance reservation, we could pull into one of the short queues where we were soon directed to the head of one of the several loading lines. This is a good spot to be in a big RV. You can see the path onto the ferry and make adjustments as the traffic handlers direct a steady stream of vehicles onto the big ship. After a short wait, a young lady wisely wearing ear protectors gave us the big "Gentlemen, Start Your Engines" kind of signal generally reserved for NASCAR races, and we trundled gently forward onto the waiting ferry. We were soon locked into place by the deck crew, and since the ride was a good hour and a half, we left the RV and climbed up several decks to the lounge and observation area, vast after the confines of the lower holds. These BC ferries are quite nice up top, with very comfortable seating, huge windows, and even coffee and snack bars. Refreshed with some coffee and Danish, we watched the progress of the ferry through the islands of the channel and chatted with our fellow passengers.

That passage gave us some lovely views and a great opportunity to be on open water again. Even a ferry ride made us feel happy and proved to be a real treat after so much time on dry land. Arriving in Departure Bay on Vancouver Island, we returned below decks and gingerly steered the RV off the congested dock and onto the island.

We were still very concerned about the health of the air brake system on Regina Victoria, so we made a beeline out of Nanaimo and headed south to find an RV dealer. Within a few miles we found one and entered the parking lot, only to discover that this was the sales area, that it was far tighter than it had looked from the main street, and we were stuck! With the tow car on we couldn't back up, and the tow bar was at an angle that mitigated against easy removal of the Jeep. The sales staff was not pleased and directed us on a torturous route around the showroom and through what looked like about an acre of display campers and travel trailers.

Sandra followed an irritated salesman in charge, who stomped ahead of us waving his arms (unfortunately in the wrong direction). This resulted in our turning too sharply right and colliding with the raised hatch of a brand new trailer. The arm of our passenger side awning (the really big one) became stuck with a trailer's shiny door, resulting in a very tense conversation between me and the salesman.

He summoned a junior salesman, this one much more affable, who produced a very large power screwdriver. I agreed to take the Jeep off by pounding the bolts out of the tow brackets, and then helped raise the stuck trailer door to its highest possible position. The young salesman with the drill removed what seemed, to my straining arms, to be about 6,357 tiny screws (but who was counting). We ended up removing the entire door from the display trailer.

With our path cleared, we slowly backed the RV about six inches, swung very carefully left, and finally made it around the lot and back onto the road. We reattached the Jeep and proceeded onwards, hoping to find the RV dealer's service department on the same road. We found it, but without an appointment they were reluctant even to talk with us. When they did – finally – they told us they couldn't (or wouldn't) work on chassis issues but they did recommend a large vehicle repair facility a few miles further on, so off we went, the afternoon sun sinking lower and our frustration rising higher.

We easily found the big truck shop and this time received a friendly welcome. The owner was upstairs in his little office and I practically ran up the stairs, eager to find out just how bad (or good!) the news about the brakes might be. The proprietor was a delightful young man who dropped his paperwork and came right down to talk with us and assess the situation. Armed with a flashlight and his battered crawler, he slid under the big coach and we could hear him moving around underneath, muttering to himself. He soon emerged with a big smile and told us we had not damaged the brakes and there was plenty of lining left. The tires had also come through unscathed, but he did caution us to have the axle seals inspected regularly as our manic descent might have "cooked" the seals and, in time, they might leak onto the brake drums.

Sandra and I were relieved to get such good news, especially as I had been checking my bank balances to see how to pay for a major brake job! Sandra asked him if he could also inspect our leveling jack system, as we had been living all day with the system's annoying warning light/sounder in the cockpit. He readily agreed and we were able to produce a full schematic of the electrics for that system. The chap was unable to diagnose the exact problem, but we ran the jacks up, and with no issues, he concluded there was probably nothing drastically wrong with the system. The solution was to remove the fuse from the jacking system while we drove. This meant having to get out of the RV and put the fuse back in if we were to use the jacks, but it stopped the light and the annoying little "gong" in the cockpit. This was a splendid solution unless it was raining.

Our new friend also suggested adding more hydraulic fluid to the jacking system, so I found the mysterious large key whose sole function was to unlock only that compartment on the RV. Topping up the big reservoir appeared to solve the problem, at least temporarily. We discovered that this solution doesn't last long if the jacks were employed regularly, but it gave us peace and quiet in the cabin for the short haul. After many profuse thanks and a "contribution" to their coffee fund as a thank you to the owner and his staff (they never asked for any payment) we were off – finally - to enjoy Vancouver Island.

As we drove through the lovely countryside we admired the beautifully tended fields and the many rows of orchard trees, most laden with ripening apples. The late afternoon was sunny and bright and we drove south at peace with the world and once again in love with the RV life. By sunset (late in these parts) we arrived at the big RV park just west of Victoria that was to be home for some days. We needed to shake off the road weariness that we had begun to feel and it would be good to be in close proximity to such an elegantly urban setting as Victoria. This was a city that offered fine dining, beautiful architecture, pleasant climate and the urban green space Sandra and I both love. Our campsite at the RV park was quite a large pull-through with a leafy hedge screening one side for privacy. The site even featured a brick paved patio just outside the coach door. We unhooked the Jeep and made our way into Victoria for dinner.

Following what had become a pattern, we opted for a Chinese restaurant in the Chinese sector of Victoria. After checking that it looked busy (always a good sign), we hunted for a parking space. This precipitated a mild case of "city shock" as we had spent months in mostly tiny towns where parking meters were unheard of and parking was, one might say, very casual. But there was a space just two blocks from our intended eatery and, happily, I had not entirely lost my parallel parking skills. We walked back to the restaurant and discovered we were moving more quickly than usual, perhaps out of nervousness at being in "a city" again. Sandra, a center-city Philadelphia urban guerrilla in an earlier life, knew just how to walk to look as though she owned the sidewalk, a skill I have never developed. Following her lead and attempting to look acceptably nonchalant appeared to work.

We arrived, got seated, placed an order and waited….and waited…. and waited! Finally the meals came…sort of. Well, Sandra's came first, followed by mine about 15 minutes later. This made for an awkward dining experience. The food was actually good, but watching each other eat was odd. During our long meal we noticed a number of big tour buses making their slow and careful way through the narrow street beside our restaurant. Curious as to where they might be going in such profusion at 10:00 at night, we paid our bill and decided to follow in their wake. We returned to our Jeep, waited for a huge tour bus to pass, and quickly slipped in behind it. We followed the bus over a long bridge and then promptly lost it (and found ourselves lost as well).

This was no problem as we had nowhere we had to be and it gave us a great chance to see some very upscale Victoria real estate. We were in an area of elegant houses and very expensive looking mid-rise condos. I have no idea what those condos might cost, with their beautiful views of the lighted harbor spread out beneath their decks and patios, but I suspect it is more than either Sandra or I have in pocket change! We drove up and down the winding streets, simply enjoying the evening and the charming views of the city and the harbor below.

Driving around for a bit, we found another way back into the old part of the city and wound slowly around the harbor and past a number of beautifully illuminated public buildings. Victoria is a pretty city, both by day and by night. The city hall is especially noteworthy, as it looks like a very large Christmas decoration, illuminated in white lights from ground floor to high roof top. It is an appealing sight late at night, and a very welcome landmark for two out-of-towners trying to re-orient themselves. That evening we also found the famous Empress Hotel where we vowed we would take High Tea during our visit. We stumbled upon the Natural History Museum, the handsome Visitor's Center and the imposing Municipal Art Museum. Frankly, it felt really good to be back in a city big enough to have museums and concert venues and all the other trappings of enlightenment that we had missed more than we had actually realized.

The next day we decided to make a side trip, this time in the Jeep alone. We took one of BC's frequent ferries out to neighboring Salt Spring Island, one of the many channel islands bordering the big island of Vancouver. The car gave us a way to take Smokey along and also a method for getting entirely around the perimeter of the island. Salt Spring is a pleasant little island, and its main town is filled with restaurants, boutiques, and innumerable galleries displaying some fine artwork and crafts from the local creative community. We were lucky to have come on Saturday, the day of the big town market with extensive displays of the local cheeses, honeys, jams, home-baked breads and pastries, woven woolens and lovely jewelry (Sandra can never resist a good pair of earrings made by a local artist).

As we drove slowly around, I came to appreciate a big poster in a shop window depicting a cartoonish walrus slapping his sides and saying "And you thought you'd find a parking space in Salt Spring on Saturday…?" But finally we found a space, right next to a gallery housed in an old church. We browsed through several cheerful display rooms and eventually selected original pieces of artwork and clothing as our first souvenirs of Salt Island…a lovely little water color and a beautiful scarf Sandra added to her collection.

Strolling out of the church-turned-gallery, we wandered right into the midst of Salt Spring's annual Gay Pride Parade. We had parked in the lot that was the gathering/starting point of the parade and could interact with the participants as they groomed, preened, adjusted costumes and practiced their various marching acts. There was even a (fairly) good brass band to lead off the festivities. With careful timing we managed to escape the lot just before the start, beat the marchers into downtown, find another parking spot, and watch the parade unfold from our new vantage point. The participants appeared to be having a great time, and the audience flanking the parade route enjoyed the entire sunlit event.

Soon it was time for some mid-day sustenance, so we found a quiet little café and snagged an outdoor table right at the harbor's edge. The fish and chips were excellent and we savored the warm sunshine on our faces and feeling the cool breeze blowing across the lightly rippled waters of the little marina and harbor. After lunch, we strolled through town to the pretty city park where the farmer's market was in progress. After sampling a variety of the local delicacies, a favorite was a cheddar-like cheese made from goat's milk. What made it even better was that the goats providing the milk were all nannies residing on Salt Spring Island. "Can't get more local than that". We also sampled the local sausages and checked out the street food vendors (mostly variants of Thai or Italian basics). There was a good selection of locally produced craft items and jewelry, reassuring somehow, in a world economy that was not in good repair. People with skills were still creating beautiful things and offering them for sale each Saturday to those who somehow, in a bad economy, found money to buy these bewitching objects. I admired these local artists and hoped they would get the support they deserved and needed.

After exhausting the market, we walked toward our car, stopping at a local ice cream parlor that also made. heavenly chocolate products right in their back room. Needless to say, we just had to sample both ice cream and chocolate. Finally replete, we returned to the car, wiped all the stickies off our fingers and drove slowly around the whole island. What was interesting was that we had been on the road long enough now that we were asking ourselves, "Do you think you would like to live here?" We actually called about a couple of properties that were for sale and stopped to check on several rent/buy RV pads.

We were taken aback to find that a small RV pad could run upwards of $72,000 (U.S.). We also quickly discovered that not only were prices for homes higher than expected, and found out the climate was normally a good deal cooler and wetter than we were experiencing that beautiful Saturday. Since cool and wet are not my favorite adjectives for describing where I want to live "when we grow up", as Sandra puts it, we decided we'd probably pass on this area for permanent residency. This was, interestingly, our first conversation about where we might like to actually end up as we grew older. We hadn't spent more than a few days to a week or so in any one spot for quite some months now, and my own view was to use the RV as an "Ocean Front Condo" if and when we wanted a bit more stability.

Sandra, on the other hand, was probably leaning more in the direction of a house where she could display her antiques and her large collection of original artwork, much of it lovingly acquired in her wanderings in Mexico and Central America. I'm not against anything so permanent as a house, mind you. It is just that I'd have some mental adjusting to do. The items I still had could certainly find their place in a home for the two of us – a piano, my sheet music, and all of my walls of books and classical CDs. At the same time, talking quietly that afternoon and evening, we realized that both of us thoroughly loved RVing and would greatly miss our nomadic lifestyle if Regina Victoria decided to roll on without us!

We enjoyed the grand tour of the island, making us appreciate what a beautiful place Salt Spring Island really is. Finally making our way to the ferry landing, we took our place in line to catch the next boat back to Vancouver Island. While we were resting, there was time to walk Smokey a last time and get more of the great local coffee (hot and very strong) to sustain us back to the RV. The ferry ride was full of sun and bright water, capping a blissful day of island adventuring.

The next day we determined to celebrate the coming end of our Canadian adventures with High Tea at the Empress Hotel. We both dressed up a bit for the occasion, me in a good silk tie and tweedy sport coat and Sandra in a very charming green silk suit with suitable jewelry from her large collection. Parenthetically, one advantage of a large motor home is that you have the closet space to bring along dress-up clothes if you so choose (I still regret not having my tux from time to time!). I personally think we looked quite good – we still cleaned up well even after months on the road.

The Empress has several seating times and we chose the 4:00 spot, as we remembered from our travels in England that was pretty close to high tea time in the Olde Countrie. As it was just a few minutes wait for our table, we had time to enjoy the entry area, which is adorned with lovely antique sofas and tables and filled with historical photos of this very grand old hotel. The framed pictures showed the famous people who had stayed here (including Queen Elizabeth II when she was still the young Princess Elizabeth) as well as many scenes depicting how the public and private rooms had looked three-quarters of a century ago.

Ushered into the tea room, we were greeted by our waiter who gave us menus and helped us make selections from the extensive tea offerings. Our server was the soul of courtesy and unobtrusive good service and wonderful hot tea soon arrived. After a few delicious sips, the beautifully presented sandwich and sweets caddies appeared (silver, of course!). While small, the delicious finger sandwiches were extremely satisfying and featured several of the seafood delicacies of Victoria Island. This turned out to be one of the best, if not the very best, High Teas either of us had had over many years, and compared favorably with High Tea at Bath. The salmon offerings were delicious and the pates were rich and savory. The desserts were in a class apart – decadent, gooey, creamy, chocolately divine and at least 500 calories each! We finished High Tea with sighs of repletion, and left nothing to be boxed as a take-home. But our waiter bestowed upon us a fun parting gift – a nicely wrapped assortments of the Empress' best teas, ready to be enjoyed later in the RV.

After that much rich food, we decided some exercise would do us a world of good, so we strolled (there is no hurrying after a High Tea of that magnitude) through the rest of the sprawling Empress. We were struck by the beauty and elegance of the main dining room, and Sandra recounted the story of how her parents had gone there for years to celebrate New Year's Eve. In those days, the dining room had been even bigger (it is now divided into two parts) and there were great logs blazing in the fireplaces to ring in the New Year. We were impressed by the beauty of the wall paneling and the huge carved ceiling beams.

One can only imagine the Very Important People who dined well here and the many deals (marital, political, commercial) struck at these snowy-white-clad tables. We asked if we could wander through the dining area and were told to go right ahead. Sandra led me to the back of the room, where a huge stone fireplace commanded the wall. Here, at a table by this fireplace, her parents had often celebrated New Years, with kilted bagpipers piping in each dinner course and huge Yule logs crackling in the great stone hearth. One could imagine the charm and gaiety reflected from the silver sconces adorning the long walls as well as the rows of fine wines and liquors resting comfortably on the long polished oak tables arrayed along the sides. This must have been truly fine dining, where the ambiance counted for as much as the reportedly superb food.

We finished our walk through the hotel with a visit to their little gift shop, purchasing a box of teas wrapped in an attractive linen tea towel with the Empress' scone recipe printed on it. This would make a fun gift for my step-daughter's upcoming birthday. The gift shop lady was happy to wrap it and have it shipped so, mission complete, we continued our walking tour of the area. Victoria's harbor and marina were a beautiful sight in the afternoon sunlight, and we strolled slowly, hand in hand, working off our just-acquired poundage. At this point we decided to take in a movie, something we hadn't been able to do very often over the past few months. We love movies and always try to find the local theatre to patronize. Surprisingly, many of the towns to our north had either no movie houses at all, or else the one or two that they once had were now closed, often converted to offices, or, more strangely, to resale thrift shops. Perhaps a sign of just how bad the economy had become in many rural areas?

Fortunately, Victoria had several good movie palaces, two of them quite near the Empress. We enjoyed the verve of the young lady staffing the ticket booth at the first theater we came to. When asked what her competitor down the street was showing, she laughed and replied, "Oh, they never show good movies!". Since we were in no hurry, we walked over and surveyed the competing theater's lineup. Finding nothing of great interest, we sauntered back to the first cinema. As we came to the ticket booth the young lady squealed, "We win!"

After the movie we returned to the RV park and took Smokey for a long walk as he would be confined a good deal the next day. We would be returning to the Lower 48 for the first time in months. We booked the 10:00 morning ferry to Port Angeles, Washington, and needed to be at the dock in plenty of time because of the large size of our rig.

CHAPTER 14

A Returning

The process of getting back to the U.S. produced something akin to culture shock. The U.S. maintains an immigration and customs operation at the port in Victoria. Once our rig was parked in one of the many long lines waiting to board the ferry, a U.S. Customs and Immigration officer came to visit us in the RV. The agent we drew was quite a pleasant lady who asked us some questions about where we had been and where we were going, but mostly inquired as to all the possible kinds of illegal plants and foodstuffs we might be bringing into the U.S. Convinced we were not hiding illegal polar bear sausages, she said we would have to take our passports to have our identities verified. Interestingly, it was okay if I went and stood in line for both of us.

Armed with our passports, I shuffled along slowly in a serpentine queue that wound rather vaguely around the parked vehicles and ended in what appeared to be a double wide trailer painted an unappealing gray. One at a time, we entered passport control and stood solemnly in front of a U.S. agent. The officer at my window barely looked up as I showed him the travel documents. Head down, he simply waved me along and I quickly exited back to the RV. The whole experience seemed designed to let us all know that we were entering a Very Important Country.

Given the number of people crossing to the states, we had plenty of time for one of Sandra's delicious gourmet "snacks", which involved her bringing forth from secret hiding places in the coach an impressive assortment of rare cheeses, smoked delicacies, unusual crackers and breads and potables that frankly, I didn't even know we owned. After this scrumptious repast we were in a much better mood and ready to tackle the not-inconsiderable challenge of getting the RV safely tucked aboard the ferry to Washington.

Our ride to Port Angeles would be aboard an American-owned/operated ferry system. As we drove slowly onto the ship, we heard a loud and disturbing bang from underneath the coach. It sounded as though we had bottomed out quite hard on the ramp. Sandra yelled a question out the window at a bored looking attendant who simply said, " I can't hear you over your engine" and walked away, pointedly ignoring us. We found our place alongside several big semis, shut down, decided to deal with the bang later, and went up on deck to enjoy the view of Victoria's pretty harbor as we left Canada. Our ship soon ran into a thick (and icy cold) fog, so we retreated to a sheltered spot and continued watching the operation of the ferry. At one point, our ferry captain must have seen something untoward, because he suddenly threw the big engines into reverse and made a very abrupt stop! We were never able to see what prompted this maneuver, but after a few minutes in idle, the ferry crept slowly forward, danger apparently averted and never explained.

As the fog lifted, we proceeded slowly into Port Angeles, Washington…home (again) to the U.S. We drove Regina Victoria carefully off the ferry, the Jeep swaying behind, and headed into Port Angeles proper. Here, with Sandra driving the big rig at the speed limit, we were soon passed on either side by irritated drivers, some of them hostile enough to give us the middle finger salute. Welcome home, I thought! We hadn't seen this kind of rudeness in many months and were both shocked by it. Twice now returning to U.S. soil, we were struck both times by how much our fellow citizens littered and by how impatient they can be.

Leaving Port Angeles as quickly as possible, we made our way down the highway to the much smaller town of Port Townsend where Sandra had several friends from her early inn keeping days and where there was chance of seeing the local wooden boat builders in action. I've have been an avid reader of *Wooden Boat* magazine for years, and Port Townsend was frequently mentioned in stories and with photos. Port Townsend had just hosted a big wooden boat festival, so I was hopeful that at least some of those beautiful creations might still be hanging about after the recent show.

Even though I was not, at the time of our trip, a boat owner, wooden boats showcase a level of meticulous, time-honed craftsmanship rarely seen anywhere else these days. They also represent a real, tangible link to our own maritime heritage. And they are simply beautiful, needing no other reason than that for their existence. I can gaze at them for hours and have twice attended the big Wooden Boat Show in Mystic, Connecticut, when three days is barely enough time to see all the marvels of wooden construction. And Port Townsend is a kind of West Coast Mystic (but with lots more rain).

Since it was getting on in the afternoon and all the ferry activity had left us a bit weary, we decided to stay the night at Old Fort Townsend State Park. We had called earlier for a reservation and had been assured that the park had full hookups and spaces adequate to house our size motor coach. When we got to what we thought was the correct park, we found the roads narrow and the full service sites could only hold 24-footers. Unhooking the Jeep and driving up a steep hill to check out these sites, we hoped the signs might be in error. Nope…I could barely get the Jeep around some of the turns, so we pulled into one of the bigger no-service sites and simply dry camped.

Because of low hanging branches and several decorative boulders that proved to be tricky, we managed to add several more scratches to our over-abundant supply. Finally nosed in and settled for the evening, we had a fine view of a rolling lawn and trees bordering a little lake just a few hundred yards away. Trying to figure out what had gone wrong, we spotted a park maintenance man and asked him how such a site mix-up could have occurred. He said there were TWO parks, with almost the same name, about a mile apart. To further add to the confusion, they shared the same phone number! Oops, I thought…this time the mix-up wasn't my fault. We were tucked in safely, had lots of food and water, and best of all, Smokey could have a really nice run as a reward for sitting all day cooped up in the RV. The little fellow went bounding away over the freshly mowed lawn, reveling in the chance to stretch his legs and run for all he was worth. He is always such a joyous sight when he is running free.

In the morning, feeling greatly refreshed, we drove the short distance into Port Townsend and found an RV park right at the marina. What a perfect location!…plus, close to a number of beautiful wooden boats moored there, and with views of a large expanse of open water. It was great to have wide spaces to park in, room for the Jeep, and with a vista of the Sound close to the front of the rig. Being so near the marina provided an opportunity to visit all the wooden classics that were still on hand after the big show. I spent hours walking up and down the docks and talking to as many owners/crew as I could. I loved the beautifully finished cockpits, sumptuous cabins ,and acres of shiny bright work. The attention to detail on the part of both builders and owners was clearly evident, as was the common love of fine lines and pleasing proportions.

These boats all "looked right", purposeful, without the strange modernist lines of the new fiberglass fleet to be seen at every marina around the world now. Walking away, I found myself looking back and thinking, "That really is a pretty boat...they got it right." And it didn't matter if the boat in question was a three-master or a small, exquisite sailing pram. Only the size and the sheer volume of detail changed. The sense of fine fit and finish was the same. These were boats that made you long to take ownership. Being around such watercraft is a spiritual experience. Such boats cut through the petty, plastic facets of our existence in this, the Age of the Consumer. Building wooden boats is all about patience and skill. Long practice with old and very fundamental tools turns a stack of lumber into a nautical creation that can speak to us directly about older and more basic aesthetics. Seeing a beautiful and functional wooden boat is also a cause to celebrate early human technologies where man met sea, not to dominate, but to use and appreciate. There is much to be said for techniques that for over 5,000 years have allowed humans to cope with a force of nature as powerful and fundamental as the open seas of our planet. Boats, especially those propelled by sails or oars, are so basic a part of our human history that we sometimes fail to appreciate how truly innovative our ancestors were.

After a long session of contemplating the wooden fleet still assembled in Port Townsend, it was great to take Smokey, now newly named "Chihusky", for a long walk along the rocky beach fronting the marina and RV park. The next morning we set off to visit Sandra's friends from back in Arkansas who had moved here some years ago. We discovered how very expensive real estate prices were in such a desirable small town, even if it was in a rather remote corner of a big state. Sandra explained to me that one winter several years before when she rented an apartment for a month with the idea of possibly moving there, she noticed that everyone in town, male or female, wore either drab brown or gray and that if she wore anything bright and colorful, she'd stick out like a sore thumb and probably be considered a woman of ill-repute. Plus, she thought it would be totally boring to wear drab for three or four months a year.

The town of Port Townsend is nestled along a pretty harbor off the San Juan Straits. Climatically, it shares the area's predilection towards fog varied with light rain, heavy rain, torrential rain, and occasional glimpses of warm sunlight. In honor of our visit the weather gods commanded a long period of sunshine, so we enjoyed blue skies and warm days for most of our stay.

We reveled in the chance to stroll around this picturesque town, taking in the many art galleries, bakeries (my downfall!) and cozy restaurants that lined the streets near the waterfront. Since we love to patronize locally-owned eateries, we had breakfast the next morning in a delightful creperie with a commanding view of the harbor. The aroma of yeasty goodies wafted out the door as we approached. The crepes and eggs were delicious and the coffee superb. I don't know if it is the Starbucks factor or a genetic predisposition, but citizens of the Pacific Northwest brew some great coffee. Even some of the fast-food chains have exceptional coffee which really surprised me, coming from the Midwest where fast-food coffee is barely a step above warm, colored tap water.

By the next morning we were ready to "git travelin'" again, singing the Willie Nelson version of 'On the Road Again" as we headed out. Dogs are terrific music critics, and Smokey loves that song, wagging his little tail vigorously in time with the music. Heading west along the very top of Washington State, we turned the big rig towards Neah Bay.

Alongside the Straits of Juan De Fuca, the road is sometimes narrow and twisting but with enchanting views of the Straits to starboard and even (when clear) of Vancouver Island off in the distance. On the way, we stopped at the little hamlet of Neah Bay, the self-anointed "Oyster

Capitol of the World". I mention this because every little waterfront community in this entire part of the world bills itself as "The (fill in the name of a sea creature) Capitol of the World". We found a long space into which to tuck the RV and chose a restaurant with a huge barbeque cart out in front, smoke rising into the clear sky and wonderfully savory smells drifting across to where we were parked.

We ordered the huge "Oyster Combo" to share and I had raw oysters for the first time (they go down nicely when coated with a bit of Tabasco sauce!). The combo also afforded a chance to taste fried oysters, oyster cakelettes, and Oysters Rockefeller, plus some barbequed oysters hot off the big front grill. All in all it was a memorable oyster feast, leaving us replete and ready to tackle the remainder of the day's drive along the north coast of Washington. Driving as far as possible towards the very tip of Washington State, we were stymied by an end to the road just short of the point we wanted to reach, so retraced our path and parked the RV alongside the road on a level spit of land overlooking the busy little harbor of Neah Bay.

Dry camping is wonderful when you have a good load of water and propane on board, and empty waste-holding tanks (it's less fun when the proportions are reversed). The spit made for a perfect camping spot and we stayed a second night taking in the working fishing boats as well as the big freighters threading their way through the straits and heading towards the big ports along the west coast. The play of light on the islands just north and east of our position was truly beautiful. Smokey and I took a long and meditative walk along the shore, concluding that life was good and that I was exactly where I needed to be, something my recovery program has taught me to recognize.

I carried my camera along on this walk and tried to frame careful photos, concentrating on light and composition. Having been an active amateur photographer in the days of Rolleiflex twin lens reflex cameras, and having shot with everything from a Leica to a Speed Graphic Press Special, I'm not yet completely comfortable with all of the digital post-processing one can achieve on the computer. I appreciate the value of Photoshop and other programs of that ilk, but I still prefer using the camera as the primary tool capturing the image/effect that I want.

As a college student, I shot zillions of campus photos and served as features editor for the college yearbook. I had owned a very large flash gun (didn't have anywhere near enough money to afford one of those fancy strobe units real photographers had draped over their sagging shoulder). The flash gun took screw-in flashbulbs about the size of a common 60-watter, and when they went off, everyone blinked, even people standing behind the camera!

Like many amateurs, I had a home darkroom and loved printing the day's shots. I savored the strange aroma of darkroom chemicals, the dim green or red lights that kept the films and prints from fogging, and the excitement of finally turning on the main lights and seeing the fruits of several hours of work. It was true, in that pre-digital age, you could manipulate the final prints. All of us knew how to "dodge" or "burn in" areas that needed less or more light, but essentially what you shot was pretty much what you got on the final print. Many of us grew up with the stunning imagery of Ansel Adams, shooting with a huge (often 8X10) view camera that gave but one chance to get it right! Margaret Bourke White taught us that double lens reflex cameras were a lot more portable and could go anywhere (with subtlety). As with all the larger format cameras, you had time and plenty of image area to get it right, but if you didn't, there wasn't much to be done after the fact.

Looking at my beach and shore photos on the computer that evening, I felt I had succeeded in capturing the images as I had seen them, and a few looked the sort I would like to print out on good quality paper. Every once in a while I surprise myself and find a creative well. Often I can't get the wanted effect, and the result, while technically fine, seems hackneyed, stereotypical… an image I have seen a dozen times before in galleries or magazines. I am finding a new sense of artistry in my photography… something more important than I would have suspected.

There is a wonderful new feeling of artistic empowerment in my life that I don't think I have experienced in quite this way before. Now when I look at my photos on the big laptop screen, I experience more frequent "ah ha" moments; what I saw and what I wanted the camera to "see" came together just as I had hoped when I tripped the shutter. Of course, it is also possible that I am too lazy to learn all that digital post-processing technology! If I get it right in the viewfinder I am "done".

After two days of absorbing the beauty and the majesty of this rugged bit of coast, we pulled up stakes and continued slowly back towards Callam Bay. There we picked up Highway 113 heading southwards towards a rendezvous with famed highway 101, that long ribbon of west coast macadam that runs from Washington State clear down to the Mexican border. Our plan was to head south taking in the delights of the Pacific coastal regions. We were in love with the Pacific Northwest, or "Nor Wet" as several local wags we met called it. Because Sandra had grown up in the Palo Alto area of California, she had seen most of this scenery before on family camping trips. I had not and was simply spellbound by the size of the trees (impossibly tall) and the grandeur of the coastline. I was quite surprised as a mid-westerner by the number of huge, lovely, and largely deserted beaches that we found in Washington and Oregon. I had imagined the whole coastline looking something like Carmel as seen through the lens of a Sunday afternoon pro golf tournament.

Our first stop down the Washington Coast was Pacific Beach where we stayed in the commodious state park near the edge of the Pacific Ocean. Being so close to the vast blue Pacific was a tremendous treat for both of us. We had camped along bays, inlets, harbors and sounds all over British Columbia and Alaska, but to be right on the magnificent Pacific, itself, was a true gift. Here we were directly on the ocean and could catch its moods, the tidal changes, the differing looks it gave morning and night. Even the air had a different quality – the clean, sharp tang of salt air blown for thousands of miles without touching land or people, a tang untainted by a town, a cannery, or the diesel perfume of large fishing vessels.

We could feel the full glory of wind and tide. This was the Pacific remembered from my California grad student day, the Pacific that spoke to Sandra of a childhood spent among the tidal pools and rock-strewn beaches near her first-remembered home. The two of us need to be by an ocean for our physical and spiritual well-being and are happiest with a huge body of salt water in close proximity. Sandra's seven-year spiritual odyssey sailing (mostly alone) in the Pacific in her 35-foot Ericson imprinted a love of the sea and its creatures. Dolphins once rescued her, whales comforted her, fish played with her. Salt air and salt water possess a restorative power, a balm for body and spirit. Sandra is more specific than I am about which coast she prefers. She is clearly a child of the Pacific.

I tend to favor the Atlantic and its numerous beaches replete with bird life and shells to be collected. I also like the historic towns along the lower reaches of the Atlantic coastline, especially St. Augustine of which I have fond childhood memories from family vacations. But the Pacific has a much more varied coastline, and the visual beauty of the beaches, with their supporting cast of giant redwoods or pines, makes for a rich aesthetic experience. The "left coast" is certainly more varied overall than the lower Atlantic coast, but we haven't yet made our way (as we plan) up the northern Atlantic coast through Maine and into Nova Scotia and Newfoundland. That'll make for an intense RV adventure!

One memorable stop in northern Washington will always stand out in our memories… the Hoh Rain Forest, part of the vast Olympic

National Park and reportedly one of the largest still-standing temperate rain forests in North America. With a rainfall of over 175 inches per year, it's a very damp place, and this was something we just had to experience. We were lucky in visiting this time of the year because the park was largely empty and we were able to camp paralleling the Hoh River, itself, which winds for many miles through this magical wet kingdom. Home to rare mosses and ferns, the park also hosts fauna ranging from the endangered banana slug to spotted owls, raccoon, deer and even elk who feast on the rare mosses adorning the huge trees. Several tree species grow to over 250 feet in height and sport massive girths of more than 25 feet in diameter.

We found the pervasive damp quite restful. Over several days of boondock camping alongside the river, we were able to take long walks and re-acquaint ourselves with the majesty of huge trees in a primordial setting reminiscent of Tolkien's Dark Woods scenes. Brooding, dark and filled always with mist, the Hoh Rainforest is both calming and mysteriously unsettling. After a few days, the chill became penetrating and our spirits needed some release from the constant gloom and the towering forest giants looming always overhead.

Returning to the coast and a more open countryside, the weather in this area in October was cool and damp but we both simply reveled in being there with each other. After talking with fellow campers and the rangers at the last park where we were, we shifted our base a bit south to Ocean Shores, an interesting little town right on the water and sporting a lovely big beach we were told you could actually drive on. That bit of information really made my day, as I have always wanted secretly to be a "dune racer" and had once entertained thoughts of buying a VW dune buggy in a rather lurid shade of reddish orange. Here was my chance to catch up on missed college Spring Break opportunities. Once in Ocean

Beach, we headed right for the beach and a driving adventure featuring sand and sun!

While in a cute beach town, it would be fun to look around and find out how much real estate cost there. To that end, we picked up one of those ubiquitous "real estate for sale" magazines while breakfasting at a delightful café on the main drag. Right next door to the eatery was a real estate office, so after some terrific omelettes and great coffee, we walked over to the office with questions. The receptionists found an available agent for us to chat with, and a few minutes later, we were seated in the office of – wait for it – Hannah from Montana (who was known locally as Montana Hannah). She was very pleasant and knowledgeable and after we gave her a price range, she offered to show us a few properties. We agreed and selected one in particular. We were sensible to the fact that she wasn't going to make a sale that day and we certainly didn't want to waste much of her time.

Hannah showed us the house just a few blocks from the beach and a couple of minutes outside of town. It was really one very big room with two small bedrooms, but it was a size Sandra and I could easily deal with and actually afford! We had only begun at this point to think about whether we would want something "fixed" as our abode. But, we do know we love oceans, with mountains a close second in terms of livability. On the other hand, we love the RV and the constantly changing scenery we get to enjoy as we journey on. It was a very interesting experience, however, to actually look at a house with at least some of our wish-list requirements.

We also spent some time using a list that Hannah gave us of lots for sale where we could have up to a year to build a bungalow or little cottage. You can also use a lot to put an RV on for up to 90 days per year, something I had not encountered before in my real estate career. This was also the first time either of us had seen lots equipped with pads for RVs that weren't part of an RV park or mobile home community – an intriguing concept and one perhaps unique to Washington or the Pacific Northwest. One of these lots appealed to both of us and we were rather tempted to make an offer. Our cooler natures prevailed, however, and we figured we had far too many other places to see before taking such an important and fairly permanent step.

Ocean Shores is a fun community, although it appears to lack anything approximating a "down town". Little town centers are something my beloved and I both enjoy greatly – quaint shops, coffee houses, little movie theaters, galleries. Many of the communities along the west coast lack this kind of central district. Instead, they feature a collection of small malls and fast food restaurants gathered on each side of whatever the local highway happens to be (frequently Hwy 101 in this part of the world). The upside to all of this, of course, is that the Pacific Ocean, in all its splendor, is usually just blocks away .That can certainly make up for a lot of sins of omission in town planning.

I am inevitably fascinated by why, in these essentially post-WWII communities, so little thought appears to have gone into creating anything approaching "town character", for want of a better term. There is little sense of cultural identity beyond the affinity of most residents for ocean-based sports and recreation. They are largely interchangeable towns as, of course, is the case in many other parts of the U.S. The major difference is in the nature of the shops you see along the main drag. You just don't see wet suit and surfing shops elsewhere than along the coast, and there are certainly far more seafood restaurants than steak houses.

One thing about the beach around Ocean Shores is that you can drive on it (well, perhaps not in a large motorhome). We unlimbered the tow car and tried beach-driving once again. What I found interesting is that the beach is actually regarded as part of the state and local highway system and normal rules of the road apply. How this works on a road that essentially disappears several times a day was a bit of a mystery to me, but people in all sorts of vehicles, from old family sedans to competition-size monster trucks, parade up and down the sand, all tooling along just feet from the salty water. It's a kind of civilized Daytona experience. We had an absolute blast driving along the beach at sunset, stopping constantly to take "setting sun" photos or just standing by the Jeep quietly holding hands and feeling awestruck at the beauty of the ocean and the huge descending red sun. We even waited for the fabled "green flash" that appears just after the sun sinks below the horizon, but on this day, we didn't see it (or maybe we blinked at the wrong time).

Smokey, of course, thought the beach was grand. He loves to run off lead where permitted, exploring everything as fast as his 6-inch legs will let him. He actually can achieve a remarkable turn of speed over the sand and appears to love to run and run just for the sheer joy of it! When we call him back, he pivots and comes charging back full tilt, ears back, tail up in a tight curl, mouth open as though laughing in his exhilaration at being freed from home and leash. I used to course sight hounds in a previous life and I must say that Smokey could give some of them quite a run for their money. And all of that energy is wrapped up in a little ten-pound gray and white Chihuahua body. He is truly our little friend and both Sandra and I cherish his companionship. It is a joy to see him stimulated with new sights, new sounds and especially new smells as each day is a new adventure for us and for him..

Smokey has become much more independent and self-assured since we began this adventure, and when we walk him in town or at a state park, I am reminded of Sandra's friend Lawrence Ferlinghetti's poetic line, "The dog walks proudly in the street." He has become a very proud little fellow, indeed, and relishes our many outings when he can be included.

CHAPTER 15

The Left Coast

Beach-walking and beach-sitting (on huge driftwood logs) became a favorite part of most nice days. It was October so the days were getting noticeably shorter and the temperatures cooler. Still, there were days that were "t-shirts and shorts" days although the Pacific waters were too chilly to think of swimming without a wet suit. A few hearty West Coasters, fully encased in their rubberized protection, had their surf boards out and were shooting the curls (such few as there were) but the beaches were mostly empty now. They have become wonderful places to find and enjoy solitude.

Sandra and I are people who like (and frankly need) time to be alone and just think, and we have found the Pacific coast ideal for communing. There is a marvelous rhythm to the sea that puts us right with the world. We think about feelings and how to express them to each other. The wonderful sea provides a backdrop against which we can "think out" our more personal inner experiences. We also love to play what Sandra terms, one of our "games" where we will tell each other the 20 most important things that we like about the other person, or we will play the "gratitude game" where we each go through the alphabet from A to Z and find something starting with each letter for which we are grateful that day. I find I am often grateful for zebras! This also helps us to come to grips with the reality of two older people in a new relationship, two people in an RV heading wherever we want to go next. And, of course, there are always the wonderful 12-step meetings that we find everywhere we go, with welcoming smiles when we tell our new friends about our adventures on our honeymoon in the big coach.

After a week of wonderful days in Ocean Shores, we moved southwards to Long Beach (Washington, that is). Here is a town that *does* have some character, in a northern "surfer dude" kind of way. At least it has a stretch of Highway 101 that looks something like a downtown. There are several blocks of colorful one- and two-story storefronts and restaurants, including several that serve terrific breakfasts for most of the daylight hours. As breakfast is one of my favorite meals to eat out, we tried all of the "Breakfast Served All Day" places and were surprised at how consistently good the food was and how varied the menus were.

The campground where we stayed was, once again, a private one, run by an elderly couple who were the very definition of friendliness. They even invited us into their "home" on site to see their Bluebird road bus conversion. The gentleman was one of those whom I admire greatly...a man who seemingly could fix anything and who had enough tools on hand to make me believe he probably could *build* almost anything as well. He proved extremely helpful when we discovered, after an evening's hard rain, that we had developed a leak in our bedroom at floor level on the slider side of the coach. This is never good news, especially as sliders can leak in an almost infinite number of ways. But Mac (I had now gotten onto a first-name basis with the manager) offered to come over and take a look at our problem.

He ambled over with a couple of hand tools, inspected the big slider extension and pointed out the glaringly obvious – the thick rubber seal that was supposed to prevent leaks was neatly (and incorrectly) tucked back into the slider, completely defeating its purpose. Mac got to work on this and showed me how to pull the rubber out while working a large screwdriver carefully behind it. This proved to be a satisfactory temporary fix and continued to work until we could achieve a more permanent solution.

We also took the time to look at some more real estate (yeah, we rarely heed our own advice) and we had begun thinking about a site on which to park the RV during the nicer months (read summer here). We stopped in a typical mom and pop real estate operation on Main Street and got some info about lots in areas that would accept an RV part of the year .Armed with a little map and our GPS, we took the Jeep exploring. It was always fun and often instructive to get off the "main drag" and explore the other side of these little towns. We drove up the peninsula looking for some of the listed parcels. We finally found at least one of them in an area of modest beach houses that were still priced surprisingly high in the opinion of this parsimonious mid-westerner. There were some very pleasant, if uninspired, beach properties but nothing that really called to us architecturally as neighbors for the RV. These were plain and functional places, but the views of the sea were generally quite good. This was in an area of the west coast where the dunes were not so high as to block the views of the ocean

That evening we had dinner in a fine Chinese restaurant (probably our second favorite type of food after Thai) and talked about further real estate ventures. One of the nicest things about being married to Sandra is that she has a keen and inquiring mind and we usually have a very broad range of topics to discuss over our meals together. One fundamental question we had to ask ourselves is where did we want eventually to settle down, or did we even want to settle down at all? We already owned an inn and several houses in the Midwest, any of which could serve as a base for further adventures. But did we really want to go back to suburbia? Part of the reason for this long trip was to discover areas we had never visited before, to find new perspectives, new ways to view the world and man's relationship to it. And while Sandra had some familiarity with Washington and Oregon, being a native Californian whose parents loved to take the children on auto adventures, much of this was new to me.

Although I had done a Master's at Stanford, I had never been farther north in California than Sacramento, so I was enchanted by this wonderful Pacific Northwest scenery. We joked with each other at dinner that, in fact, we had found very few areas of our travels thus far that we didn't find appealing for at least one reason, and usually for a lot more. Generally, we found lots to like and admire in terms of both scenery and people. For me, at least, climate was something of a weighty factor in making long-term habitation decisions. I don't' really like cold and damp. I also don't like extensive rain in quantities which I regard as excessive. (Sandra teases me that excessive, in my case, is anything much damper than the Atacama desert!) But, I had come to like the rather dry Yukon although I am not at all sure I could for long tolerate temperatures that regularly dipped to -40 F, even if it was a "dry" cold. At a certain reading, cold is just bitter. Period.

Over dinner, as we enjoyed some excellent steamed dumplings and egg rolls, we concluded there were just too many places we wanted to yet see to burden ourselves with more real estate, but we should continue to assess the markets we were passing through. That lead us to the egg drop and sweet-and-sour soups and reflections on which of the many Chinese restaurants we had dined in had the best soups. My vote was a Chinese eatery in Whitehorse, Yukon Territory with the richest egg drop soup (my favorite) I've ever had. It was chock full of delightful surprises, including a delicious little noodle made right on the premises. Interestingly, Sandra, with her cast-iron palate, usually has the hottest possible version of the hot and sour soup, and her vote also went to the restaurant in Whitehorse. She has actually had more really good sweet and sour soups along our odyssey than I have had good egg drops soups. Most egg drop soup tastes a whole lot like the Lipton's powdered chicken noodle soup (as advertised each day on the Arthur Godfrey show of my childhood), only cut with more than the recommended amount of water.

The fun thing about Thai and Chinese restaurants we were able to try on the Left Coast is that the cuisine is a bit different than one finds east of the Mississippi or in the deep south. We've tried a number of new (to us) dishes, often involving interesting blends of sea creatures we hadn't known about while living in the Midwest. Our culinary base was being considerably expanded (as was my waistline!). In particular, since we are not eating beef, we have tried a number of chicken and fish dishes we hadn't experimented with before, as well as new ways to cook pork. We love to hit the local ethnic restaurants in whatever little towns we find ourselves, particularly if they seem to have a good number of customers. Sandra always keeps a sharp eye out to avoid eateries where the only vehicles are parked in the back and probably belong to the chef and the waiter. This is never a good sign if it is prime lunch or dinner hour.

Because we were staying at an in-town RV park, we couldn't easily walk to the beach, so next morning we took the Jeep with Smokey proudly riding on Mama's lap, tail wagging madly, for a drive on the beach. The Washington State beach here is broad, long and very drivable (in a Jeep, at any rate). We drove several miles down the beach from our little entry road, parked, and let the Smokester out to run. He took off like a tiny gray rocket, paws churning on the uneven dunes (which he seems to prefer to the much scarier open beach down by the – gasp, shudder! – cold Pacific water). Sandra and I watched our little fellow running and playing, then set off after him, hand in hand. Autumn is rather a magical time of the year on the Washington coast, with still-warm days and enough sunshine to make beach-combing fun. Unlike the more southerly beaches, there are few shells to be found and those that we did pick up were largely the dinner leftovers from the amazing number of sea and shore birds who call this part of the Pacific Rim home.

The next day, a Sunday, we decided to venture north along Willapa Bay to the tip of the peninsula. Located here is the town of Oysterville, which may, for once, truly *be* the Oyster Capitol of the World. The town itself has several streets of lovingly preserved or restored houses that had belonged to 18th century Washingtonians who settled here and developed the oyster trade. The houses reminded me of the sort Sandra and I had exclaimed over in historic Saybrooke, Connecticut, just the prior year. Surrounded by verdant gardens and painted picket fences, these homes bespoke solidity and comfort without ostentation, a theme echoed in many seafaring towns on several continents. And Oysterville still has oysters, quite a lot of them, in fact, judging by the towering heights of some of the shell middens dotting the landscape.

We stopped at the big oyster packing plant at the edge of town. Sandra wanted oysters to take with us in the RV, and as I had developed a taste for the little bi-valves, I was game. The young lady working the counter in the retail operation was quite knowledgeable about these small critters, demonstrating how to shuck one and explaining the types and sizes currently available. Sandra and I watched the shucking demonstration, looked at each other and decided that shucking our own oysters would probably result in the loss of one or more valuable digits. We opted, instead, for several quarts of table-ready oysters with an extra bottle of really good sauce.

I liked this store because you could walk right out the back door and onto the long wooden dock where the counter girl's father unloaded his oyster catch each morning. Willapa Bay oysters appear to be a better managed resource than we found in other coastal areas, meaning that there is actually hope for both the oysters and the oyster men (and women) whose lives revolve around each other. The health of the oysters here is also less threatened by pollution and agricultural runoff found in many other areas. This coast line is sparsely settled and the local demand for the product is not, perhaps, as high as in areas such as the densely settled Chesapeake Bay.

After a few more idyllic Fall days in this beautiful Washington coastal area, wanderlust came calling and it was time to head south again, crossing the long bridge over that very deadly river, the Columbia. From the high (and scarily narrow) bridge, we could see the strong currents and shifting sand and gravel bars that had claimed so many vessels, big and small, over the past 200 years. Crossing bridges is often a bit problematic in a large RV; the lanes are narrow and there is always the chance of unexpected cross winds. But we made the crossing uneventfully and arrived soon after at our first Oregon town, Astoria. I had never been to Oregon before, so was quite excited to see this landscape.

Our first order of business was to find a Bank of America in order to pay a bill. Using the GPS, we wandered (read blundered) into the heart of Astoria and finally found the B of A situated in a temporary home – a corrugated trailer deep in a tiny parking lot. This presented a substantial problem – no way was our 60-feet of vehicle going anywhere near the front of that bank. We turned down a side street, which quickly became one-way the wrong way. Another turn was in order, this time to the left, which resulted in our parking along a curb with about half the rig sticking out into a traffic lane.

Sandra ran into the bank, while I sat in the coach with the engine running, ready to take off the moment she returned or if the local constabulary suddenly showed up. When Sandra reappeared, we decided the road ahead looked nearly impassable unless we could quickly execute another turn and get the rig back onto the main drag. Surveying the route ahead had become a necessary survival skill during our adventures, so walk it I did, trotting up to the corner and peering around to see where it ended. Satisfied that I could somehow nurse Regina Victoria around the turn, I jumped back in and pulled into traffic, working my way quickly left and around the turn, down a short street and back onto the highway we had exited some minutes before.

Getting onto that highway was the last challenge, as mid-day traffic was very heavy. Fortunately, in time there came a major break in both directions and I floored the accelerator, bringing the big Cummins roaring to life. What that meant in practice was that I achieved the acceleration of an elderly VW microbus running on three cylinders but, like rank, sheer bulk hath its privileges and no one saw fit to challenge me as I pulled into the traffic pattern. Continuing southwards, we soon left Astoria and picked up our favorite highway, US 101. This wonderful road brought us back to the coast, and it soon became clear why Sandra had often spoken of " the rugged Oregon coast,". for rugged it is.

Leaving the broader sandy beaches of Washington behind, one soon begins to appreciate the sheer beauty of the rocky coastline that Oregon provides. It is visually stimulating, and the cries of sea birds mingled with the smell of the Pacific as we cruised slowly along with the side windows wide open. This is a "take no prisoners" coast, with huge spires of granitic rock arising just offshore. Such rock formations are the remnants of a very ancient coastline, slowly and methodically worn away until only the incredibly tough and resilient underlayment still remains. These imposing vestiges of an ancient past continue to defy wind and wave as they have for untold millions of years. This is a fascinating geology and it sent me digging around in the cupboards of the RV for my well-thumbed old college geology text.

The coastline of today's Pacific Ocean is dramatic in Oregon. High rocky cliffs peer down at sandy or rock strewn beaches at their feet. The spray here is visible far above the ocean as waves crash resoundingly against unyielding rock formations just yards offshore. Along the Oregon coast it is necessary to stop often. Every photo op seems better, more breathtaking, than one just a few miles back. But there was one obligatory stop that first afternoon in Oregon that had nothing to do with natural wonders – the huge and famous cheese factory in Tillamook.

The biggest employer in the county, the factory has been making great cheeses for more than a century. Today the dairy is a sprawling, ultra-modern facility, but when Sandra first came here as a child with her parents, she remembered it very differently. In those days, you could take a tour of the "assembly line" that let you actually peer over the shoulders of the workers as they stirred or chopped or wrapped. In fact, she saw one workman wielding a huge machete-like knife open a gash in his hand when momentarily distracted. Shrugging off the injury, he continued his routine, bleeding slightly into the cheese.Nothing wrong with a bit more protein in the cheese! (But those were pre-OSHA days as well).

Today, the tour is mostly done through instructive videos, although there is a large viewing area high above the tanks and the packaging areas. Separated by large glass windows from the highly sanitized production floor, today's visitors can view the huge stainless steel tanks that each holds over 60,000 gallons of milk on its way to becoming a variety of cheeses. Of course, there is quite a large retail operation next to a parking lot big enough for us to easily pull the RV and tow car in and even find some shade. The store is crammed full of wonderful cheeses and we couldn't resist taking several varieties home for further "research".

We had a very late lunch in their café and enjoyed, naturally, huge grilled cheese sandwiches and, since this is the Pacific Northwest, a cup of clam chowder to begin the repast. Because this is a place with lots and lots of milk, I was betting they made ice cream. Lo and behold, they did! We each had to have a sundae to finish lunch. I had grown to like Marion berries, so had the rare treat of a Marionberry sundae, their subtle earthy flavor complementing the rich vanilla ice cream…truly a memorable gustatory experience.

Suitably stuffed with high-cholesterol goodies, we motored sedately south, back to the coastline and onwards to the little town of Manzanita, where we hoped to find Nehalem State Park. Our road took us past a new subdivision, a very old cemetery, and several indeterminably aged and weathered beach houses. Finally, we found the rather artistic entrance to the park itself: two huge timbers surmounted by a third that looked as though it could contribute enough board feet to make a small house. A few hundred yards in and we came to the park guard shack, closed as was so often the case. But we pushed on in, turning into an area that looked promising but turned out to be "reservations only" with a scattering of rentable yurts for that "authentic wilderness experience".

Armed with some fresh instructions, we found another RV loop. Dropping the Jeep, we went exploring, finding on the far side of the loop a very nice camp site (and oddly for this time of the season, practically the only one left). It was located on the ocean side of the campground and just inside the large dunes that form so much a part of the Oregon coastline. Once parked, we plugged in and heaved a large collective sigh of relief. The day had been long and we had had quite a number of driving adventures, so we were more than happy to be settled in.

From our site it was about a third of a mile walk to the beach and the ocean, so tired as we were, we put Smokey on his lead and set out to catch a glimpse of the extraordinary sunsets these parts produce.

The walk was steeper than we had thought, but we made it in time for Doggie Boy to enjoy a run on the dunes and for Sandra and me to stand close together marveling at the beauty of yet another Pacific sunset. These moments were a major part of what our trip was about. They were visual experiences you could photograph, but sharing with a loved one is a thing of memory. Such images can be hauled out from the recesses of our minds whenever we need reminding of what this adventure was about. No camera is as able as the human eye to render the full dramatic effect of the sun inching into the broad Pacific

There is something about the sheer size of the scene that only our retinas and brains can really invoke. For over 10,000 years humans have stared at this same scene and it is still overwhelming in its scope and the sheer intensity of its color palette. We stood quietly and watched the sun finally slip below the horizon – always quickly at the very last. The sea birds, having followed the sun to ask it to stay a little longer, gave up and returned to their rookeries and accustomed places along the dunes, or sat bobbing quietly in the tidal waters as the light slowly faded for the day.

The next day was quite pretty and we decided to take our laptops outside and work on our writing projects. This is always fun, as we get to read what we have written to each other for comment and critique At day's end we decided to celebrate a good run of literary production by driving back into Manzanita. This evening we watched the sun set from the comfort of a convenient park bench, set just at the junction of town and beach. It was fun to be there with others watching the sunset also. Even the motel across the street had a full complement of guests standing on the balconies, wine and cocktail glasses in hand, waiting for this nightly Pacific ritual. As Old Sol cuddled into the ocean's embrace, a cheer and loud clapping arose from the spectators at the motel. The rest of us quickly joined in and our solar neighbor was sent on his nightly journey with much goodwill. But the miracle of that sunset was that we got to see the fabled "green flash", which appears just as the sun sinks below the horizon. This phenomenon is so rarely seen that Sandra, in seven years of sailing in the Pacific, had never seen it before this magical evening.

Having worked up a substantial appetite, we drove back through the few blocks of the little town looking for an interesting eatery. In this case it turned out to be an Italian restaurant/pizzeria. Sandra and I love non-chain pizza, so we decided this had to be the place for dinner. It turned out to be a good choice.

The starter salad was big enough to be a meal in itself. After RV fare, it is always good to get fresh greens, and these were so crisp that I suspected the kitchen had a lettuce plot just outside the back door. I was reminded of a wonderful scene in one of C.S.Forester's "Horatio Hornblower" adventures where the assembled captains of the British fleet on blockade duty off Toulon were ecstatic that their admiral host was able to produce a dish of real greens for their dinner. After living on ship's biscuit and salted meats for weeks and months on end, the assembled company of senior commanders almost drooled over fresh veggies!

The Manzanita pizza was a real find - wonderful crust, judicious use of tomato sauce, freshest ingredients, and lots of grated Parmesan cheese as an added fillip. Heavenly simple – Italian pizza at its very best! This was very much the kind of pizza that Sandra and I remembered from our own separate journeys to Rome and Florence. We savored every bite of that pizza, and when we were done, just had to each have an espresso as a suitable "dessert" How much more Italian could we get in the middle of Oregon?

The next day, we went back to enjoying our camping experience and took several long walks. I "hitched up" Smokey and we walked all the way around the whole campground, ending up at a "horse camp" just off the main camping loops. The horse camp contained sites large enough to back a good sized horse trailer in and park it for the duration. A distinctive feature of these campsites was a very sturdy corral made of thick logs with a central division, making them suitable for up to four horses at each site. Being a horse enthusiast, I could understand how much fun it would be to bring your equine friends out to play in such a beautiful setting. I only regretted that I didn't have a horse along with us so that we could all share in a nice trail ride through the dunes and down to the ocean. Most of the campsites were empty, but a few had horses standing solemnly with tails swishing. The sights and smells of the horses made me miss the quarter horse I used to own, but somewhere on this journey, I promised myself, I would treat myself to a rent-a-ride pony just to get back in the saddle for a few hours.

That evening, we decided we deserved a really fine dining experience. Having heard of an excellent restaurant in the immediate area, we decided that would be our choice this evening. With the address in the faithful GPS, we sallied forth, dressed in our best (that is to say, RV best). Smokey asked to stay home so he could listen to his favorite classical music on Regina Victoria's excellent sound system. After driving through several nearby towns, we began to doubt the Garmin, but as usual it was right. We crossed a river and there, seemingly in the middle of nowhere, was an unpretentious little inn, warmly lit and with lots of parking. We were the only diners at first, but a slow and steady influx of other couples told us that we had made a good choice.

The dining room was softly lit and our table was perfectly situated to afford a view of the Coastal Range in the distance, with the inn's herb garden in the foreground. The service was first class and our waiter suggested the filet mignon, the house specialty. As our beef treat for the month, the filet sounded wonderful. Since we only allow ourselves beef once a month, we try to pick something quite special for that rare meal. Dinner began with a savory vegetable soup followed by a tossed salad of local greens; then came the filet, cooked perfectly and presented in a lovely plate scape. We thoroughly enjoyed it and even found room for a homemade dessert of marionberry cheesecake and rich strong coffee.

While lingering over dessert and coffee, we had a chance to chat with the co-owner whose husband is chef. Sandra and I were both impressed at how much knowledge of food and wines the owners had imparted to the wait staff. These were all people who shared a passion for the details of fine dining and we applauded their efforts in this seemingly remote part of the Pacific Northwest. Before we departed we also had the chance to eavesdrop on an adjoining table, whose occupants were the local purveyors of fresh produce for the inn. It was instructive to hear about what was fresh and in-season and what would soon be past its peak and not worthy of a good restaurant. All in all, this had been a wonderful "dress up" evening with a fine meal and classy service. It doesn't get much better than that, especially when your garnish is the local mountain scenery!

We stayed in Neaham Bay State Park for the better part of a week, enjoying the local 12-Step meetings available in the little town, making new friends, and, as always, getting good advice from our fellow RV sojourners. Reluctantly, we finally decided to move on, only to discover, for the first time in over 10,000 miles of travel, that we had engine/transmission problems. Leaving the park, we noticed that the big rig's Allyson was behaving oddly on hills, seeming to hiccup slightly as it changed through its six speeds. This was worrisome, but nothing compared with the next issue which occurred a few miles out of town. The engine coolant light flashed on and off, then stayed lit. With a large diesel engine, this is not something to be ignored, so we pulled over as quickly as possible and went around the back to assess the situation. Opening the big barn doors that hid the engine, I found the coolant reservoir, which appeared to be just slightly low. I mixed water and antifreeze and administered a therapeutic dose to the Cummins, hoping that we just had an overly-sensitive warning system and that all would be well.

Given this worrisome combination of problems, we decided to head to Lincoln City and stop early. The drive to this charming little town was a nail-biter, as Regina Victoria seemed less and less able to go up even small hills. The engine was losing "oomph", the tranny was continuing to feel notchy, and the engine cooling light blinked on and off (but apparently had enough coolant to remain reasonably content for the time being). Once in Lincoln City, we found a very nice Good Sam RV park, booked a large pull-through space, and gratefully shut the engine down for the day.

That evening we chatted up a neighboring RVer, a lady whose husband was a retired over-the-road trucker. She suggested that part of our problem might be a dirty air filter and that our performance might improve if we took it out and thoroughly cleaned it. This was a capital idea, but a review of the literature available in Regina Victoria didn't make it clear where the air filter was located. Here again was one of those challenges facing a fellow who, in a previous life, had called for help whenever a mechanical issue loomed.

As I pondered the problem, I suddenly remembered a large, round black housing that ran between the engine area and the big electrical compartment on the left rear end of the coach. I opened that housing and found the outboard end of the big black cylindrical box I had noticed earlier. "I can do this", I thought once again. Removing many clamps, I gingerly extracted the biggest air filter I had ever seen. Needless to say, it was filthy. Thousands of miles of Canadian and Alaskan dust clogged every inch of its surface. Hopefully, our neighbor was right and cleaning this huge "lung" would help restore our performance. Much pounding and inhaling of dust later, I had the filter clean enough to at least help the engine breathe better, although this surely wasn't the only problem the engine faced (not to mention the vagaries of the transmission). Lacking a spare filter, the temporary fix would have to be enough and we made a note of this on the growing list of repair issues.

We had made an appointment for routine servicing with Beaver Coach, in Bend, Oregon, which constituted a sizeable detour from our planned coastal route but Beaver came highly recommended and visiting Bend would give us an opportunity to visit with Sandra's nephew, who lived there and whom Sandra hadn't seen in years. Bend is a good 190 miles inland and the length of the journey worried us a bit, but we thought the engine probably wouldn't get any worse and the transmission troubles, while annoying, were no more than that at this point. Next morning, after getting in a quick round of laundry at the RV park, we set off for Bend. Starting out, we ran primarily on level ground, so the RV was able to keep up with traffic. Once we turned inland at Newport, however, we quickly realized we had "A Big Problem." Worse, we were going to have to climb some of the highest peaks in the Cascade coastal range before ever setting eyes on Bend. From Corvalis on, the trip turned ugly. By now, the rig had slowed to about 12 mph while going up any grade. The long, steep passes leading up the Cascades meant that we sported a constant stream of irate motorists behind us, each eager to pass as quickly as possible. We became increasingly afraid to pull off in order to let others pass, as the RV seemed less and less willing or able to get going again from a dead stop. It was a very long and very frustrating afternoon.

Haltingly, ever so slowly, we climbed painfully from sea level to over 4000 feet. Since it was Friday afternoon, I decided to call Beaver coach and see if we could spend the weekend in their lot, as our appointment was for the coming Monday. We found a big pull off area and I got out of the RV, hoping to find better cell coverage than I had from inside the rig. I had to walk far back down the highway until I could get enough cellphone bars to make contact. It must have looked a bit strange, watching this white haired man walking along in the late afternoon chill dressed in a Yukon t-shirt and khaki shorts, yelling at a cell phone held high over his head. I was finally able to connect, only to find out that my service manager contact was gone for the day.

Oh boy, what to do now? I decided to talk to the other service writer who was helpful but we kept losing our phone connection. By the fourth try at communicating I could sense that he was becoming a bit restive, eager to close shop and get on with his weekend. One more try, I thought, and this time, by shouting and literally running backwards, I made myself understood. I was assured that we could spend the weekend in their lot and given detailed instructions on how to find their place, what gate to use after hours, and how to find a parking spot with water and electric hookups. This was almost too good to be true, I thought, sobered by the realization that we could have missed this connection if I had called even five minutes later.

We still had at least two or more hours to go at our present pace, even though we were only about 50 miles from Bend. Sandra put the rig into gear and we tried to accelerate onto the climbing, winding highway. No luck! Regina Victoria simply said" no!" and refused to enter the stream of traffic. We held our breath as Sandra eased off and tried once more. Success…slowly we lurched forward into traffic and upwards towards Bend. Eventually, the road leveled as we reached the high desert. Nearing Bend's city limits I set up the GPS, plugged in the address info for Beaver Coach and navigated while Sandra piloted through traffic. We turned down a street paralleling the showroom and then entered a vast empty parking lot. Concerned for a moment, I looked up and there above us, on a hill, was a most welcome sight – a row of big RVs, all plugged into electricity and sitting just outside the huge doors of the Beaver Coach service bays.

We decided to unhook the Jeep so we could back into the last available spot on the lot. Then we had to ask, could Regina Victoria make it up one more hill, this one a rather steep driveway leading up to the parking area? Sandra rolled back as far on the lot as she could, then gunned the big diesel. Our poor sick girl coughed asthmatically and very slowly gathered way. I decided to walk, then trot, in front, willing our motor home to make it up this one last hill.

"Come on Regina, just one more hill to climb! You can do it, old girl." Lumbering, coughing, she climbed slowly and then we were up on the level...she had done it! With rapidly fading twilight my bride nursed the rig into our assigned parking spot and I hooked up the amenities. Done for the day! It was very comforting to know that help would be available on Monday.

Sandra's nephew lived about 25 miles south, in Sun River, and sometime earlier, we had debated whether to stay in his driveway or a local RV park. Our breakdown solved that problem and provided us with a place to stay at the RV repair place right in Bend (little did we know how long that stay was going to turn out to be!). Once we were a bit rested, Sandra gave her nephew a call and he agreed to meet us for dinner. Allen met us at the RV (he had been in Bend on business) and after a "tour" of the RV, we went to a local Thai restaurant for dinner. The food was excellent and I appreciated the chance to chat with Allen whom I had not met before. It also gave Sandra a chance to get re-aquainted with him as it had been over 10 years since last they had seen each other. After dinner, we returned to the RV for some very much needed R&R. We were exhausted and even Smokey was too tired to be his usual ebullient self!

The next day, we rested and spent time catching up on our business emails. I also took time to phone and get us tickets to a concert that Allen had thought we might like. It featured the David Gusman band and was to be held in Bend's old Tower Theater in the historic downtown that

Sunday evening. Gusman had apparently once played with Jerry Garcia (who is buried in the cemetery just behind Sandra's childhood home in Menlo Park) "back in the day" and now had his own touring bluegrass-style band. He played mandolin and served as the lead singer. Sandra and I both thought this would be a nice break from our usual diet of classical music, so I got us the best tickets still available which turned out to be balcony side box with individual chair seating, my favorite way to see and hear concerts.

The Tower was originally Bend's premier movie house in the early days of cinema, an opulent testimony to the popularity of that newest rage, the talkies. Like so many of its brethren, it had gradually fallen into disrepair and neglect, until it was finally rescued from the wrecking ball in the 1990s by a group of civic-minded Benders who restored it to its former glory. Now it served as a performance venue and seemed especially well suited to a band like Gusman's which filled the stage with sound and colorful motion.

The band had a delightfully eclectic sound, featuring bluegrass along with good shares of Basso Nova beat and even some fusion jazz licks thrown in. It's a group that plays very comfortably together, with David plucking some amazing chords from the mandolin. All of the musicians behind him were first class and most numbers featured sub-stantial solos by one or more of these sidemen. I was particularly taken with the flautist who appeared to play while being in perpetual motion around the stage. Sandra found him a bit distracting, but I marveled at both his finger work and his footwork!

Going to a live concert is clearly high on our list of priorities and Sandra and I talked on the way back to our RV about making a greater effort to find more live music, especially our beloved classical concerts which we were really beginning to miss on our long journey. Before leaving on our odyssey, we had both often enjoyed symphony and opera performances as well as chamber music, live theater (St. Louis has a very rich and active theater culture) and even occasional pop concerts. We had brought a lot of classical music CDs with us in the RV and often sang or hummed – badly – to each other as we rolled along.

Sandra also mentioned that having the Tower sold out on a Sunday evening was quite a testimonial to the management savvy of the current ownership. Being as involved as she has been professionally in the arts, she had seen other old restored theaters fail because their owners had not exerted enough effort to book name acts. As a result, their audiences dwindled to the diehard or dispirited few who had nothing better to do or needed a warm place to get out of the cold. She pointed out that it was often possible to book name acts, as she had done, if you catch them when they are travelling nearby or are on their way cross country between high revenue sites.

When Monday morning came, we were up bright and early. I had already talked to the shop manager who was prowling about the parking lot over the weekend, so I had some idea of how things proceeded with the service department. At Beaver, customers are to have their coaches ready to go into the service bays at 8:00 sharp. That meant disconnected from electricity and water, antennas stowed away, sliders in, etc. At five minutes before 8:00 a.m., I was in line at the service door…in fact, first in line, a tribute to my Teutonic heritage. When the service adviser door opened, I popped through like Alice's white rabbit, ready to see my adviser, Ken, with my lengthy to-do list. Ken was a delight to work with - orderly, calm and efficient. He was exactly what was needed that Monday as I went through my several-page list of maintenance and repair items. The engine would be our top priority, but Beaver didn't have Cummins diagnostic equipment, so they would start by changing all the fluids and filters, in the hope that would remedy many of the low power problems. After I had detailed our Alaska and Canada experiences, Ken opined that the problem might well be incredibly dirty, clogged filters. In this he was correct as they turned out to be, in his words, "disgusting".

Additional issues included a leaking bedroom slider, both TVs that had stopped working, the water system was leaking from some low point in the compartment where the relief valves were located, the bedroom needed an inverter outlet installed, and the leveling jacks were leaking somewhere, meaning the jack warning light (and its annoying sound) were on again most of the time in the driving compartment. Additionally, the 7-KW Onan generator needed servicing, a process that would take both time and money. And, of course, we had the stumbling transmission and the issue of how badly we had scored the brakes descending those incredible grades in British Columbia.

We were assigned our own tech, Jeremy, a young man with the patience of Job, who came out to the coach and went over every one of our service items with us, making notes and commenting on possible fixes. By 9:00 we were fully checked in and Jeremy drove the coach into the cavernous service bay to begin work. I had naively (very naively) assumed we would be here a day or two at most. Wrong! That was a serious error, as Ken explained, noting that the leveling jacks problem alone could take weeks to resolve.

"Why?" I asked.

"Well," as Ken put it, "nobody keeps these in stock. We can't stock every part for every motorhome here, and the re-builders who work on the jacking systems don't even begin to make the actual parts until an order is placed".

"Hmmmm," I mused. "How long could that take?" I asked in full innocence

"Oh, two or three weeks minimum," was Ken's cautious reply.

I was, once again, amazed at how hard it could be to get parts for something as seemingly mundane as a motorhome. I could get parts for a Lamborghini faster than this, I thought. I asked Ken if he could just have his techs look at the jacks and ascertain how bad they were. He promised to do that and later in the week reported the jacks were leaking from several points but would continue to function if used gently. He also found all the necessary parts numbers so an RV dealer somewhere down the road could order the hardware and have it available when we finally planned to stay somewhere for a bit.

Gradually, the shop worked its way through our list, with a few big surprises that caught us a bit off guard. The first was that the generator badly needed its 1000-hour overhaul, at a price of some $1300. Oops! Oh well, that was alright because we used the genset a lot while dry camping which we loved to do whenever local rules permitted it. The other big surprise was that the front tires were pretty well shot and would cost $600 each mounted and installed, plus more dollars for necessary new hubs. These were crucial items with which we readily concurred. Along with all the other work to be done, the week was looming longer! Oh, and we also needed new front brakes.

On the fun side of things, with the Jeep off tow we spent one lovely sunny day driving south of Bend to the magically beautiful Crater Lake. This high altitude lake (over 4000 feet) is a brilliant cobalt blue, set deep in a ring of mountains. The lake itself occupies the crater of an extinct volcano that once spread vast quantities of volcanic rock over the high desert surrounding the lake and its basin. Personally, I love high deserts and always find the air there just a bit cleaner and sweeter than anywhere else. We could distinctly smell pines, an aroma I often associate with this type of topography. In fact, we stopped in a large pine forest on the way to the crater to let Smokey run free, unfettered by his customary leash He took off down an old logging road in the forest and we could see he was just ecstatic. His tail was curled up tightly, a sure sign that he is happy, and he seemed delighted to be the first dog to have an opportunity to mark so many trees at one time.

Essentially an urban dog, Smokey was finding his outdoor self on the trip and he seemed to be reveling in the chance to get out and play in nature. It was always great fun to see him exploring a new bit of the great outdoors, nose down to the ground like a tiny bloodhound and moving as fast as his little legs would take him. He is quite an athletic dog for his size and age. Large fallen trees seem to offer no obstacle as he vaults them in the style of a Moses Malone. It is quite astonishing to see this very small dog suddenly pop over a downed tree and continue on as though out for a café stroll with his peeps.

Once at Crater Lake, we began hiking around the various observation points, each offering a superb view of the lake from different perspectives. I discovered a trail leading from the parking/observing area to a mountaintop lookout where a fire observation station was located. I decided that I just had to see the view from up there and take some good pictures for our collection, so I told Sandra I was going for a hike up the mountain. She wished me good luck and told me, "Write when you find work."

The hike was listed on a signpost as being about a 45-minute hike round trip with approximately a 500-foot vertical ascent. That sounded doable, so off I went. After a few hundred yards, I realized that altitude and not being in great shape might make this a much harder climb than anticipated. But as I trudged upward the views over the lake and the surrounding desert just kept getting better. Twice, I stopped for a brief rest, then continued on. I didn't feel that I was breathing especially hard, but my legs were feeling quite leaden by the three-quarters mark. Determined to get all the way to the top, I pressed on.

Finally reaching the summit and climbing the last few yards up to the base of the fire tower, I was tired but quite exhilarated because the views from there were everything one could have hoped for. I was up over 5,000 feet and could see clearly for many miles in every direction as the clear desert air made for incredible visibility. I took picture after picture until my camera's card read "full", and then started back down. Nature came out to greet me in the form of three squirrels busily gathering pine nuts and sloppily devouring them. I passed a number of beautiful jays and also saw a very large insect, almost the size of a small hummingbird which I did not recognize and have not been able to identify to this day. It made a very loud droning, rasping sound to announce its presence.

Encountering several couples slogging their way up the mountain, I assured them the views from the top were well worth the climb. When I finally rejoined Sandra in the lower observation area, she confided she had been a bit worried about me. But she seemed genuinely pleased I had made the effort and had scored a small personal triumph, another of the little rewards that accumulated on this trip as I got to know more about myself and what I actually could accomplish.

We continued our parking lot camping adventure for the remainder of the week, appearing at the service door each morning at 8:00 a.m. to let the service department know we were ready for the day's work. One of the fun parts of staying at Beaver was the chance to see all the shiny new motorhomes on display in their extensive showroom. Sandra and I naturally just *had* to take a tour through all of those beautiful coaches. Equally naturally, I just had to buy one! Thank goodness, saner heads prevailed. As we thought about such a costly purchase, our faithful Regina Victoria looked better and better. And truthfully, you can only make one of these behemoths so big – I think 45 feet is about the upper limit. That's 7 feet longer than our coach, and I remembered the many times we had had difficulties backing Regina into a tight camping space. I just couldn't imagine what it would be like with a 45-footer. My suspicion is that these really huge coaches thrive primarily in sunny southern RV parks that are designed to accommodate big rigs. Many of them probably don't actually see much road duty and it is a certainty that they can't fit into many state parks, our favorite venues. In California, only five state parks could accommodate even our size RV.

When Friday came, we were eager to leave, but the generator, our last major repair item, still wasn't finished. Finally, Friday afternoon, the parts to fix it arrived via UPS. Could this important accessory be finished in time for us to leave that day? Getting it repaired turned into a three ring circus, with several techs working on the big Onan in unison. They actually performed a beautifully choreographed dance around the mechanism, adding filters, changing oil, installing new parts and generally polishing the old girl to a fare thee well. Soon the generator was humming along, quieter than we had ever experienced and ready for another 1,000 hours of faithful service. With the generator slid back into the nose of the RV, we were ready for a final test ride conducted by two of the techs, with Sandra and me along as observers.

It's always a bit of a nail biter when someone else is driving the motorhome, but we had no concerns this day. Our driver had been an over-the-road trucker for many years and his terminal point was often the narrow streets of lower Manhattan, so the open spaces of Bend were a no-brainer for him. He took us for a short drive around town and helped us to bed in our new brakes. During our test ride, we discovered that the ABS light was coming on regularly. Our second tech jumped out and got into the electrical compartment where he did mysterious things that halted the display light. We weren't sure the problem was solved, but at least it was fixed for the nonce. Ken stayed late to check us out, and since it was getting quite dark by then, he allowed us to stay another night in the parking lot, snug and hooked up to electricity and city water. He also told us how to use their pump-out station when we left the next morning.

Saturday morning, we fired up the diesel and enjoyed the sounds of steady deep rumbling from the rear of the coach. All gauges were in their accustomed normal range. Satisfied that things were very much improved, Sandra popped off the air brakes and set out for a return to the beloved coastal highway.

CHAPTER 16

Homecoming

By the end of our stay in several beach-front campgrounds, we were ready to move on south through Oregon and reach California which would be a kind of homecoming for Sandra (born in Palo Alto) and a chance to revisit where I had begun my grad school work (Stanford). We had often talked about how much both of us liked California and about the many experiences we had had there. So now we found ourselves vaguely "antsy", willing to push a bit on the road to actually be in our desired destination.

At the same time, Sandra was beginning to suffer some real discomfort in her left knee. We'd both been aware there was a problem with her leg which had surfaced on our trip to Prague just before our marriage, but she has a strong constitution and seldom complained. However, she was beginning to limp and descending from the coach was becoming more difficult and clearly uncomfortable for her. We had a long talk one evening and decided surgery was probably the only viable option at this point. Whether the knee could be repaired or whether she would need a complete knee replacement were questions only an orthopedic surgeon could answer. We both knew Stanford had an outstanding medical program, so that became our next "must go there" destination. Besides, she had been born in the Stanford (Palo Alto) Hospital and figured she'd feel comfortable returning there.

In the meantime, we had some lovely scenery to enjoy on the way south. The Oregon coastline is spectacularly different from that of Washington State. It appeared more rugged,somewhat more like the California coast I remembered from my grad student days. Tall, jagged rock outcroppings just offshore provided a rugged interest that added to the beauty of the sandy beaches. Worn away by wind, tide and coastal rain as well as by the ever- present wind, the ancient shoreline had gradually receded and standing just offshore were the remnants of mighty rocks that had once been the hardest, most durable part of the Pacific cliffs.

This was a wonderful photo-op and we took full advantage of it, pulling Regina Victoria over frequently and jumping out with cameras clicking to capture yet another incredible, seemingly even weirder rock formation or curving coastal vista. Back lit by the descending sun, these photos of prehistoric megaliths are among our most artistic and most treasured from the entire trip. As we were photographing, we had an unspoken agreement to the effect that, "The shot through the pine tree is mine...you can have the rock over there for your foreground." We enjoyed calling shots to each other as we always then had different views of the same subject at the end of the shooting day. Frequently, Sandra's were the better composed. Her years as a Philly photojournalist and reporter made her more keenly aware of composition and of getting it right with just one shot. That said, I felt over time that mine were getting better and better and I looked forward in the evenings to seeing what I had shot and how successful I had been at getting it the way I wanted it. This was another grand lesson that had come with our travels. I was finding I had an artistic eye and even if I couldn't draw a straight line, I could take a passably artsy photo.

After wandering down the remainder of the gorgeous Oregon coast, we finally crossed into the Golden State just above Crescent City on Hwy 1/101. Since it was late in the day, we decided to stop for the night and actually found a lovely pullout overlooking the ocean. For one of the very rare times in our California travels, there were no signs prohibiting overnight camping. Usually they are everywhere, so we were overjoyed we could have this wonderful private spot to ourselves with a stunning view of the ocean right outside our windows. If we had thought the CHP would have let us, we would have stayed for several days, but realized that would be classified as "pushing our luck" really hard! The Highway Patrol officers we did encounter were uniformly courteous and helpful, but they might look askance at an older couple setting up permanent housekeeping right beside one of their busiest state highways. So the next morning we moved on after allowing Smokey to stand at the cliff's edge and sniff the keen sea breeze, looking a bit like Snoopy gearing up for the Dawn Patrol.

As we put some California miles under our belts, we decided we needed a break from the coast highway, as gorgeous as it was. Poring over our maps, we decided to stop at the Redwood National Forest for some peace and quiet; plus, we both love the giant Redwoods. Interestingly, one of the first longer piano pieces I mastered as a child was, "Among the Giant Redwoods". I always loved that little piece and had been so proud when I worked out the fingering for its big chords.

Entering the park, we found a place to ditch the RV for a short while and proceeded with the Jeep deeper into the winding roads traversing this pristine and ancient area. There are several well-marked trails that lead into the heart of the forest and Sandra and I, holding hands, walked slowly and very quietly into the deep shadows and profound silence that filled this magical space. Surrounded by trees of staggering height and unguessable age, I was awestruck. We were in the presence of living things that had been here when the great mosque of Cordoba had been dedicated, the first crusaders had set forth from Western Europe, the first universities had enrolled their first students in Paris and Bologna. The chronicle goes on and on. This very tree I was leaning against has been here absorbing the rains of the Pacific Northwest since Caesar first marched into Gaul – and that is a very humbling thought, indeed.

That day marked our six-month wedding anniversary and I can't imagine we could have found a better place to spend the day than among the Redwoods, talking very quietly. Sandra reminisced about her child-hood and her parents. Redwoods were always a part of her growing up, a place for family picnics, teen adventures, and finally a place to scatter her parents' ashes as they had wanted - funerals without fuss, with only the impossibly tall trees and a loving daughter to memorialize Mother and Father.

The quiet and repose of the Redwoods had worked their magic on us and we were soon ready to tackle again the Golden State's most famous roadway. Proceeding southwards at our slow (I prefer the word "careful") pace, we decided it might add to our adventure if we left Highway 101 and took one of the little connecting roads across the hills and down to the road that ran right beside the Pacific ocean, county road 211. So, after stopping for fuel and some lunch at Eureka, we headed south towards Fortuna. About a mile before that little town we turned right onto highway 211. Soon after, we began one of the most frightening and most rewarding parts of our whole trip.

If I had any illusions about this road being any easier than highway 101/1, I was quickly proven very wrong, indeed. Signs warned that this road was not for large tractor-trailer rigs with kingpin-to-rear lengths spelled out in detail on a closely spaced succession of signs. I did some quick mental arithmetic and decided our configuration was different enough that we should give this a whirl. Sandra took the wheel, and I rode shotgun, my head on a swivel watching the big side mirror and craning backwards to see out the windows behind me. My job was to keep track of where the Jeep was, as it frequently disappeared from view around the curve the coach had just traversed. We were quickly rounding curves that were tighter than any we had encountered before.

Sandra was driving Regina Victoria at walking speed. The road was not only twisting madly but was also exceptionally narrow and lacking either shoulders or guard rails. To add to our worries, the gradients were steep so Sandra was either riding the air brakes hard or trying to accelerate up the next steep hill. This was the trickiest road we had been on since the infamous "Top of the World" highway between the Yukon and Alaska. In terms of difficult curves and switchbacks, 211 quickly climbed the charts to top honors in the *Truly Scary Highways* category.

After what seemed like endless miles, our nightmare materialized. We entered a curve so tight that we could not get the Jeep to follow. Full stop! Sandra set the brakes, turned on the emergency flashers and we got out to examine our possibilities. Because we couldn't back up with the Jeep in tow, we determined we would have to remove it right where we sat. This was not going to be easy. We were out of cell phone range so no way to call a wrecker to assist.

The only option I saw was to try and wrestle the Jeep loose with the tools I had. Selecting a heavy hammer and my largest screwdriver, I had to beat loose the two heavy, thick rods holding the tow bar in place. We had been forced to this extremity a few times before in our journey and it was not a fun process. It is a difficult task if the car and the RV were at even slight angles to each other with both on level ground. Here on this remote back road, pointing downhill, the two vehicles were at a 45-degree angle to each other. I truly hoped that this would prove to be another of those challenges that I could actually overcome – another "I Can Do This" moment... because if I failed, we were going to have to wait for help while, meanwhile, completely blocking a county road.

With the brakes locked on both vehicles, I found a large rock and wedged it in front of a Jeep tire. I did not like the quickly suppressed image of white-haired Senior squashed between tow car and heavy rear bumper of RV. Preparation complete, I pulled the retaining cotter pins and began to pound on the first of the two horizontal rods holding our combo together. It was just as bad as I had thought it would be. With the full weight of the Jeep binding the rods in place, I could only bang away with the hammer against the screwdriver, slowly backing the rod out. It took ten minutes of sustained pounding to get the first rod loose. Even though the day was California coastal cool, I was dripping with sweat.

After a short rest to get some feeling back into my arm and hand, I then tackled the other rod. This proved more difficult as it now bore the whole weight of the Jeep. I began pounding again... nothing happened. Getting more desperate, I rummaged in the RV's vast rear locker and found a small sledge hammer. Not sure if using this would shatter the screwdriver, nevertheless, I was determined to get these rods out before I simply couldn't swing *any* hammer. The sledge finally did the trick. The additional weight against the big screwdriver finally budged the rod, and then it was a matter of trying to hit accurately with the sledge (and softly cursing) until rod number 2 popped loose. A few taps freed up the remaining mechanical bits and Jeep and RV were separated again!

I was arm-weary, but proud I had been able to "get'er done". We quickly decided I would follow Sandra in the Jeep which made her driving job easier with only the big rig to watch out for. We proceeded along 211 until we came through the village of Petrolia, which featured a large hog farm just off the highway. From there on it was downhill to the Pacific coast. And this proved another magical moment in our travels.

Our little back road ran right along the Pacific shore, just yards from beach and surf. We pulled off at a wide spot near a little bridge to rest a bit. After brewing some fresh coffee, we sat staring at the beach, taking in the sun and the sparkling blue water. And then we decided just to stay there. Nothing said we couldn't and our little site was absolutely pristine in its beauty. We let Smokey out for a first run on the beach and he scampered off to check out the resident shore birds. We were camped just beyond a small one-lane bridge which effectively slowed down any vehicles so we would not have to worry about speeding vehicles barreling past our rig in the dark of night.

That evening, we pulled our lawn chairs out from under the RV and just sat soaking up the gorgeous sunset. California was as magical as we both had remembered. The Pacific hills ranged above our site to the east provided a warm golden and green contrast to the blue of the Pacific. Adding to the visual delight, the hills were populated by beautiful, sleek cows, among Sandra's favorite creatures. She was captivated by the landscape we had stumbled upon and spent the fading light photographing our bovine neighbors contentedly munching their way up and over the hills above. As the light was quickly fading, the last cow over the ridge turned and looked back at us below, as though wishing us farewell and good night. That night, we slept the sleep of the just or at least that of the very exhausted!

During the night I awoke and went into the forward cabin of the RV. Looking out the window towards the ocean I could see the moon sparkling on the waves and lighting the incoming high tide. This was what I had come back to California to see…a coastline that in other parts of the state was overbuilt and overcrowded. Here it looked as it must have hundreds of years ago when the first Spanish settlers drove their herds northward from Sonora and Baja, California. This was an area of vast Spanish land grants, *fincas* running to many thousands of acres, the land of the Franciscan missions that still dot California. If I let my imagination have free play, I could just see Don Diego riding through the surf this night.

We spent three very relaxing days tucked into our spot along the coast, with only a very occasional truck or car for passing company. This was truly a remote part of the state, and yet only a few miles from one of America's busier highways, California 101. Having braved the torturous mountain roads to get here, we were rewarded with splendid isolation and a sense of solitude that we hadn't experienced since our days in Canada and Alaska. We worked on our writing projects, listened to classical music CDs, caught up on our emails and generally found this one of the most beautiful spots we had camped in. Listening to the surf and taking long walks along the beach with Smokey proudly leading the way made this truly memorable.

Finally, a friendly county sheriff stopped by to check that we were okay. We told him we were and didn't indicate how long we had been camped there. I took his visit as a warning that we probably should be moving on. So we folded up the lawn chairs, poured some coffee into the travel mugs, and headed out. We decided to keep the Jeep off the hookup until we discovered what the remainder of 211 was like on our meandering way back to Highway 101. I followed Sandra in the Jeep, and after a few miles decided the road was not quite so grueling as it had been farther north. We attached the faithful toad again so that we could ride together and enjoy each others company while motoring slowly through this spectacular bit of the coastal range. My banging and hammering on the critical rods had left them none the worse for wear. One of them, I knew, was custom machined from the head bolt of a huge Cummins truck engine when we had lost its predecessor in a parking lot, so I was pretty sure nothing I could do would damage *that* piece of carbon steel. The other rod was the original and seemed made of equally tough stuff.

By evening we were still running close to the water's edge. We decided to stop for the night in a small campground that appeared to be maintained by the county although there was no sign of personnel or any place to pay for the overnight experience. We had our pick of campsites and chose one near a little stream. It was quite a charming setting and we enjoyed being among the trees for a change, although we missed the booming of the high-tide surf that we had grown used to. The site was large enough that we didn't have to back in or unhook the Jeep, so we had time to play with Smokey in the gathering twilight of late Autumn. He loves his evening romp, especially if he has been confined to the RV all day.

Once the big diesel is silent, Smokey seems to know that a walk is at hand. He bounces up and down, uttering little grunts and assorted squeaks that tell us he is more than ready for us to open the big side door and let him out. At full speed, he flies down the steps and off to see where his people have parked his home this time! Satisfied that we have picked a good site (one with lots of things to mark), he will circle back and invite us to go exploring with him. If the area is deemed safe, we let him roam off lead and he rewards this trust by frequently looking back to check on where we are.

Highway 101 in California is, and always has been, one of my favorite roads, full of curves and breathtaking views over the Pacific from high atop the shoreline cliffs. I remember reading about it in "Sports Car Country" in an early copy of *Road and Track* magazine, and I was immediately hooked, wanting to try it for myself. It is a treasure of a road if you're driving a sports car, as I used to "back in the day". Then I had an Austin Healey 3000 six-banger with sliding removable windows, so low to the ground that it dragged its complex exhaust on every driveway I ever entered. Driven hard, it was supposed to make co-eds weak in the knees, although I think that only worked for James Bond in his Bentley.

(Check out Fleming's Casino Royale and the chase through the forests of France for some of the best driving scenes ever.)

Fifty years on, and driving a whacking great motorhome, Highway 101/1 proved to be a far greater challenge. It is still absolutely beautiful, but the twisty, curvy bits become a good deal more intimidating when the driver is perched high in the air with about 60 feet of vehicle trailing majestically behind. As I got us underway the next mornng, there was a momentary temptation to imitate the bus driving scene from the original "The Italian Job" movie, one of my favorite heist flicks. In the concluding scene the gang, having successfully pulled off their brazen robbery, escapes in a large tour bus. Uphill and down and around the tight curves of the winding Italian coastline the huge bus rockets, tires screeching, gears winding madly, and everyone on board laughing and popping Champagne. I was tempted (ever so briefly) to try a similar driving style. Age, slower reflexes and what I like to think of as "mature wisdom" came to my rescue and we proceeded carefully 'round the never-ending series of curves and switchbacks.

This kind of driving is probably the most difficult physically, as it requires constant attention to the coach. Sandra does this better than I do and often handles the scarier stretches of these more difficult roads. The little-travelled roads of Canada and Alaska, while demanding, could be negotiated at slower speeds. The main problem up in the North Country was keeping a sharp watch for coach-swallowing holes and tire-shredding shale. On California's coastal highway, there is the looming problem of traffic. California motorists do NOT like to be held up. Accustomed practically from birth to travel on high-speed freeways, some only slow marginally on roads I regard as "country" at best. Therefore, we always had to be watchful we had not grown a long tail of fuming motorists as we negotiated the hairpin turns. We tried our best to pull off and let our train pass wherever we could find a spot big enough, but sometimes these safe zones were miles apart.

After a morning of Highway 101, we reached Leggett, California, and made our way over to the famous Coast Highway, California 1. To me, as a historian, this is a fascinating stretch of road. Back in my doctoral student days at USC, Dr. Manuel Servin had been a major player on my thesis committee. He was editor of the California History Journal. And, of course, even though I was a Europeanist to my fingertips, "Manny" had insisted I read his beloved journals. In doing so, I came to see the close connection between my specialty, Spanish Medieval history and his, Early Spanish California. Highway 1 was, to some degree, the Mission Trail, as well as the path by which early land grant settlers had moved slowly up from Spain's Mexican holdings to open this wilderness that was 17th century California. I always liked to imagine that the many cows we saw grazing along Highway 1 were descendants of the early herds brought north by the grandees who held those valuable grants from the King of Spain.

Marked as "scenic" on every map I had ever studied, California 1 deserves that moniker and much more. It is truly one of the world's great drives. Even in a big RV it is a delight to take in the vast sweep of the California coastline. Perhaps that should read *especially* in a big RV. Regina Victoria put us up high, and with her enormous expanse of windshield, gave us a picture window view of this spectacular geography. The road is winding, but that, of course, is the charm. Here one can see the Pacific (always on the right heading south) crashing against the rocky coastline.

The views ahead are constantly changing as each curve and dip reveals yet another facet of the ocean's interface with land and sky. Primal elements are combined, then combined again in some new way that is frequently breathtaking and always hypnotic to watch. Even on a flat calm day the Pacific breakers surge in a way that invites surfing. Driving along the rocky coast, the viewer is reminded of the sheer power of the Pacific as it hurls itself against rocks – huge boulders that have withstood its advances for more millennia than we have walked upright.

As we drove south, we began to notice more traffic. This came as a bit of a shock to both of us, as we had spent the past months pretty much being able to say, "No one in front of us, no one behind us." Sandra, in particular, does not like traffic. Much of her adult life has been spent in cities with public transportation, or alone on her own sailboat in the Pacific, or in a small town in the Ozark Mountains. I remember one of our worst traffic nightmares was driving Sandra's original 30-foot RV around Chicago during a weekday rush hour. This was before I had become an experienced big rig driver, so all I could do was scream, "Watch out for that truck on your right!", or "You're too close to this traffic sign … we're going to hit it!" It had been an extremely trying afternoon, made complete by a rear tire blowout. We were compelled to pull off the infamous Dan Ryan Expressway, call for help, and sit it out with cars and trucks whizzing past just inches away. Finally, a very big wrecker showed up and towed to us to – of all places – the police impound yard. At least we felt very safe that night!

Taking our time driving the Coast Highway meant we would need to find places to stay for the night that weren't state parks. We had discovered that only a few such parks in California could accommodate a rig our size, so we began to search for alternate overnight sites. We were past the point of being able to camp right along the coast as we were entering more built up areas, so one night we decided to try California casino camping. We had stayed at First Nations Casinos in Canada but not, thus far, at a similar venue in the U.S. Examining all our maps, we found one located about where we wanted to be at day's end.

Sandra and I like camping in casino parking lots. They are usually huge spaces which means we have plenty of room to swing the RV with tow attached and find a comfortable parking spot. Many of the casinos we have seen actually have reserved RV parking areas, with long slips for big rigs and even shuttle service to and from the casino. Some of those in Canada have an attendant who will direct you to an appropriate space and even serve as flagman, wig-wagging you into your site for the night. And many will also allow RVers to stay for several days, on the assumption that you have nowhere else to go and nothing else to do but gamble or eat. So it's a win-win from all angles. Another plus is casinos didn't charge RVers anything to stay until only recently when some started charging a nightly rate.

Once we were in our spot for the night, we headed into the casino for dinner. Casino food is not usually gourmet quality, but you generally get a lot to eat for the price and the people- watching is some of the best! I find it particularly interesting to watch those playing the slots. There is an intensity, a concentration (and an odd sense of aloneness) that I don't see elsewhere. It's as though every sense is critically tuned to the finger that pushes the button or pulls the lever (becoming much rarer). Players seem hypnotized by the motion of the little icons whirling and then clicking into place – a winner or yet another loser. A loser simply results in another coin or token dropped into the slot, another push or pull, another quick sip of the beverage of choice, another quick surge of hope.

I enjoy playing the penny and nickel slots, but as soon as it becomes mechanical I stop, fearing, I suppose, that I will become addicted to this in some blind way. Being in recovery and recognizing how thin is the line I can cross, I do tend to watch behaviors that uncomfortably mimic mine from the past. Sandra does not especially like casinos. She will eat with me and even play a few slots, but the general level of alcohol consumption and some of the more obstreperous behavior makes her uncomfortable.

By morning, we were ready to rock and roll, heading back down Highway 1 and singing old Beach Boy songs to each other. Sandra was the first girl surfer in Santa Cruz and always keeps a watchful eye out for the best surfing waves. We drove all day, enjoying the scenery and the sheer pleasure of Regina Victoria performing flawlessly. That evening we stopped at the small and charming town of Fort Bragg, staying at a private campground close to town. We enjoyed watching the town in the twilight as the lights came on, and after a bit of searching, discovered a cozy restaurant where we wolfed down another terrific seafood dinner. That night the three of us snuggled into the big bed in the Regina Victoria's aft compartment and slid into sleep with visions of approaching San Francisco occupying our thoughts.

The next day was gorgeous and we got an early start, fortified with delicious omelettes from a little eatery we had found during our walking tour the night before. We stopped to fill up the big diesel tank, then headed back south on Route 1, delighting in the sea breezes as they wafted through the side windows of the RV. Traffic slowly but surely began to increase, and from the GPS and our map readings, we knew we were getting closer to the fabled City by the Bay (or Baghdad by the Bay as famed newspaper columnist Herb Caen named it.) Finally, we rejoined Highway 101 above Sausalito. A few more miles and we rounded Mt. Tamalpais.

There in front of us, spread out in intense Kodachrome, was our favorite city – San Francisco. The early evening light set off the Golden Gate Bridge and its brilliant orange-red that is instantly identifiable by travelers worldwide. We literally caught our breaths, so stunning was the view. I had never seen the city so clearly lighted – the Bay Bridge, affectionately known by locals as the Necklace of Diamonds, on the left, the Golden Gate Bridge to the right, and the most beautiful city in

America squarely between. And then, very softly, as if by secret signal, we both began to sing "San Francisco, Open Your Golden Gate". We had arrived – we were THERE!

Crossing the Golden Gate, holding hands across the big cockpit as we had months ago on our first night out of St. Louis, we both knew the adventures and the lessons had only just begun!